BEING INFORMED

BEING INFORMED

John Swain

JANUS PUBLISHING COMPANY
London, England

First Published in Great Britain 1995
by Janus Publishing Company,
Edinburgh House, 19 Nassau Street,
London W1N 7RE

Copyright © John Swain 1995

British Library Cataloguing-in-Publication Data.
A catalogue record for this book is available
from the British Library.

ISBN 1 85756 104 X

All rights reserved. No part of this publication may be reproduced,
stored in a retrieval system or transmitted in any form or by any means,
electronic, mechanical, photocopying, recording or otherwise,
without the prior permission of the publisher.

The right of John Swain to be identified as the author of this work
has been asserted by him in accordance with the
Copyright, Designs and Patents Act 1988.

Cover design Linda Wade

Printed & bound in England by
Antony Rowe Ltd,
Chippenham, Wiltshire

Contents

Foreword		vii
Introduction		xi

Part I   Settling In
1. Hendon Training School — 1
2. West End Central Police Station — 9
3. Aide to CID — 16
4. Detective Constable — 24
5. Liaison with the US Navy — 37
6. Building a House for Myself — 44

Part II   Making My way
7. Transfer to the Company Fraud Squad — 67
8. Detective Sergeant in the Flying Squad — 74
9. Posted to Brixton — 94
10. Return to the Flying Squad — 108

Part III   Promotion
11. Promotion to Detective Inspector — 123
12. Upwards to Detective Chief Inspector — 141
13. The Stanley Butcher Murder — 152
14. The Murder of Rokaya Bibi Hazari — 168

Part IV   At the Top of the Ladder
15. Detective Superintendent at Southwark — 179
16. Back to the Flying Squad — 192

Part V   Moving On
17. Retirement Time — 217
18. Into a New Profession — 222
19. The American Experience — 236

Foreword

I was rather surprised and not a little flattered when I received a request from John Swain to consider writing a foreword to his book *Being Informed*. When one joins and then makes your way through the Police Service there are certain 'giants' of the organisation who, although one might not work directly with them, just cannot be ignored: their reputation ensures that everyone knows of them and their names crop up over and over again. John Swain was one of those people. His entry into the Metropolitan Police preceded mine by a decade and he was therefore well established long before I began to think in terms of promotion myself. Indeed, John Swain, having already given service to his country as a successful soldier during the war was already a Detective Inspector while I was still a Constable.

Nonetheless I knew well the name of John Swain, which seemed to appear with regularity whenever there was a big or exciting job happening – something which everyone wanted to get involved in. But your name doesn't appear on these important and exciting (and not unusually, dangerous) events by accident. You don't just chance upon those big jobs, and reputations don't grow on trees: they have to be worked at and worked for, and John Swain got his rewards, commendations, promotions and above all, his career satisfaction, because he, in turn, gave everything he could to his chosen profession.

This book is a fascinating account of how young John Swain realised his ambition of following his father into the Metropolitan Police, and later into the elite Flying Squad. It covers his whole career from the early days at Hendon Police College and on his first uniform duties at West End Central Police Station (which covers the heart of London's West End including Mayfair, Piccadilly, Regent Street and Soho – embracing areas of Chinatown and 'Clubland'), Brixton, Southwark and his various postings to the Flying Squad.

As I read through the book so a number of those other giants of the service stepped out to greet me, and it is not surprising that someone like the author should have worked in the company of these other formidable and successful detectives. Names like the late Vic Gilbert, Commanders John Lock and Don Neesham, the unforgettable and famous Tommy Butler, Mike McAdam, Nicky Birch, and a host of others including Professor 'Taffy' Cameron, one of that fine band of pathologists with whom I also had the privilege of working during my investigative days. He introduces them all to the reader who may not have had the pleasure of meeting them in real life, and reminds those of us who knew them of their great talents. I was particularly pleased to see reference to Henry Dowdswell, a man whom I admired very much but who sadly died whilst a serving Detective Inspector. It was Henry who had shown great courage when the trap was being sprung to capture the I.R.A. terrorists responsible for many murders in London (later to become known as the 'Balcombe Street gang' following the week long siege when they held a middle aged couple hostage before surrendering). Had it not been for Henry who, unarmed, continued the chase whilst the taxi he had commandeered was hit a number of times by the bullets of the fleeing terrorists, they might never have been captured. His actions were publicly rewarded in the Honours list and this is an indication of the calibre of person with whom John Swain worked and of which he was one: all of them courageous, determined, single minded – but as they would also admit, occasionally fallible, crime fighters.

John captures the atmosphere of the demands on the young police officer and particularly on the young Aide to C.I.D. when recounting in anecdotal fashion his early efforts to get into the Criminal Investigation Department. But, if anything, he probably plays down the enormous pressures which were on those who were endeavouring to compete for the coveted few vacancies which occurred from time to time. He explains how at times as he rose through the early ranks of the service he was on the horns of a dilemma, searching and working to arrest the more lethal type of villain was time consuming and could well have prevented him from producing the quota of work that would satisfy those whose eyes were fixed on a target governed by statistics. Keeping pace with the desires of his superiors for the prosecution of the quantity (and quality) of what he lightly calls miscreants, places enormous pressures on the aspiring detective: and we know to our dismay, and to the grief of the Service, of those who allowed their better judgements to be overcome because of these pressures and the perceived imperative of propping up what was an inadequate criminal justice system in their efforts to capture the villain and protect the public. It is these pressures which John, through his loyalty to a Service he loved, perhaps understates. Maybe it is also because his own high standards would never break any compromise with his professional and personal integrity.

The reader will judge the quality of the man, his thoroughness and determination, and not least of all his fairness as he or she reads through the chapters. His humour shows through clearly as does his humanity when he generously notes his admiration for an 'habitual and incorrigible rogue' for her loyalty to her husband.

There are many lessons to be gleaned in these pages for the aspiring young police officer and I wouldn't pre-empt a good read by trying to list them but how good it was to read his advice about listening to everything a suspect has to say — however insultingly it may be put — and never losing one's temper: as he puts it 'when one of my "customers" lost his temper with me, I was always the ultimate winner'. Throughout the book the reader will be much taken with the author's 'feelings' when he knew in his heart that something was not right. Although this is often called the policeman's 'hunch' there is always a good reason for such a feeling, often generated by observation of some small detail which because of the experience of the investigator does not ring true; but he sounds a very clear warning note to the up and coming detective that 'feelings are not evidence'. Never in John Swain's career did he forget that to maintain a successful prosecution one has to have credible and admissible evidence.

This is a book which will interest police officers and non police officers alike, but for my part I was glad to see the inclusion of a chapter on 'supergrasses', comments on the extreme brutality of some criminals (this is the reality of life), and also the most difficult and vexed question of the 'nobbling' of jurors. One could go on but I won't spoil the readers enjoyment by doing so.

John Swain has been a great detective and I am delighted he has decided to tell his story for the benefit of us all. Perhaps he always had a touch of the author in him, the reader will notice the reference to his ability to write shorthand — that is like one's reputation: you don't wake up one morning with such a talent, it takes hard work, dedication, and devotion to the task in hand — and that is the measure of John's life. He has always given of his best and because of that he succeeded. His dedication to the police service, and to the public he had served for so many years, was publicly recognised just prior to his retirement when he was awarded The Queen's Police Medal for Distinguished Service.

It is typical of John Swain that he left one successful career and then carved out another with his private investigative work. In the last few pages of his book he says he has many good years of work left in him yet, and one can have but little doubt that he will be as successful in the future as he has been in the past. One thing is for sure, his zest for life will ensure that he enjoys every minute of it.

Sir Peter Imbert QPM DL
(Commissioner of Police of the Metropolis 1987 – 1993)

Introduction

From a very early age, I had only one aim in life, to be a successful detective like my father, John Swain senior. He was born in Birkhill, Coupar Angus in Scotland in 1893 and started work as a farm labourer, then went on to be a railway clerk, and later joined the Dundee Police as a uniformed constable. When war broke out in 1914, he was one of the first to leave the Force and volunteer for armed service. He joined the Scots Guards, was soon in France and in 1916, after injury, was returned to the Guards Depot at Caterham, Surrey. There he met my mother, who was then working at Kenley Aerodrome. In 1919 the couple married and I arrived on the scene in August 1920. By this time father had joined the Metropolitan Police and had moved to live in Shoreditch in the East End of London.

I had never seen my father in uniform and learned that he was in fact a detective. I only learned this after seeing him return home late one afternoon, unsteady on his feet and with red bleary eyes. Apparently my father with some colleagues had raided a house where some wanted men were hiding. The villains had pelted the officers with 'pepper bombs' – prepared bags of pepper. This did not do the eyes a lot of good, but the villains were all arrested.

I was about seven years old when we moved to Battersea. My father, then a Detective Sergeant, had been moved to Lavender Hill Police Station. Soon he was studying for further promotion and spending a lot of time poring over a very large volume on law and police work.

Things were changing for my father, but they were changing for me also. Some of my school chums began to act rather strangely towards me. About once a week as I came out of the school gate four or five of the boys would be waiting for me. A fight would follow, sometimes I lost, sometimes I won, but it was always a fair fight. I was never struck with a stick or implement or kicked, and never had to deal with more than one boy at a time.

I found that I was beginning to assess the opposition more accurately. On one occasion I was approached by the boy who was reckoned to be the toughest in the school, Jim Stockwell. I ran. I arrived at my front door, which was opened for me by my father. 'What's the hurry?' he asked. I told him my problem and was told that I had better go and hit Jim Stockwell, or he would give me a bigger hiding than Stockwell would. I did as I was bid and earned not only the respect of my father, but also that of my school chums, including Stockwell.

On leaving school, I found work as a junior clerk in various offices, all very boring. I just had to study in order to pass the police entrance examination when I came of age. My life was therefore divided between my work, study and cycle racing, which I took up in order to keep fit.

In late August 1939, when war was the principal subject of all gossip and news, and with little opportunity of getting into the police until hostilities were over, I volunteered for the Territorial Army. I joined the London Welsh Regiment, Royal Artillery, and was called up that very day. War was declared a few days later, on 3rd September 1939, and I started to learn to be a soldier. I had taken quite an interest in the mechanics of the guns and became the Battery Sergeant Fitter. My superiors, highly satisfied, sent me to the Military College of Science to learn more. I passed muster and was promoted to the rank of Staff Sergeant in the Royal Army Ordance Corps.

I was posted to the Second Infantry Brigade Workshops at East Dereham in Norfolk, which were later to form part of the Royal Electrical and Mechanical Engineers. We travelled to Scotland, thence to North Africa, and I became involved in the North African campaign and in the battles in Italy, including the Anzio beachhead landings. Subsequently I earned promotion to Artificer Sergeant Major. From Italy I moved to Palestine, and served in Syria, Lebanon and Egypt. Throughout this time I never lost sight of my determination that I was going to join the Metropolitan Police in my home town, London, as soon as I could get out of the army.

I was offered an army commission if I stayed on, but refused pointblank. My mind was made up. Many thought that I was crazy not to take up the offer, but my ambition to become a police officer was too great. I was later demobilised from the army, happy in the knowledge that I knew where I was going from there!

PART ONE

SETTLING IN

1
Hendon Training School

Joining the police force was the only matter truly on my mind and something that I just had to do soon. It was all very well going round meeting my old peacetime friends. Even visiting relatives seemed like a waste of time. There was always the nagging thought in my mind, what if I don't get into the police? I might fail the education examination. I could not imagine that I would fail the physical examination, although one never knows, especially after being in foreign parts for so long.

My mind was in something of a turmoil. When my father came home from work, joining the police force was the first thing I wanted to talk about. He, of course, had other ideas and would lead me into discussions about all the interesting places which he felt I might have visited during my overseas service. It was often well after midnight before we got to bed, that oh so comfortable bed I had left behind way back in 1939. As I lay down on it for the first time it felt really wonderful, but I had the greatest difficulty in getting to sleep on it. I had slept on all manner of uncomfortable things in many different places in the past few years and would probably have got a better sleep if I had just curled up on the floor.

I got in my application to join the Metropolitan Police within a very short time of returning home. On 12th April 1946 I attended the Metropolitan Police Recruiting Office in Beak Street, Soho, for a medical examination, and interview. This was followed on 17th April by an educational examination. I felt happy with both. Then came the waiting period, because, satisfied as you might personally be with what had taken place, there was always the unknown to take into consideration. For the best part of the following three weeks I found myself turning over in my mind everything that had taken place in connection with my application; but then the letter of acceptance came, and I received orders to report to Peel House in Regency Street, Victoria, in Central London, the Metropolitan Police Training School. Here I was fitted out with a uniform. After the smart uniformed turnout I had got used to in the army, the hurriedly issued police uniform left much to be desired. On 3rd June 1946 I was sworn in by Sir Maurice Drummond and at the same time offered up a silent prayer: 'Thank you, Lord, I've made it at last. '

That very same day, I believe twenty of us were taken by coach to Peel House, Hendon, on the outskirts of North London. I knew very little about this establishment. It was, however, the new recruits' training school, and I was fortunate enough to be in the first class of recruits to attend there. We were in a historical class of recruits, the first to be trained at what was the Hendon Police College, originally formed for the training of selected constables, who would pass out at the end of their course as Junior Station Inspectors. It had been the brainchild of the famous Commissioner of the Metropolitan Police, Lord Trenchard, but many had disagreed with that scheme, and it had at the time been abandoned.

The course lasted until early in September 1946. I passed the examinations, but the pressure and discipline we were subjected to was a very sound lesson to us all.

One of our first surprises was to find that we actually had a Drill Sergeant. This just had to be a joke. To a man, every member of that class had been either a commissioned or a non-commissioned officer in one or other of His Majesty's Forces. We found the notion somewhat degrading. Sergeant Duffy was the Drill Sergeant. A former Scots Guardsman, he was fairly short by Guardsman standards, but what a voice he had. He did not victimise any of us in any way, but he was very strict about his particular orders.

Our first experience of him was when we were all lined up in front of him for the first time on the parade ground at Hendon Training School. He introduced himself, and came over as a smiling and most pleasant man. But before our bold sergeant had finished his smiling introduction, I had decided that I would not trust him.

He made us stand stiffly to attention. No problem. We had been doing that for the past six years. He then walked round us. Now he looked mean, and I found myself likening him to that mythical figure of Ajax defying the lightning. He was definitely intent on exerting his authority on us and projected himself as an utter bully. As he walked round the back of us, he tapped everyone on the neck and barked 'Haircut', 'Haircut'. Then returning to the front of us he told us what he thought of us. We were then taken to our respective rooms and told to stand by our beds. We were told how to stack our blankets and spare kit. Nothing new about this, but we found ourselves asking whether we had joined a new brand of kindergarten. Notwithstanding all this, however, we were all sufficiently disciplined to do as we were told. We all had a haircut, and stacked our kit in the manner directed.

The following morning the bold Sergeant Duffy did a further tour of inspection. Over half of the class, including myself, were ordered to have yet a further haircut. He was not interested in the fact that we had already had a haircut as ordered. His answer to this was to take off the peaked cap he wore and show us what he thought a haircut should look like. It was almost laughable. Quite frankly, you really had to look hard to establish that he did have hair on his head at all.

From the parade ground, we were all marched into the Commandant's office. All of us, the whole class. The Commandant was told by the sergeant that he had given us orders the previous day to stack our kit in a particular manner. We had disobeyed that order by not stacking our kit in the prescribed manner. We were shocked. Things were being put over in such a petty and childish manner that many of us were beginning to wonder just what sort of organisation we had offered to join. The Commandant put on a stern face and let it be known in no uncertain terms that he was cautioning us on this occasion, but, if it happened again, we would never complete this course and become Police Officers.

The following day, after yet another haircut, we paraded again. The same procedure was repeated. Sergeant Duffy did his inspection. We all waited for the shout of 'Haircut', followed by a tap on the neck or shoulder as he passed behind us. None came. He returned to the front of the parade and proceeded to address us in an unfamiliar and almost fatherly fashion. He was fully aware that he was talking to former officers, some of whom had been of high rank, to former regimental sergeant majors and other senior non-commissioned ranks of the various armed forces who had now decided to join the police force. Discipline in the police was far more strict than in the forces, he said, and as we were likely to be loosed off on to the streets of London within a few months, where we would be the servants of the public, he had been obliged to bring us all to the same level.

He did not exactly correct the phrase, 'servants of the public', but went on to enlarge on it. Indirectly the public paid our wages, he said. Our duty therefore was to look after them and to protect them. They in turn could, and would, come to us with their problems. Even children would come to us when they wanted to cross the road or were lost. One important part of police discipline is to ensure that when a constable is allowed out on the street, he is able to talk with anyone, be he a king or a tramp, in his capacity as an officer in the Metropolitan Police. As far as he was concerned, he intended ensuring that when we, or any of 'his' recruits went away from the training school, we would be moulded into a style of person who was the ideal police officer.

I don't think that we believed what had been said to us during the first month at the training school, but we did learn to have a very great respect for our Drill Sergeant. As other classes joined the school, we saw them being moulded into his ideal in the same manner as he had handled us. By the time we left, Sergeant Duffy was our best friend, and there was not one of us who did not have absolute admiration for the manner in which he undertook his task. He took down colonels, squadron leaders, naval commanders and regimental sergeant majors from their ivory towers, dusted them and turned them into constables.

There was only one break in the continuous round of study, when my father made a remark to a London Evening News reporter, who had spoken to him about his impending retirement in early August of that year. He had mentioned that although he was leaving the force, another John Swain would shortly commence duties on the beat. He kindly referred to me as a 'chip off the old block'. The reporter could not resist turning the phrase into typical journalese and seized upon those words. When he put the article into his newspaper, in August 1946, he quoted me as the 'Six Foot Chip' who would take the place of his father when he retired in a few weeks' time. Needless to say I then found myself the subject of much ribbing from my fellow students and instructors on this very touchy point.

The course at Hendon was no easy matter for me. My head at the time was full of things military, as I had spent the previous six years virtually as an engineer, supervising others, repairing, servicing and lecturing on guns of all description or perhaps, to be more precise, artillery pieces, some of which were huge and very intricate. Now I had almost to return to my school days, learning law definitions parrot fashion, and acts of parliament by act and section. We then had to be able to interpret accurately a criminal act and associate it with the particular section of an act of parliament; learn the powers of arrest applicable to a particular offence, while remaining aware that in certain circumstances there is no such power; and on top of all that be able to sit down and write a description of exactly what action should be taken in an instance that had been placed before us.

I was indeed glad that I had been fortunate enough to be posted to Hendon for my studies. There was a large sports ground at the rear of the college. Here, during the course, on any evening or period of spare time, a number of students could be seen; each one alone, perhaps walking backwards and forwards and talking to himself. For my part, I did a lot of this. We were required to stand up and quote from acts of parliament at the drop of the hat, without notice of any description; to quote a section of an act, or recite a particular definition of an offence, parrot fashion. I found, in common with many others, that the only way I could hammer home these quite often long definitions was to repeat them to myself aloud; the open sports ground was ideal for that.

Then there was the important business of learning how to give evidence. Under normal circumstances one does not think about this matter, which is, however, a subject of vital importance to a police officer. It is not until you are actually called upon to stand on your own in what has often been described as one of the loneliest places in the world, to say your piece from the witness box, that you realise just how difficult this task can be. From that rather awesome place, you say your piece in all truth, perhaps from notes made at the actual time of the incident. Then from the defence side, up gets a little man who makes a very spirited attempt to prove to everyone else in the court that you are telling lies, that you could not possibly have seen what you say you did; then makes all manner of aspersions on the manner in which you have conducted yourself, either during the course of gathering the evidence or in giving it. Believe me, it is all very frustrating.

Fortunately for me, in addition to my artisan work in the army, I had also lectured quite a lot on matters concerning the guns I was involved with. Lecturing was a subject that I felt I knew well. I knew my subject, and certainly it gave me the necessary confidence to stand up in front of others and say what has to be said, with ease. At Hendon, I was in for another shock. In the mock-up court, with one of the instructors acting as the magistrate and another instructor taking the part of the prisoner in the dock, I found things a little strange. There was a whole lot more to giving evidence than just repeating what I had written in a notebook. A probing cross-examination from an expert is something that has to be experienced to be understood. Most of us were quite at home standing in the witness box and saying our piece. Then the questions came, and it was very quickly demonstrated to us that an expert examiner could soon induce the uninitiated to make statements quite contrary to the evidence in his notes, or that given by others.

This was a most valuable experience, which made us all realise that when we put evidence together in any case, it had to encompass every truthful fact covering the matter under review: evidence against the accused person and evidence in his or her favour. Verbal statements were always to be written down at the time. The maxim of date, time, place was hammered home to us. The evidence we were giving in the mock court was from notes that we as recruits had made in our own handwriting from an incident acted out before us earlier. In our ignorance we had made our notes without the knowledge of just how easy it is for the expert to locate the mistakes and omissions they contained.

Then came the subject of observation, brought home to us in a simple, yet extremely thorough, manner. With no notice whatsoever of what was about to take place, we were all enjoying a period of revision, reading through our notes and study books. The instructor was busy reading up on something or other and leaving us to our own devices. One at a time we were told to go to a specific room to see a named instructor. There he spoke to the individual on various matters. He talked to me about my army service in Italy. It was an interesting chat, but seemed pretty pointless. Talking of course was forbidden during these rare revision periods, and the returned student silently took his place in the class as another was called out. When the last student had returned to his seat, the instructor got up from his seat with a sheaf of paper and walked round the room, handing each of us one sheet. 'I want you to write down everything that you saw in that room' was his next remark. There was an audible groan in the classroom. He then returned to his chair and continued reading. We did exactly as bid and each compiled quite a list, without any discussion.

Then came the shock. Comparison was made between the lists of articles we had noted and a list of what was actually in the room under consideration. Between us we had only noted about a quarter of the articles present. We were warned that such tests would be repeated periodically during our stay. It was also pointed out to us that this was the type of exercise that could happen to us as serving police officers, when we would visit a scene of an incident for some reason or other and later be required to state what we had seen.

As the course continued with more subjects, more surprises and even more acts of parliament and regulations to be learned; each coupled with more of the dreaded definitions to be instilled into our very tired brains, I for one felt that my head was going to burst. Evenings were spent studying, and my rare journeys home at weekends were spent either reading up on a subject or repeating to myself a definition just learned. Once home, it was out with the books again. I regularly felt that I could absorb no more, yet somehow managed to retain my sanity.

Just before the course ended, our class was taken by coach to New Scotland Yard to have our finger prints taken. This, we were told, was for record purposes, for our own protection and the protection of investigators as we progressed through the service. The possibility of any one of us leaving a fingerprint or fingerprints at the scene of a crime that we were called to was never overlooked. By having our fingerprints taken and put on record, they could be eliminated from those of suspects at the outset. This explanation was accepted by us all.

On our way to Scotland Yard, I explained to the sergeant instructor in charge of us that my father was the Divisional Detective Inspector at Cannon Row Police Station. I asked if I could call on him before returning to Hendon. The sergeant agreed to this, but warned me that the coach would leave at 4 p.m. sharp, and I had better be on it.

Walking into Cannon Row Police Station, I hoped that I would remember exactly where my father's office was. I also hoped that he would be there, for I had given him no prior notice of my call. He was there and was delighted to see me. There was, however, another gentleman sitting in the armchair in his office, who looked at me in a most hostile manner. He was obviously very surprised at my unannounced intrusion. I found his piercing stare most disconcerting. I could not recall a previous meeting with a stranger that had affected me in that way, and he had not even spoken. My father certainly looked surprised, and perhaps his words reflected this. 'What the hell are you doing here, son?' he asked. I told him that I had passed the course and that I would be posted to 'C' Division in London's West End the following Monday.

There was a short period of silence as my father turned away to speak to the gentleman sitting in the armchair. 'This is my son. He has been in the army and has just completed his course at Hendon. He starts in 'C' Division on Monday. There is no room for two of us in the job. I shall be putting my papers in.'

Mr Rawlings, the gentleman present, was a very senior Detective Superintendent, a very rare rank in those days. Judging by the effect he had had on me as I entered my father's office, he must have been quite a detective. He got up from his chair, shook hands with me and said, 'Good luck, son. ' Then turning to my father he said, 'I suppose there comes a time when we all have to leave the force, but think it over, Jock. ' He then turned and left the office. What a true statement that was, a statement I knew that I would have to make sometime in the future.

2
West End Central Police Station

On 2nd September 1946, I reported to West End Central Police Station for duty. As Police Constable 372 'C' I was quartered in Trenchard House, in Broadwick Street, Soho. The police station was on the edge of fashionable Mayfair, whilst the section house where I lived was almost in the centre of Soho. I felt that this was going to be a very interesting posting. My instructions were to report for duty at 5.30 a.m. the following morning at the police station in Saville Row, and also to acquaint myself with the section house sergeant, the house instructions and the facilities.

The quarters were good. I had a room to myself and a canteen always available. I felt that I was going to enjoy this. Nevertheless, anxious to get on with my new job, I awoke at 5 a.m. and very soon dressed myself in my uniform. While doing so I realised what date it was: 3rd September, the seventh anniversary of the outbreak of war! My thoughts went back to Shirley Park Camp and the first uniform I had worn, and in my mind I could hear the sound of the sirens that I had heard way back in 1939. I had come a long way since those days.

I very soon found one problem that would give me some trouble for a while. I had to adjust my eating habits to my new vocation. Breakfast to me had always been a most important meal. I had been brought up to it from an early age, and my love of a good breakfast had never been disappointed whilst in the army. At Trenchard House, between 5 a.m. and 7 a.m. the best one could get was a cup of tea and some buttered toast. Within an hour my stomach would rumble, and I knew that this was a matter I would have to do something about.

At that time I was doing what is fondly referred to in the police as 'learning beats'. I therefore put my problem to the various senior constables who accompanied me during those first few weeks. There was, however, no immediate solution. 'You will just have to get used to it. You will get a refreshment period later' was the general response. I never did get used to starting the day on an empty stomach, and within a few weeks had remedied the situation, if not perhaps strictly in accordance with regulations.

Though I had a high expectation or plenty of excitement, life was, in fact, getting somewhat boring for me, particularly in the cold nights of 1946, after spending so long in the Mediterranean area. I found that I had difficulty in keeping warm despite comfortable warm clothing and boots. I began to wonder whether I had done the right thing in leaving the army. My heart, however, was set on the Criminal Investigation Department, and that was what I was going to work for, though my enquiries indicated that the probability of getting into that exclusive department for a few years was most unlikely. All that was left for me to do was to work hard, damned hard, to justify selection into the CID, and I reconciled myself to doing just that.

I was, no doubt, very fortunate to have been posted to the West End of London whilst on uniform duty. Probationer police constables straight from training school are not let loose on the streets of London immediately. The reasoning behind this restriction is not made known at the time, and it is something that is not appreciated by any of the new recruits. Those unsaid reasons, however, soon become very evident and proved to be a most important part of police training.

During that probationary period, I found myself in the company of police constables who had held extremely high ranks in the various services. This did not surprise me at the time, for I had found this variation in service ranks among my colleagues in my class at Hendon. What I did not know then was that some of those wise old constables into whose care we were placed would, before I left the service myself, become chief constables of county police forces and deputy commissioners and assistant commissioners in my own force.

PULLING RANK IN SHAFTESBURY AVENUE

On one such tour of duty, I was posted with an older and very experienced constable. He was an interesting man who discussed domestic matters and sport widely. He gave no indication that he had been in any of the services and showed no intention of being drawn into that subject during our conversations.

On this particular evening, we were walking along Shaftesbury Avenue towards Piccadilly Circus, when a slight accident occurred behind us. We stopped and looked on. It was between a London taxi cab and a private motor car, and there was quite obviously only slight damage to one or perhaps both vehicles. It was, in fact, something that we need not get involved in if all went well. We turned and walked slowly towards the scene to hear the driver of the private motor car refuse to give particulars of his insurance to the taxi driver. Seeing us, the taxi driver called us over. The driver of the private car was making life difficult for everyone by standing on his rank as a major in Eastern Command. He was dressed in civilian clothes, and my colleague, who was conducting the conversations asked to see his army identification particulars. This he refused point-blank.

The polite and conciliatory tone of my colleague changed immediately. 'For your information, young man', he said, 'I was a colonel in the Commandos until very recently, and from your very stupid attitude I cannot imagine you being an officer of any description, let alone a major. If you don't come to your senses and produce your insurance particulars as required, or evidence of them, and also your army identification, you will be coming to West End Central Police Station with us and we will take this matter further.' I was shocked and could hardly believe my ears. I had never even realised that my colleague had been in the army. The cab driver stood by quite open mouthed, whilst the driver of the motor car went as white as a sheet.

The required papers were produced, and we all went on our ways, not, however, before the driver of the car had received a very severe warning on his future conduct, at which point he stood in front of us stiffly to attention. To say that he left us with his tail between his legs would indeed be a gross understatement. As for me, I found it very hard to equate this extremely quiet man with whom I had been walking the beat with a colonel in the commandos. Some months later I found confirmation that my guide on that particular night had in fact held that rank and had been engaged in the memorable raid on the Lofoten Islands during the war.

Not long after this incident I was released on to the streets of London on my own, as a uniformed police constable. Now I found that I became extremely disappointed in my apparent inability to arrest a criminal. I had my quota, if I dare say it, of arrests for minor offences such as obstruction, begging, drunks and minor assaults. The criminal, however, was somehow avoiding me. I stopped many suspects, questioned and searched them, but only managed one positive arrest for an actual criminal offence.

My friend at this time was Police Constable Bert McGowan, PC 172 'C'. He had similar ideas to myself about getting into the CID, and together we discussed our apparent shortcomings. We both came to the conclusion that we were having difficulty in projecting ourselves as 'thief catchers' and decided to have a look round Soho when off duty. We lived there. We knew the area better than most people, and we had nothing to lose, we thought! It was not long before we had some positive useful arrests.

Shortly after our successes, we were sent for by our superiors. As far as we were concerned, we were going to be complimented for our efforts. To our surprise however, we were told in the strongest possible terms that we were neither expected or permitted to carry on working when off duty. At first I could not see the justice in this direction, for I had already received a commendation for arresting a wanted burglar whilst off duty. Fortunately, my army experience had taught me that orders were orders and there was generally sound logic in whatever my superior said. We both attempted to analyse what had been said to us. One point emerged quite clearly. Our activities and ambitions had certainly been noted. We decided there and then to restrict our activities in line with the directions given.

In June 1947, having managed to justify my existence in the eyes of my superior by arresting some quite interesting criminals, I applied for consideration to be posted to the Criminal Investigation Department. An officer was not permitted to make this application before completing one year in the service, and that year took a while to pass. I heard nothing official about the application and made discreet enquiries to ascertain what had happened to it. I was quietly informed that my name had been placed on the list of applicants for consideration and that in due time I would be called up for an interview. I contented myself with the albeit unofficial assurance.

I was indeed impatient to get into the CID and to get on with CID work, and quite frankly thought of nothing else whilst going about my various duties. The most fortunate point that I should mention here is that what makes police work so very interesting is its variety. You never truly know what is round the next corner, or what the next person who speaks to you is going to disclose to you, or oblige you to do in the line of your duty. To the young uniformed officer, this is the most important part of his training, for if he cannot cope with those unpredictable incidents as they are thrust upon him, he will never be an efficient police officer.

THE STORY OF OLD JOHN

One incident that I am unlikely to forget from those days occurred when I was on beat duty in Piccadilly, near Green Park. It was August and hot, and I was walking one afternoon with the traditional measured step in the direction of Hyde Park Corner. My thoughts were, in truth, miles away, directed towards the Divisional Detective Inspector, Bob Higgins, and his office, which then held my application for consideration for admission into his department.

Traffic is usually thick in the Piccadilly area during working hours, and this day was no exception. Suddenly I heard a screech of brakes from behind me, coming quite obviously from a number of vehicles. I stopped and looked back. Everything seemed quite normal. Traffic was moving again, although somewhat slow in places. There was no evidence of even a minor accident having taken place. I did notice, however, a strange-looking individual, a man in a dirty white jacket, walking on the other side of the road, away from me. His trousers were tucked into what looked like hooped football socks and he was bouncing a tennis ball in the way that children do, as he walked along. I changed my direction, and walked back towards Piccadilly Circus.

Quite suddenly, and without warning, the man walked into the roadway still bouncing his ball. Then, rolling the ball to the ground, he dribbled it in and among the moving vehicles. He then quickened his pace, and weaved from one side of the road to the other. There was the sudden squeal of brakes again as cars nearly knocked him down, and he was on the other side of the road, back on the pavement once again and bouncing his ball as before.

I quickened my pace along Piccadilly. Then he did exactly the same thing again, bouncing his ball into the traffic amid varied squeals of brakes and shouts from irate drivers. In and out amongst the cars he went again, but unfortunately for him, on this occasion he came to a halt at the gutter on my side of the road. Picking up the ball at the kerbside he rolled it in my direction. I picked up the ball and stood in front of him. If ever there was a cartoon for Punch magazine, this was it. A stern-looking, but very young, policeman standing in front of an old man, probably sixty-five to seventy years of age, who looked every bit like a very naughty schoolboy caught in the act. This strange character was about five feet two inches tall. His head was sunburned and bald. Across the top of his head was a pair of glasses, secured by an elastic band under his chin. Underneath his white jacket he was wearing a very bulky and very dirty white polo-necked sweater. His trousers were riding breeches and he was wearing red and white hooped football socks, tucked into what looked like very large and old army boots. He was also wearing white mittens. As he stood in front of me he seemed somewhat unsteady on his feet, and his breath certainly smelled as if he had had a good fill of liquor of some description. 'You had better move on,' I said, 'and not in the road with this ball.' I waved him on his way. He turned and started to walk off. Walk! Stagger was more like it. This man was very drunk by my estimation, and I felt sure that if I did not arrest him he would cause serious injury to himself or some other innocent person. He had not taken more than two or three steps before he bent down as if he was going to roll the ball that I was still holding into the roadway once more. My mind was made up. I arrested him and took him to West End Central Police Station, where he was charged with being drunk and disorderly.

At Bow Street Magistrates Court the following day, 'Old John', as I will call him, was quite the centre of attraction. His dress was exactly as I have described it, but whereas on the previous day he had little to say for himself, he was now extremely verbose and caused quite an uproar in the normally sedate atmosphere of the court. The case was called at 11 a.m and the hearing was in front of Sir Laurence Dunne, the then Chief Magistrate. Old John simply bounded into court and up the steps into the dock. Then to everyone's surprise, waving a woollen mitten in the air, he shouted, 'I deny it. Absolutely.'

The charge against him had not even been read out to him. 'What?' said Sir Laurence. 'Absolutely,' replied Old John. With some difficulty the Clerk of the Court managed to read out the charge of drunkenness. 'Deliberate lies,' shouted the prisoner, pointing an outstretched and mittened finger towards the dome of the court. Finally, and with some difficulty, he was coaxed to remain quiet as I commenced to give my evidence. Halfway through, however, he suddenly shouted to the magistrate, 'the police are six a penny. I will take this case to the House of Commons.'

Then followed a period of cross-examination of myself, conducted by the prisoner from the dock. I think it was the first time I had ever been subjected to a spirited examination of my evidence, and at the outset I was quite worried. Then as suddenly as the cross-examination had started, he thumped the rail of the dock with his fist and shouted 'Ha! I have a commentary to make. Where is the witness box? Where's the bible?' As he shouted this he bounded out of the dock and round to the witness box. I made way for him.

Picking up the bible, Old John held it aloft and gabbled out the words of the oath written on the card in front of him, in a manner that could not possibly be understood. He was told to read the oath slowly and distinctly by the Clerk of the Court. Giving the Clerk a most withering look, he carried out the instructions in a very loud voice, finishing with words not printed on the card, 'And I mean it too.' The evidence that he gave went along with almost everything that I had said, with one exception. He would not admit that he was drunk. He was, he said, a professional walker and a professional footballer, something that his general appearance truly denied.

Old John was finally called back to the dock. There he was found guilty and fined ten shillings. He left the court in the same flurry that he had arrived in, and although he was often seen in the West End of London dressed in similar attire, he apparently kept away from drink. He was also seen bouncing his ball along the pavement at times, to the amusement of pedestrians and drivers alike. Fortunately, however, he refrained from bouncing it into the roadway.

3
Aide to CID

In October 1947, I was posted to the Criminal Investigation Department on temporary attachment. This was normal practice for every constable after about twelve months in the service. The object was to let junior officers know how the CID operated and what the actual work involved. I received positive instructions, I answered telephone calls, took messages and read reports, most of which I did not truly understand. This may seem to some like a waste of time, both for the officer and the service. There is, however, another side to it. It gives the CID officers some idea of what type of person you are. Certainly, for my part I had the feeling throughout this attachment that I was being very thoroughly examined and assessed.

This was a heaven-sent opportunity for the lazy officer to do just nothing. I decided that I would make sure that those watching me would find that I was not entirely useless and not scared of work. On one occasion I noticed a sergeant typing a report, using the time-honoured 'one finger system'. I felt that here I could at least do something useful. I offered to assist by typing the report for him at his dictation. He at first doubted my ability and to some extent quest-ioned my cheek for even asking if I could assist him; but ultimately agreed to let me assist him. On completion of the report he was clearly very grateful.

That lunch time, whilst the sergeant was taking his meal, I answered the telephone for him. It was from a man in a nearby hotel to say that a man, McClosky, whom I knew from the report that I was typing, the sergeant was looking for, was in a certain hotel near Piccadilly Circus. I no doubt should have told the CID officer nearest me of that call. I did not. I had typed out the report with the sergeant,

I had very thoroughly read the papers on the matter and I had seen photographs of the two men involved. I went to the hotel and arrested McClosky. The sergeant was delighted with my action when he came back from lunch. At the same time, however, he warned me about the misguided enthusiasm of my action, pointing out that by rights I should have told the nearest CID officer and left the matter to him. Fortunately for me, the assistance I had been giving the sergeant in typing his report produced something of a bonus for me. He was sufficiently pleased to mention what I had done, and the assistance that I had given him, in glowing terms to the Divisional Detective Inspector, Bob Higgins. He in turn congratulated me and arranged for my period of attachment with the CID to be extended whilst we completed the case.

McCLOSKY AND DOBSON

The cunning of the villains in this case truly amazed me. The prisoners, John McClosky and Peter Dobson, had been together in prison. Whilst there they had met a woman Prison Visitor and given her the impression that they were reformed characters. Prison Visitors in this context are volunteers, who attend prisons with official blessing, to spend a little time with certain prisoners to discuss domestic matters with them and, where practical, to assist them in their rehabilitation.

On release from prison, having obtained the telephone number and address of this well-meaning lady, McClosky telephoned her to ask if she could come to the Mayfair Hotel and meet a prospective employer. The good lady was eager to assist in any way she could, and they met as arranged. They waited together for some hours until it was quite obvious that the alleged prospective employer was not going to keep the appointment, and parted company. Whilst McClosky was impatiently awaiting the arrival of the supposed employer, Dobson, knowing full well that the coast was clear, broke into the woman's home in West London and stole everything that he could find with a saleable value.

McClosky, having said farewell to the kindly Prison Visitor, made his way to a pre-arranged meeting place to examine the spoils with his partner. The two men then hawked the loot around jewellers and second-hand shops in London's West End.

In another incident the two men went into a church not far from Piccadilly Circus. McClosky entered the church alone and spoke to the verger, saying it was his intention to change his religion for the faith of this particular denomination. The verger was pleased to be able to assist. He led the way to the altar, and together they kneeled and prayed. Whilst this was going on, Dobson was watching from a suitable distance, waiting for the right moment to strike. Once he saw his colleague kneel to pray with the verger, he quietly crept into the church behind the couple, proceeded to roll up the very expensive carpet runner that was laid out in the aisle leading to the altar and walked out with it. When McClosky had finished his prayers with the verger, he shook hands with him and left. The verger did not even notice that the carpet was missing from its place in the aisle. This was the first criminal case that I ever became heavily involved in. Having arrested McClosky, the next step was to arrest Dobson and recover some of the property. To this end, observation at the hotel in Piccadilly paid off. I arrested him as he came into the foyer, and the surprise of his arrest was such that to my amazement he immediately decided to tell all, even to informing us where they had disposed of their loot. The result was that we recovered much of the stolen property very soon after it had been sold to the unfortunate receivers.

I later gave evidence in this matter at Bow Street Magistrates Court and subsequently at the Central Criminal Court, the Old Bailey.

For me this was a taste of what I truly wanted to do. Moreover, the overall result was very satisfactory. McClosky was sentenced to three years' imprisonment, Dobson to two years, and I received a Commissioners Commendation for the work I had done in the case.

My application to be considered for permanent engagement in the Criminal Investigation Department seemed to die. Or was I just a little too impatient? I found myself involved in all manner of duties that precluded me from arresting criminals: traffic duty; station duty; ordinary uniformed duty; and a short spell in the typing pool of the process section, typing summonses. Someone had obviously got word that I could use a typewriter, but I did not join the police to be a typist. Then, quite out of the blue, I was sent for by Bob Higgins. After a short interview, Bert McGowan and I were posted to the Criminal Investigation Department as Aides to CID. At last I had one foot on the ladder.

Work as CID Aide in those days was a very strange in-between situation, at times most frustrating. You were a uniformed officer on loan to the CID in plain clothes, to assist them to catch thieves. Your future rested almost entirely upon results produced and your professional demeanour. The result was that you worked as hard as possible, with little or no care about how many hours you put in. In the back of your mind during this time was the fervent hope that you would be accepted by your new-found colleagues, who had considerably more service, and in due time become fully taken into the department. You still kept your divisional number, which was displayed on the uniform now locked away, a number that you were obliged to quote when giving evidence and also to place beside your signature on statements and other official documents.

Our duty was to catch thieves and lawbreakers, but not to carry out investigations or type reports. It was a matter of arresting a prisoner, bringing him into the station and satisfying the duty CID officer that you had the necessary evidence to justify the charge. The person was then charged and you wrote out your statement of evidence which you handed to the duty CID officer. Having completed all the formalities, you were expected to leave the station immediately and continue your search for other criminals.

I was posted to duty with an old hand named Ron Peters. Ron had been an Aide for many years. He was one of a small band of time-serving Aides, retained in the service to guide, instruct and even dispose of those seeking preferment to the Department. He knew the West End of London inside out and seemed to know everyone, villains, businessmen and just plain passers-by. From him I learned a great deal about the activities of the criminal fraternity who were operating in what Londoners refer to as the Square Mile. I had not been working long with Ron Peters, when we were walking through Shepherds Market in Mayfair one afternoon. There he spotted a man leaving the doorway of Gino's restaurant. Ron suddenly shouted, 'Hey you, stop! Police!' The man was gone, running as if the very devil was chasing him. 'Go and get him, John, I want to talk to him,' he said. I was very fit in those days and took off after the disappearing figure. I had no idea what this man had done, but my training to obey the last order given was still very much in my make-up. From Shepherds Market he turned into Curzon Street, over Park Lane and into Hyde Park and then into Knightsbridge.

I was fit, but so was this unknown character. I was not gaining ground. Every time that I thought I had gained a few yards, he would cross the road, cutting through the traffic, and we were back to being almost the same distance apart once again. We turned into Brompton Road, where he seemed to slow down, and no doubt so did I, for I was almost exhausted. I caught up with him outside Brompton Oratory after a run of about a mile and a half. We were both puffed out, to say the least, and I for one was extremely glad that he gave me no trouble.

We both walked back to Shepherds Market. There I found Ron Peters leaning up against the wall where I had left him. He was puffing away at a cigarette and talking to Jock MacHattie, the proprietor of a nearby antique shop. 'Where the hell have you been?' exclaimed Ron. I did not answer this question, I might have lost my temper and I don't do that very often. He said no more, and we just went off to West End Central Police Station with our man. There I discovered that he was wanted in a number of divisions and districts for housebreaking and burglary. All news to me, but Ron Peters knew from the fleeting glance he had of the man in Shepherds Market.

Before long Ron Peters took on another Aide to CID to instruct and assess. As a result I was permitted to work together with my friend Bert McGowan. Our principal operation was arresting people stealing from motor cars or buildings in the area. We also stopped many suspects under the provisions of Section 66 of the Metropolitan Police Act, which resulted in arresting a number of persons wanted for different offences.

ASSAULTED IN SOHO

One such 'Stop' very nearly ended my career. It was on 19th October 1948 when Bert McGowan and I were patrolling Soho. We rarely walked together, for in those days we were expected to be smartly turned out, even as Aides, and two large, well dressed, or perhaps I should say, large, smart men together in Soho could only be police officers.

Bert McGowan and I were patrolling in our usual manner, on opposite sides of the road, well aware that if we walked together we had little chance of success. We were keeping an eye on each other and passers-by. As we walked along Old Compton Street, I took it upon myself to stop a man who was walking towards me. As was the usual first step in those days, I told him that I was a police officer and asked him to produce his National Registration Identity Card, which everyone in those days was expected to carry. He produced the document without comment or argument. McGowan, seeing me stop the man, crossed the road and stood by. The Identity Card had a number on it which indicated that the holder had been in one of the services. This man looked as if he could have been a soldier and was not the slightest bit concerned about being stopped.

All the same, I was not happy with him. Don't ask me why. Just a feeling, call it what you will. I said to him, 'So you were in the army?' 'Yes,' he replied. 'The Artillery?' I asked. 'Yes, that's right,' he replied. I was now quite sure that the man was lying. Making a point of examining the identity card a little closer, I said, 'Looks like the 19th Field Regiment to me,' fixing him straight in the eye. 'Cor,' he said, 'that's right. How the hell did you know that?' I was now convinced that the identity card was stolen, for I knew that this man had never been in my old regiment. 'I think you had better come along with us,' I said.

I got no further. My would-be prisoner struck McGowan on the chin and knocked him down. That of itself was something of a feat, for Bert McGowan was an ex-commando and by normal standards quite a hard man. As I went to grab the man he gave me a violent push in the chest which lifted me off my feet. I careered backwards to be struck by the radiator of a passing motor car. Very fortunately for me, the driver was alert. He stopped almost immediately, whilst I scrabbled at the front of the vehicle, struggling to keep it away from me in my attempts to prevent being run over. My new suit was torn, and my hand was bleeding. I was absolutely hopping mad at having been caught so easily unawares.

Whilst McGowan and I were re-orientating ourselves, our quarry had made off across a bombed site. I saw him take a fence in a single leap: there was no doubt about it, but our suspect was a very fit and strong young man.

I took off after him. I was very fit myself in those days and could have caught up with him very quickly. Experience, however, had taught me, both in my younger years at school and whilst in the army, always to assess the opposition before taking action. As my temper simmered down, I found myself loping after this character and in my mind attempting to work out just what sort of individual I had got mixed up with. I could run better than most young men. I was fairly strong. I could box quite well, but I could never have knocked Bert McGowan down in the fashion I had just witnessed, let alone push away a man my size in the manner I had just personally experienced. My mind was made up. I was going to run this man into the ground. The less wind he had in him when I decided to get level with him the better.

We were running in Wardour Street, he turned left into Darblay Street, right into Poland Street and then left into Great Marlborough Street. He was slowing down, which pleased me. Perhaps he was not as fit as I thought. Then, as he turned into Argyle Street, he stopped suddenly, turned and shaped up to fight. At this point I became very worried. My left hand was bleeding profusely and I had very little feeling in it. I found myself hoping that it was only cut from hitting the radiator of the car in Old Compton Street.

There was no sign of Bert McGowan, so I decided to spar round this man to keep him in Argyle Street, praying silently that Bert would show up any minute. My state of mind was undoubtedly read by the opposition and he took a flying kick at me. That was his big mistake. I caught his foot and lifted him high in the air. As he crashed down on his back, Bert McGowan came puffing round the corner, and I was very, very, glad to see him!

Our prisoner was soon subdued, and we took him to West End Central Police Station. There it transpired that the National Registration Identity Card had been stolen during a burglary and that our prisoner was Thomas Tantony, an escapee from a Borstal Institution. At the Central Criminal Court some weeks later, he was sentenced to two years' imprisonment for housebreaking and assault on myself and Bert McGowan.

My greatest concern in this case came after Tantony had been charged. I had paid £28, a great deal of money in those days, for a suit to keep up with the expected dress. I was wearing that suit when I was struck by the passing motor car in Old Compton Street, and the result was that the right shoulder was badly torn. I had it invisibly mended, but it took me some while before I could convince the powers that be that the damage had been caused in the strict course of duty and get them to pay for the repair. This may sound rather penny pinching, but that repair cost more than two weeks' wages in those days and considerably more than a couple of months' plain clothes allowance. My army demobilisation pay was all that I had in the bank, and I was already digging well into that to keep up with the required standard of appearance.

4
Detective Constable

Our successes thus far had been sufficient to recommend Bert McGowan and myself to appear before a selection board for interview and consideration for appointment to the Criminal Investigation Department. In the event I had to undergo two interviews, but happily I was successful in both and as a result was posted to Gerald Road Police Station, then 'B' Division, covering Belgravia, as from 17th January 1949 as the junior member of the CID staff.

There I found myself working under Detective Inspector 'Nosher' Hearn and Detective Sergeant Charlie Case among others. The Detective Inspector had earned the nickname 'Nosher' from his expertise in the boxing ring and his ability to arrest the most violent criminal without difficulty. As for Charlie Case, he had the reputation of being able to sense a criminal in a most uncanny manner.

I had much to get through, but I was extremely happy in the knowledge that I could learn a lot from these tried and tested experts. Now it was no longer a matter of going out and catching thieves in the street. I now had to record allegations of crime reported at the station and follow the matter through by investigation to a satisfactory conclusion. I also had to receive from the Aides to CID the prisoners they brought in to the station, and process them. Life was full of surprises, and changes, but I knew that I would soon adapt myself to this totally new existence.

After a few months at Gerald Road Police Station, I was quite suddenly posted to New Scotland Yard, Central Office, on 20th May 1949. I could not work out what had brought about this unusual and no doubt highly interesting posting. George Hatherill was the

'Superintendent Central', a very important post, in fact the very nerve centre of the famous Yard Murder Squad. He was a large impressive man who chain smoked and gave the impression when he spoke to you that he knew the answer to every question he put to you, long before he actually spoke. He was in charge of a group of superintendents, many of whom were legendary names in those days; Bob Fabian, Jack Capstick, better known in the underworld as 'Charlie Artful', and Jock Black, to name but a few. These officers for the most part were sent out to provincial and colonial police forces to assist in the investigation of complicated murders and other serious offences. Also within the Central Office, C1 Department, were groups of officers or squads, dealing with drugs, currency, customs and fraud. In addition we were then in the process of setting up an office which was to be the forerunner of Interpol.

Quite a responsibility. These officers, specialists as they may have been, had other important tasks that they were called upon to carry out with little or no warning from time to time. The Scotland Yard Murder Squad Superintendents were quite legendary in their efficiency in producing results. The unsung heroes, however, were more often than not the band of officers who were on what became fondly known as 'the London End'. These were officers, usually from a particular Superintendent's squad, who carried out painstaking and sometimes most boring enquiries in the London area on behalf of their boss, who was engaged either in the provinces or somewhere in the colonies. These enquiries often seemed quite pointless, but irrespective of this, no time or effort was ever spared to find the answer.

My ability to write shorthand had been noted, Hatherill said, and the Divisional Office of C1 needed a shorthand writer. I was not too keen on this, but I had to keep my tongue between my teeth. I took my shorthand and typed my reports for about three weeks. I was good at it and enjoyed my work, but found myself becoming extremely disenchanted with the thought that I looked like being an office-boy-cum-shorthand typist for a number of years. A number of years? Goodness knows how many before I gained promotion. Then my thoughts went to the point of whether one could in fact qualify for promotion as a detective after being the holder of such a mundane job. Even on promotion, I had been told, I could be retained in this very important, but to my mind, hole-in-the-corner job. Job satisfaction was in those days a cliché that I had heard bandied around, but had never given much thought to. Now I was getting job dissatisfaction. I did not like it and I had to say something to someone, but who?

George Hatherill was not the sort of man one would want to upset. He had a personality which to his junior officers seemed to smoulder. I found myself once again weighing up the opposition. I came to the conclusion that he was not a bad-tempered man despite the fact that he looked as if he could explode any minute. I had to find the right moment to speak to him.

On the next occasion when I had completed his dictation, he definitely seemed approachable. I told him very carefully indeed that I was more interested in investigating crime than being a clerk-cum-shorthand typist. He sat silently looking at me, his face quite expressionless. I waited for what seemed an age, literally quaking at the knees. Then he smiled. That of itself was rare and probably scared me as much as his silence. 'If you want to be a detective, you shall have your chance. See me in the morning,' he said. With that he turned to the papers on his desk and waved me out of his office.

The next morning, I arrived at the office to find the sergeant, Bill Tennant, sitting at my desk. 'I don't know what you have been up to,' he said. 'All I know is that you have got to report to Bob Fabian and take your gear with you.' I passed no comment further than to say, 'OK,' and left the office.

As I walked along the corridor to Mr Fabian's office, I was very happy indeed. This was indeed a very famous detective. He was, in fact, a man whom my father had worked with as a young man. I knocked and entered his office. 'Morning, young man,' he said, putting out his right hand to shake mine. Fortunately for me I had heard about the strength of Bob Fabian's right hand, and how he loved to crunch the hand of a new member of his team, irrespective of rank. I also knew the counter-move to this action. I pressed the centre finger of my right hand against the centre of his wrist. 'Cunning monkey,' he said. 'Did your old man teach you that one?' I said nothing.

My new boss was indeed famous. He had an outgoing personality, and was able quite easily to mix with lords and villains. He was a great talker and had the ability to make all in his company either laugh or go silently into deep thought on the subject under discussion. As an

Investigator he was without doubt one of the best. I used the word famous, because by the time in question, 1949, he had solved a number of quite startling and unusual murders. These cases had been seized upon and publicised by the press, who had dubbed him 'Fabian of the Yard'.

I felt that at least now I could look forward to becoming involved in some interesting investigations. My shorthand knowledge, however, had become well-known, far better known than I ever would have appreciated. Not that I was all that much of an expert, but very few CID officers possessed that knowledge. It was therefore something that senior officers often required to use, and they lost no time calling upon me to assist them in some most unusual cases.

SITTING IT OUT WITH CLAUDE BAKER

Such a situation arose shortly after I joined Bob Fabian's team. A very wily old detective, Chief Inspector Claude Baker, sent for me. Having enquired how my shorthand was, he threw a cushion to me. 'Hang on to that, you're going to need it,' he said. At the same time he was rummaging around in his desk drawer. He came up with a doctor's head lamp, the type that has a strap to go round the head, an adjustable light in the centre of the forehead and a wire to a battery that you put in your pocket. 'You will like this one,' he said. 'Get yourself a new notebook and a supply of pencils, and be back here in ten minutes.' I hurried out of his office, somewhat excited, but trying hard to work out just what he was up to.

Having gathered up the necessary stationery, I returned to Claude Baker's office. As I walked in he stood up and reached for his hat. 'OK?,' he said. 'Yes,' I replied. He said no more, handed me his briefcase and walked out of the office. I followed. I had no idea where we were going or what we were going to do. Clearly my boss had a lot on his mind, and I had no intention of disturbing that train of thought. We walked into Whitehall, round Parliament Square and into Victoria Street. Mr Baker still said nothing. In Victoria Street we entered a block of offices and went straight to the Chairman's office. We were made very comfortable and sat listening to the Chairman as he unfolded his story. This was a very large company of civil engineers who deal in contracts coming to millions of pounds.

In this instance, a man purporting to be a King's Messenger, who quite positively knew that a contract was out for tender to a number of concerns, had approached this company with an offer that would ensure that they obtained the contract. The contract entailed extending the arm of a particular Far Eastern harbour by about a mile. This company could do the work and had the necessary stone-crushing equipment. The Chairman went on to detail how it would be necessary to mount the stone crusher on the harbour arm, excavate rock from the sea bed, crush it, turn it into concrete blocks, then drop the blocks back into the sea and slowly move on until the job was completed.

All of this was a little over my head. The crunch came, however, when the chairman said that the alleged King's Messenger, had assured him that he could secure the contract for his firm for ten percent of the estimated profit. This as you can well appreciate could have come to a few million pounds. At this stage, the Chairman looked at his watch and said that the man would be arriving at his office in a few minutes.

Looking at me, Claude Baker said, 'This is where you earn your wages.' He got up from his chair and took me over to a cupboard in the corner of the Chairman's office. Here I took the cushion out of my briefcase, now realising why he had given it to me a short while earlier. Mr Baker laughed. 'You've got the idea, John. You will have to sit on that box and take down everything that is said between the Chairman here and this King's Messenger chap. Everything, my lad, and don't miss anything out. You should be able to hear alright.'

I sat in the cupboard, with the lamp round my head, and was able to hear a test conversation in the office. The suspect duly arrived a few minutes afterwards, and I proceeded to scribble away. Through a tiny hole in the cupboard door I could roughly see a most impressive man of military type, with a moustache that he was obviously proud of, fingering it now and again. The conversation that followed was quite short and very much to the point, and the demand was exactly as outlined by the Chairman.

At the end of the conversation, the visitor stood up, shook hands with the Chairman and left the office. As he left, the Chairman came over to my hiding place, opened the cupboard and intimated that I might be required outside his office.

I am sure you will have noted that I have been careful not to mention names in this case, although those concerned will probably know exactly what I am talking about. We arrested the man as he left the Chairman's office. He was not a King's Messenger. He was a retired army officer and later appeared at the Central Criminal Court, was found guilty and sentenced. The company concerned did obtain the contract, but entirely as the result of their own actions and ability. The principals offering the contract would have known nothing about this incident until well after the conclusion of the case in court, for there was no publicity whatsoever released on this matter.

This was a most unusual case which I often thought about as I proceeded through the service. We had no advanced equipment in those days, and my main worry whilst at the Central Criminal Court was whether my shorthand would be put to the traditional test in the witness box. That test, feared by many very experienced shorthand writers, was having to take down the leading article in The Times newspaper at about one hundred and forty words a minute. It was not so much the speed; but the witness box is a lonely place, with the psychological effect of being closely watched by the judge a few yards away; the jury, all twelve of them probably going through a new experience; and the public gallery, people who had just come along out of curiosity, looking on. On top of all that there are the many court officials present. This was the first time that I had to give evidence on shorthand notes I had taken, but fortunately I was never questioned about those notes.

As a Detective Constable in Central Office at New Scotland Yard, one tended to become nothing more than a bag carrier and statement taker. The work, however, was extremely interesting, but unfortunately, as a young man the Detective Constable rarely had the opportunity to see a job through from start to finish. Many senior officers were away in provincial towns investigating murders and other serious offences. Those enquiries generally had a London connection, which had to be investigated. Much time was therefore spent on those 'London End' enquiries that I mentioned earlier.

The point that most impressed me at the Yard was that every individual enquiry was carried out with patience and thoroughness to the extreme. As a young man you generally knew the officer for whom you were carrying out the enquiry. On many occasions that officer was out of town, but would be returning to the Yard in the near future. It is not surprising therefore that I and my fellow constables in the Detective Constables office, often referred to as the 'Snake Pit', felt honoured to be involved and trusted to do the bidding of our superiors.

In so many cases in those days, the officer concerned had been called in by a particular provincial police force to assist them. Those forces during the period that I am talking about were very much undermanned. Few had had an increase in establishment for a number of years. They were therefore grateful to be able to turn over the particular enquiry to an experienced officer from New Scotland Yard. This of course, was another very important reason why 'London End' enquiries were carried out so methodically. We could under no circumstances lay ourselves open to accusations of inefficiency from anyone, for the good name of the Yard meant a great deal to us as well.

In those early days, our office used to house some dozen or so other offices. We were each posted to a squad, under a Detective Chief Inspector. Discipline was strict, but quite frankly that did not worry any of us, for we had all been in one or other of the armed services.

Detective Inspector Harry Stuttard was one of the senior officers on my squad. He was the one man whom I particularly enjoyed working with. His knowledge of the London underworld and in particular of the East End of London, where I was born, fascinated me.

I think what drew us together at the outset was the fact that we were sufferers in sympathy. We both had serious sinus trouble. Harry Stuttard's was, however, far more serious than mine. There was also the incident of the first report that I put in when posted to a squad from the divisional office. I knew that this first report from the new boy would be closely scrutinised. I therefore checked and double-checked it before putting it in to the duty inspector, one George Chesney. I even gave it first to my colleague Ken White to cast his experienced eye over, before daring to put it forward. He was satisfied, so was I.

Notwithstanding such care, I was very much aware of the extremely high quality demanded of reporting in this particular department. I therefore entered the Inspectors' office a little humbly, hoping in my heart that this my first report would pass muster. There were four inspectors in this office. All looked up at me, the new boy, as I walked in. I was aware of their very close scrutiny of me, but that did not worry me.

I handed my report to Mr Chesney. He placed it on his desk and read it. I say, read it. Glanced at it would have been nearer the mark. Picking up a blue pencil with something of a flourish, he drew a diagonal line, from the bottom left corner to the top right of my report and handed it to me. 'You'll have to do better than that,' he said and waved me out of his office. My heart dropped. I took the report and returned to my desk in the Snake Pit.

Ken White was sitting at the desk next to me. I gave him the report and said, 'So much for your advice.' He read the report and was quite convinced that there was nothing wrong with it. He also rather surprised me with the extent of his annoyance that the report which he had examined and agreed with, had been rejected. He further surprised me by calling over some of the lads in the office and asking them to cast their eyes over it. No fault could be found or suggested. I re-typed the report, moving a couple of words around so that I could at least put my hand on my heart and say that I had done as directed.

Once again I went to the Inspectors office and handed over my report. Mr Chesney looked at it again, then looked at me. Then once again picking up his blue pencil, he drew a line across the report as before. Having done this, he looked up at me with quite a menacing scowl and remarked that I had better learn how to put a report together if I wanted to remain in the Criminal Investigation Department.

I left the Inspectors' office once more, this time wondering what on earth I could do next. I can't say that I felt actually downhearted, as on the previous occasion. In fact, if anything, I felt bloody rebellious. I was, in my mind, clearly the victim of injustice, something that I must sort out, but how? By the time I returned to my office I had resolved on one further attempt. I said nothing to my colleagues, but re-typed the report to make it absolutely identical, to the last dot and comma, to the latest one that Chesney had rejected. I then made my way back to his office to see what he had to say about this effort.

As I mentioned earlier, there were four desks in the Inspectors' office. All had been occupied throughout this particular series of incidents. On my next entry to this sanctum, I was determined to learn what exactly was wrong with my report. As I walked over to Inspector Chesney's desk, Inspector Stuttard called me over to him. 'Is that the same report?' he asked. 'Yes,' I replied. 'Let me see it,' he said, stretching out his hand. I handed him the report. He read it and signed it. Then as he handed it back to me, he indicated George Chesney and said, 'Don't ever take your reports back to that man again. I want to see them.'

I was somewhat shocked. I had always believed that the senior officers would stick together on a point of order such as whether a report was correct or not. It was a month or more, however, before I learned what was really behind this matter. On one of my trips home, my father, always interested in how I was getting on in the service, put his usual question to me. 'How are you getting on, boy?' I told him that I was enjoying my apprenticeship as a detective. Then the incident with George Chesney came to mind. I told him exactly what happened. His reply surprised me. He had worked with Chesney many years before. He did not like working with him and told him so. He would not tell me the reason, but he never did work with him again. Whose fault it was, he would not say. One thing he did say, however, was, never nurse a grudge. Disagree with whom you like, if you are right, or believe that you are right. But if you are wrong, admit it and then forget it. The evil of nursing a grudge causes more unhappiness than you will ever know. I got the message. Working with Inspector Stuttard brought home to me how very important it was to have what is referred to as 'local knowledge'. Harry Stuttard seemed to be able to pick up the telephone and speak to a trusted contact in almost every part of London. In my case, the only such knowledge I possessed was in relation to the small part of the East End of London where I had been brought up, and the 'square mile' of Soho and Mayfair. That square mile is divided into two very separate and distinct parts: Mayfair, bounded by Park Lane to the west; Oxford Street to the north; Regent Street to the east; and Piccadilly to the south. Soho is bounded by Regent Street to the west; Oxford Street to the north; and Charing Cross Road, to the east; with Cranbourne Street which runs on the southern edge from Piccadilly to Charing Cross Road.

The two areas are as different as the proverbial chalk and cheese. In Mayfair there are for the most part respectable businesses, clubs and restaurants; whilst Soho, which also does have respectable business houses and restaurants, in addition has a veritable hotchpotch of sleazy clubs, clip joints and other businesses which can only be described as shady. You will therefore appreciate that it was Soho that I was interested in and to Soho, where I had learned my first lessons as a constable in uniform and aide to CID, that I paid particular attention.

I had built up a chain of clubs and public houses in Soho where I knew I could pick up snippets of useful information. These were for the most part places used by criminals, where I knew the licensee or club owner, with whom I had built up a feeling of mutual respect. Knowledge of the opposition is always important in business, but it is even more important for a detective. A good detective does not glean the knowledge he requires by reading books, sitting in the office waiting for the telephone to ring or calling on the more respectable establishments. He has to go to ground to some extent and study the opposition, ever conscious of the fact that he is above all a law enforcement officer!

TROUBLE IN THE MIRANDA CLUB

In the latter part of October 1950 the dangers inherent in my habit of occasionally going to ground to seek information were brought home to me. I had just completed a tiring day in London's West End, on a time-consuming and comparatively uninteresting observation. It was 8 p.m. and I had booked off duty by telephone. I fancied a glass of beer before going home and made my way to the nearby Miranda Club, in Greek Court, at the end of Old Compton Street. The club was run by 'Sandy', a retired Detective Sergeant with whom I had built up a mutual respect. I had a glass of beer, and we chatted away.

Our conversation was interrupted by the arrival of Johnny Black and a number of his 'heavies', in plain terms, gangsters who thrived on the racecourse protection rackets. Black I knew by sight, but his henchmen were new to me and a very ugly bunch they were. Walking over to me, in an obvious attempt to show off in front of his men, Black said to me in a quite loud voice, 'You had better buy the guvnor a drink.' I knew exactly what he was up to.

This was his ploy to get a local detective to buy him a drink in front of his men, to prove to them how well he was in with the police. Turning to 'Sandy' I said to him, 'Would you like another?' This was not quite what Black expected and he was most annoyed. 'For your information,' he said, 'I am the guvnor, and the boys would like a drink as well,' indicating the very motley throng that had come into the club with him. 'Sandy' silently indicated that I had better leave and started filling up glasses for the gang. Then whilst Black's back was turned, I made my way out of the club. I fully realised that whatever Black was up to, and whatever he had in mind, it was not going to be very healthy for me to stay.

On my journey home that night, my mind was in something of a turmoil. I had to report what had taken place to my superiors, but if I did, I would have to explain what I was doing in a drinking club used by criminals. Explaining my quest for knowledge of criminals would hardly be accepted from one so junior, but I had to do something. My journey home seemed to take far longer than usual. With those troubled thoughts still on my mind, it took me some while before I fell asleep.

The following morning I was up with the lark. I had made up my mind during those sleeping hours exactly what I had to do. On arrival at the yard I made straight for Inspector Stuttard's office and told him what had taken place the previous night. His response was immediate. 'That's good. I'm glad you told me lad, we can use a lot of this to our advantage, but you were very lucky not to have got yourself a right hiding with that mob.'

I accepted the last remark, but on the rest of his statement he had me guessing. 'To our advantage?' I said. 'I don't get it.' The inspector's reply came straight back at me. 'To our advantage, and to the advantage of the service, and that's damned important. If we let monkeys like Black and his mob get away with this type of stunt, the country would soon be run by them. They have got to be taught a lesson.'

I still could not see what use he could make of an incident that I was not a little ashamed of. Harry Stuttard waved me to take a seat by his desk and picked up the telephone. He dialled a number, and when it was answered, said that he wanted to contact Mary. He wrote down a number on his blotter, and dialled that number. 'Mary', he said, 'give me George's number.' He dialled George, spoke to him, and asked for Charlie's telephone number. He made seven calls in all. At the last call, the somewhat benign attitude that he seemed generally to use on the telephone changed completely. 'Johnny,' he said. 'Stuttard here. We've got to talk. I will see you outside Fanum House up at Leicester Square at six o'clock tonight, and you had better be there.' He did not wait for an answer, but slammed the telephone down. Turning to me he said, 'You and I have a meet tonight. See you at half past five.' With that he waved me out of the office.

Fanum House is about fifteen minutes' walk from New Scotland Yard. I went to the inspectors' office at 5.30 p.m. 'Plenty of time, boy,' he said. Then looking at his watch he said, 'We'll leave here at about 6.15 p.m.'

When I reported back to Mr Stuttard's office he leisurely put on his bowler hat, his coat, picked up his umbrella and we left the Yard. We sauntered up Whitehall, apparently with all the time in the world. This worried me, for I had been brought up to being prompt in everything. As for keeping a person waiting at an appointed time and place, this was unheard of by my standards. However, there seemed to be no urgency whatsoever about our journey, and I was beginning to wonder whether the meeting that I thought had been arranged earlier had been called off.

It was ten minutes to seven when we arrived at Fanum House, and Johnny Black was waiting there. Walking straight past him Mr Stuttard said in a loud voice, 'Follow me.' Turning into Whitcombe Street, we walked into the saloon bar of the Globe public house. This to me did not seem quite right. This was a public house used generally by the better class of business people in the area. On this occasion, however, it was crowded with many criminals whom I knew by sight, and a lot whom I did not know, but felt that I should. There were of course also a number of businessmen, many of whom I did know.

The next move was even more surprising. Springing on to a table, the inspector banged his umbrella down a couple of times to call for silence. He then announced in a loud voice, 'This rascal here,' indicating Johnny Black, 'has done his best to take the piss out of young John here,' indicating me, 'one of my lads. This was a very silly thing to do, and he is now very sorry. He is now going to buy everyone here a drink, for as long as you like to stay.' Then, hopping down from the table he went over to the bar, tapped his umbrella on the counter a couple of times and said, 'Mine's a large Scotch to start with.'

We remained in the Globe for about two hours before leaving, but I made good use of that time. I logged the faces of many suspected criminals as I met them that evening, for future reference. I was amazed myself how these villains were taking this whole matter. What I found most surprising was that, whereas they were between them into almost every crime in the book, the unwritten law amongst them was that you don't aggravate the police just for the hell of it.

Furthermore, the general feeling amongst these 'guests' was that had I stayed in the club that night, I would without doubt have been seriously assaulted, and that was not on under any circumstances. When I look back at it now, over forty years on, I have to admit that there was in those days some honour amongst thieves. Something that I doubt exists to the same extent today.

On my way home that night, although I had had a very interesting and enjoyable evening, I had to admit to myself that I could not see Black standing for that show-down. My thoughts were trying to work out what monkey business Master Black would get up to next.

Following my first embarrassing meeting with him and the confrontation worked up by Harry Stuttard in the Globe public house, I decided to keep my eye on his activities. But Johnny Black was never involved in further crime and became quite a successful businessman. In fact when I last saw him, about ten years ago, we had a very interesting chat about our respective vocations. He had been successful in his, but what really surprised me was the fact that he attributed his success to the day when he was, as he put it, 'cut down to size by Harry Stuttard, after our little upset in the Miranda Club'.

5
Liaison with the US Navy

My quest for knowledge of the activities of villains very often led me back to the West End of London. It was on such a trip into Mayfair that I decided to call in on the Manhattan Club, in Woodstock Street, just off Oxford Street. This was a drinking club, which I had heard was a cut above the average Soho club and was being used by some very interesting Soho characters. I say Soho characters because they were undoubtedly, as I saw it then, attempting to climb up their strange twisted social ladder by coming over Regent Street from Soho into Mayfair. The Manhattan Club was therefore one which I felt I should know more about. The owner, Jimmy Valentine, was known to me by sight and reputation, and was a cut above many similar people in his profession.

It was late in 1951. I was in the area, at something of a loose end, for the informant whom I was to have met at Oxford Circus had telephoned the office to say that he could not keep the meet as arranged. I therefore decided to pay the Manhattan club a visit, purely to expand my knowledge on exactly who was now using this watering hole. As I walked down the iron steps leading to the basement club I could hear a band playing rather loudly. Inside the small and rather narrow premises I was surprised to find it so well appointed and with an extremely pleasant atmosphere.

I knew quite a few of the people at the bar, and felt that by the time I had taken four or five steps into the club, everyone present would know that I was a police officer. At the far end of the bar, Jimmy Valentine was talking to a man whom I felt I ought to know, but did not. He was about 6 foot 2 inches tall and built like an all-in wrestler. My immediate thought was that he was a new West End 'heavy'. He interested me.

I walked over to Jimmy Valentine to introduce myself. To my surprise he seemed genuinely pleased to see me and welcomed me almost as an old friend. Turning to the big fellow he had been talking to, he said 'Meet John Swain, Tom. He used to be on the 'Manor', (indicating that I used to be stationed locally, in the West End of London), 'Now he's up at the Yard.' Turning to me, he said 'John, meet Tom Duval. He's in the American Navy. You've probably got something in common.' With that Jimmy Valentine turned and got into conversation with other people at the bar.

Tom Duval and I had quite a chat, which went on until well after the club closed. He was with the American navy and worked at their London headquarters in North Audley Street off Grosvenor Square. He was interested in my work and expressed a desire to visit Scotland Yard. On his side he assured me that he was involved in very mundane work of an administrative nature, yet unusually was equally anxious to assure me that he could probably assist me in my work. Despite my first feelings about Tom Duval, I found myself warming towards him, for my feeling was that here I had discovered someone who could very well be useful to me in my work.

Tom and I met on many occasions after that first meeting in the Manhattan Club. He visited the Yard quite regularly, and I visited his office on a number of occasions, where I was introduced to his chief, Commander Dave Reid. Dave Reid, in turn, had been a Sheriff in New Hampshire in the United States.

On one of my visits to North Audley Street I was drawn into a discussion about a very large shortfall that had appeared in the PX stock check. (PX items are the duty-free goods that serving members of the American Forces are able to purchase through their canteens.) My enquiries into their method of checking, however, revealed that in fact very little checking was done. The PX stores, probably best referred to as comforts for the troops, were shipped in from the United States to Southampton, where a large articulated American truck, referred to as a 'Sami', picked up the shipment and transported it to an American depot or vehicle park, situated on a bombed site which had been a static water tank during the war. This was located in Baker Street, and on arrival there the vehicle and contents were guarded by American marines until delivered to the North Audley Street headquarters the following day.

The empty truck was driven to Southampton, a distance of about

Liaison with the US Navy

eighty miles, by an English driver accompanied by an armed American Marine guard. The Marine had in his possession an open security padlock that snapped closed. There was no key carried with this padlock, the key being retained at the North Audley Street headquarters. When the truck arrived at the loading point in the docks at Southampton, it was loaded under the very strict supervision of the officer who happened to be Duty Officer at the particular time. On completion of the loading, the Marine handed the officer the padlock. He then secured it to the lock hasp on the back of the truck. The load was thus sealed and checked as correct, the manifest of the contents being passed to the Marine to hand over on his return to London. The truck was then driven to Baker Street vehicle park, where it was expected to arrive at a set time to correspond with the vehicle travelling at an average of twenty miles per hour. The vehicle always arrived dead on time. Everything seemed in order but there were still serious shortfalls when the contents were compared with the manifest.

Different security locks were used. They were marked to see if they had been opened after being secured to the transporting vehicle. The officer supervising the loading at Southampton was rarely the same person twice. The Marine guard differed from day to day, and the English driver was from a pool of drivers who would be directed to whatever assignment arose at a particular time, therefore these drivers should differ from day to day.

Even more worrying was the fact that the PX truck always arrived within the allotted time, taking into consideration its permitted average speed of twenty miles per hour. This permitted average speed caused us not a little concern. Make no mistake about it; to average that speed and pass through various towns on the way to London, then cover something like twenty miles of London itself, that vehicle would have to travel at a much faster speed than twenty miles an hour. Something was wrong, very, very wrong.

At that time, the vehicles used by officers from the Scotland Yard Central Office consisted of two Hillman Minx saloon motor cars, each of about ten horse power. The petrol, drawn from the police garage then at Lambeth, was standard low grade 'two star' petrol. These vehicles were thus rarely good for speeds above fifty miles per hour. As they were used for the most part in London, where there were in those days very few places where the speed limit was over thirty miles per hour, speed was not a consideration.

The route used by the particular PX vehicle was always the same by regulation. Furthermore, it was the duty of the Marine guard to insure that the vehicle stuck to that route, as prescribed at the United States Naval Headquarters in London.

After considering all the facts, and with my fairly comprehensive knowledge of London, I was confident that this was one that I could crack quickly. I booked out a Hillman Minx motor car at 8 p.m. on a particular night when a shipment was due to arrive, and took Tom Duval and Dave Reid with me to the Bayswater Road, which the truck was routed to come along. There was no sign of the truck, so we went off to Baker Street. It had arrived a few minutes beforehand. Tom said nothing. We did not want to alert anyone in the pound to our interest.

The next time the shipment was due, I got my friend and colleague Arnold Goodall, a Detective Sergeant from the Central Office, to come along with us. We went to Staines Bridge over the river Thames, on the outskirts of London, also on the prescribed route, and waited. We had about a half hour to spare, but there was no sign of the vehicle. After about one hour we returned to London, and from the outside of the vehicle pound could see the truck in its rightful place, parked inside the compound. The following day, the check-off of the goods this vehicle had carried proved once again that items were missing.

I now had to go to my boss, Detective Superintendent John Gosling, a huge and amiable man, a true country boy type. He, like myself, loved a challenge away from our normal and sometimes very mundane work. I explained what was happening and introduced him to Tom Duval. He was interested, and we got out the maps. In Hampshire, there was a former Royal Air Force airfield known as Blackbush, on the Southampton Road. We would park our vehicle behind one of the old hangars and await the arrival of the big truck. This was outside the Metropolitan Police district, and authority to operate outside our area of jurisdiction had to be obtained. It was granted, and we got into position on the day of the next PX collection.

At about 10. 30 p.m. the huge truck came thundering along the road. It passed us about one hundred yards off, but was travelling fast. We pulled out from behind the hangar and drove after it. The speedometer climbed to sixty-five miles per hour, and there was no doubt that we had passed the limit of speed that the vehicle felt like travelling. As for the truck, it disappeared from sight and must have been travelling above eighty miles an hour. We made our way to Baker Street. The truck was not there, but whilst we were wondering what could have happened, it arrived, and pulled into its regular parking place in the compound as before.

We had tried, and we had been hoodwinked. In something of desperation, I turned to John Gosling and said, 'I think we have got to hand this one over to the Flying Squad'; they at least had truly fast vehicles with which to do such a job, but I got no further. The guvnor was going a little red in the face. Turning on me he said, 'Not so bloody likely. They, whoever it is that is at it, are not going to take the "Mickey" out of us. That just does not happen to me without a fight.' I was frankly delighted, but knew that I personally could do nothing without the sanction of my chief.

In those days, I had what was known as a combination, motor cycle with a sidecar attached. I removed the sidecar and as a solo motorcyclist parked myself at Staines Bridge. John Gosling and my colleagues, together with Tom Duval and Dave Reid, were parked up by a convenient telephone near Hammersmith, still on the prescribed route. We had no radio link between us. By dint of subterfuge Tom Duval managed to rearrange the rear lighting of the truck to make it more easily recognisable from the rear.

Upon arrival at Staines Bridge, I was well prepared for a long haul. I did not have to wait long. The truck arrived about two hours earlier than the so-called twenty miles an hour, or twenty miles in the hour directed from headquarters, would have allowed. I took off after the vehicle. Within the area of Staines town this presented no difficulty. As it got away from the town, however, its speed grew well over the legally acceptable limit, and I found myself wondering what I would do if it decided to stop suddenly, for I was obliged to keep close to the tail of the truck to avoid being seen.

At Hammersmith the truck made for Shepherds Bush, where it stopped at traffic lights, and to my surprise the Marine got off. The truck went on immediately with the wheels hardly stopping and continued on to the North Circular Road, building up to an almost breakneck speed, which it maintained to Edmonton. There it turned off into a side road, then pulled up outside what in those days was referred to as a 'prefab', one of the prefabricated houses put up after the war as temporary housing.

Fortunately, a telephone box stood within sight of the truck, and I made for it immediately. I called up my associates, gave them my exact location and urged them to get over to me as quickly as possible, bearing in mind their distance from me and the schedule that the driver would obviously attempt to stick to. I then settled down to watch the activities of the driver as he climbed out of the truck and made his way to the rear of the vehicle. In a flash he had mounted the back of the truck and unlocked the prized security lock. He then climbed into the rear of the vehicle, obviously to sort out what items he wanted to remove.

His next move was to run to the prefab door, which was opened by his wife, with his arms full of items he had removed. This went on in a continuous stream and a very fast moving stream at that. I was getting worried. Where were my companions? They had better get there soon! Then just as the driver was about to shut the container doors, they arrived and no doubt my sigh of relief could be heard some way off.

The driver was most surprised at our arrival. Perhaps I should say stunned would be more appropriate. We took the driver to his home, where I doubt whether the mythical Ali Baba's cave could have outdone the contents of the interior of this neat and charming prefab. There was so much property inside that one was left wondering how the occupants ever managed to use it as a dwelling. Police tenders were sent for and the property loaded into them, every item being something from the United States destined for the Grosvenor Square PX stores for the American Forces.

Whilst this was going on, the driver had been searched. In his pocket was the fancy American security lock, still open, and undoubtedly ready to be snapped into place once he had decided that he had taken out everything he wanted. In another pocket he had a lock similar in size, but with the key still in place.

As the story unfolded, the frustration of Tom Duval and his boss was very obvious, for around the tightest plans the simplest of answers had been produced by the opposition.

American marines are smart, very smart in appearance, particularly those posted to North Audley Street. There they performed duty under the eyes of admirals and ambassadors. Their uniforms therefore were immaculate, for they were constantly under inspection.

The driver of the PX truck had done a master job with his homework and sized up the whole situation.

Firstly he had taken certain steps, probably by bribing his superiors or certain of his colleagues in the driving pool, to insure that he always got the long run to Southampton, even when it was not his turn.

His first job on getting to Baker Street, when a Southampton run was scheduled, was to take out a piece of rag and a tin of grease and rub it over the back of the truck around the lock hasp, some eight feet above ground. During the run to Southampton the normal dust and dirt of the road would stick to the grease. Thus on arrival at Southampton, no marine in his smart embassy uniform would want to climb up and hook on the lock. The driver, however, being the perfect gentleman, would volunteer to put the lock on the hasp under his view and that of the officer supervising the loading. What they did not notice was that as the driver climbed up to the hasp he would exchange the lock for his own. He knew that this would never be seen by those watching, for it was always dark by this time; and in fact this move was never noticed.

The homework carried out by the driver did not end there. He had built up an acquaintance with a club owner in Shepherds Bush, and at his say so the marines were more than welcome as good spenders. The escorting marines were therefore dropped off, then after a few drinks they would make their own way to the vicinity of the Baker Street vehicle pound. There they would be picked up by the driver at a pre-arranged time and place, after the driver had allegedly visited his girl friend, who according to him lived in the neighbourhood. The driver's story was apparently always accepted by the marine, who would be picked up by the driver as arranged. The truck would then drive into the compound with its escort, on time. The marine would report to the guard commander and then go off duty. Finally, the driver would clean down the back of his vehicle and complain bitterly to anyone who saw him doing this that the dirt on British roads had to be seen to be believed. They believed him.

The driver was charged with the thefts and dealt with by the courts. The marine was also dealt with, but to what extent I do not know. My friendship with Tom Duval, however, never looked back and even to this day we are in regular contact with each other. Tom now lives in Denver, Colorado, and regularly commutes to Washington DC to work, returning home at weekends.

6
Building a House for Myself

On 15th February 1952 the funeral of King George VI drew massive crowds of people to London from all over the world. It was indeed a sad and solemn occasion, when one could be excused for believing that criminal activity would be at a minimum. The police, however, do not take chances on such occasions and are as vigilant as ever to insure that criminals do not take advantage of the sadness of others to go about their activities.

Detective Constable Roy Yorke, later to retire as a Commander in the Criminal Investigation Department, and I were detailed to patrol the area of Horseguards Parade and the Mall, leading towards Buckingham Palace. This was going to be a boring tour of duty, of that we had no doubt. Three young men, however, who had other things to do than pay their respects to the departed monarch, were unfortunate enough to cross our path. Brian Marchant, David Dunscombe and Michael Phillips were followed for some forty minutes and watched in their attempts to steal from the handbags of women in the crowd who were waiting for the cortège to pass. The three youths were arrested as suspected persons loitering to steal. We took them to Cannon Row Police Station, where it soon became apparent that the trio had come up from Bath in Somerset and that they were suspected of other offences in that area. They duly appeared at Bow Street Magistrates Court and were remanded in custody for fourteen days.

On 5th March 1952 they were handed over to an escort from the Bath Police, and one would have expected that to have been the end of the story. Dunscombe, however, took it upon himself to return to London on 13th August 1953. The 13th, a very unlucky number for some and certainly for David Dunscombe. At that time he had escaped

Building a House for Myself   45

from one of Her Majesty's Borstal Institutions, and unluckily for him he just happened to be walking down Wardour Street towards Piccadilly at a time when I just happened to be walking up Wardour Street from Piccadilly. We met, and I arrested him once again, and he was returned to Borstal. The question left in my mind was, was this fate or was it just plain luck?

Many happenings in life are put down to luck, but when you analyse the circumstances of a particular incident, luck goes out of the window. It matters not, as a police officer, whether you are on or off duty, whether you are obliged to be in a certain place or have gone there for a purely domestic or private reason. The big thing is that you take notice, you see something that links with something you have seen or read about in the past and you are able to fit the person or object you have seen at that time in with an incident or happening in the past.

Back in 1953, Arthur Richard Thurbon was one of the most wanted men in London. His picture in the Police Gazette appeared as regularly as did the pictures of well-known actors of those days in daily newspapers. Thurbon's particular brand of crime was classified as 'housebreaking by artifice', quite a mouthful, but a crime that took quite a special type of person to carry it out. Furthermore, it was a brand of crime that I had never dealt with. This may perhaps account for the fact that I paid particular attention to his name and photograph.

The White Bear public house in Lisle Street, just behind Leicester Square and the London Hippodrome Theatre, was a watering hole where I had picked up a lot of useful information in the course of my West End investigations. It was also a public house run by the son of a very good friend of my father's in those days. His name was Wilf Brennan. Generally when off duty and on a social visit to the area I would drift in and have a pint of beer and a chat with him.

On one such occasion, I called at the White Bear for a beer. This house has quite a large bar, and as I walked in I noticed Thurbon at the bend of the bar, between the two doors. I could see that he immediately recognised me as a police officer, but the recognition went further than that, for his attention was directed not so much at me but towards the two doors leading into the bar. It would seem also that he knew me. To put matters straight, I have to tell you that I have never had difficulty in arresting anyone inside a public house. When this has happened, it has rarely been noticed by anyone else. When on duty, I rarely walked with my partner; we usually took opposite sides of the road. Furthermore, when entering a public house, we never entered together and through the same door. I carried out this procedure throughout my service, and even in those days my practice was well known to criminals in this particular area.

I quietly walked over to Thurbon, whose eyes were fixed on the other door to the bar, and told him that I was going to arrest him. There was no doubt in my mind but that he was waiting for my non-existent partner to enter the bar. I had no partner on this occasion, I was alone, but my prisoner did not know this and I certainly was not going to tell him.

Thurbon was charged with a number of offences of housebreaking and later had a large number of similar offences taken into consideration when he was finally dealt with. At the Central Criminal Court he was sentenced to four years' imprisonment.

The story that unfolded was tragic indeed. It reflected how criminals take advantage of every new situation as it presents itself. This was during a period when houses and other premises damaged by enemy bombing raids during the war were being repaired through the War Damage Commission, a government department formed expressly for that purpose. War Damage Assessors would examine and note the damage and the extent of the repairs necessary, then through the Commission put those repairs into action, following the acceptance of tenders from contractors. Such repairs were paid for by the government.

This was all very well when genuine people were involved. Certain enterprising criminals, however, just could not let this heaven-sent opportunity pass of getting into people's homes with the blessing of the householder. Thurbon was one such person.

He would note a house that had obviously been damaged during an air raid, then watch the occupants. He was looking for mainly the older women living alone or one whose husband was at work all day. His next ploy was to call at the house when the woman was alone, to check in the first instance that the war damage was being attended to. If it was, he would apologise profusely and blame the lack of communication within the office for the mistake.

If he was the first War Damage official to call, he knew that he was 'in business'. He would be truly welcomed into the house, more often than not offered the most comfortable chair, together with a cup of tea or a drink of some sort. After explaining that his job was to inspect and assess the damage and the costs of repairs, he would walk round the interior of the house with the lady and note whatever he thought should be done, together with whatever the anxious occupier might request. His interest, however, was not in the damage, but in what he could steal; also to ensure that he knew his points of exit, just in case he should suddenly require them.

This inspection was, of course, only the build-up. Next came the action. Generally one room upstairs was his first target, followed by one room downstairs. He would go into the upstairs room that he fancied and tap on the wall. Looking a little shocked, he would explain that this wall needed some attention and take the good lady into the adjacent room. There he would hand her a walking stick or other object from within the house and tell her to tap on the wall at a specific place and to keep on tapping until he told her to stop. He would explain that this operation could take about five minutes and he would call out to her when he wanted her to stop. With the occupier tapping on the wall in the next room, he knew exactly where she was. He would then go quickly through the drawers and cupboards, help himself to anything worth stealing and put the articles in his pocket.

The next move was to tell the unfortunate woman that he had noted a fault in the wall, but had found a suspected fault either in the upstairs flooring or the downstairs ceiling. He would take the woman to a point in the upstairs floor, away from the room that he had just ransacked, and explain the suspect area to her. This point would always be out of view of his intended avenue of exit and for that matter away from the room that he now intended stealing from. He would instruct the woman to tap on the floor, as indicated, in the same manner as she had tapped on the upstairs wall for him. With the floor tapping going on, he would go downstairs and help himself to whatever he felt inclined to steal and then make off. Quite often he had left the house ten minutes or so before the occupier realised that she had been duped. On other occasions the occupier did not realise that she had been robbed for some weeks.

I have to admit that I gained considerable satisfaction from this particular arrest. The victims were for the most part elderly women, many of them war widows. This was a particularly heartless enterprise.

In discussing Thurbon's activities, other matters immediately came to mind. During that period after the war, a great number of complaints were received from numerous councils and government departments about fraudulent work carried out by jobbing builders. The War Damage Commission came into its own in respect of these entrepreneurs. Work carried out on the damaged property was inspected by one of their inspectors and not until he was satisfied with the work would payment be authorised.

This was a great innovation on the part of the government. The intentions were genuine and sympathetic to the occupiers of such damaged property. Nevertheless, the procedure did lay itself open to abuse by those who had little previous experience in building and building repairs. The result was that suspected fraudulent claims by the few were passed on to the Yard for the necessary investigation. I say the few, because a great many premises had to be attended to and such claims were, in fact, a small percentage of the total number.

I had become involved in a number of war damage investigations, and as time went by I found myself able, from the complaint of the occupier of the premises, to assess the basis of my investigation. Then, by coupling this with the claim submitted by the builder and the report of the War Damage Commissioner, the probable truth of the matter would emerge. I found that my personal assessment was rarely wrong. I became involved in the prosecution of a number of recalcitrant builders and do not recall losing one case.

During this time I was living in Police Married Quarters at Sydenham, in south-east London, and slowly began to realise that if I remained in this very comfortable residence for the rest of my service, I would find myself, on retirement, obliged to purchase or rent fresh accommodation. My close association with the building business also brought home to me the fact that the price of housing was going up by leaps and bounds each year. My bank balance at that time consisted only of my army demobilisation money and did not amount to more than a couple of hundred pounds. I had to look for accommodation that belonged to me and not to the Commissioner of Police. Above all I wanted a house with a garden similar to the one I had lived in at Norbury before the war, which my parents still occupied.

An idea was born. I had two choices: either I would purchase a war-damaged house and do or organise its repairs myself; or I would build a house myself, somehow. I would need a lot of help from someone whom I could trust, someone with the necessary knowledge, prepared to assist me. I realised that I did know such a person.

Building a House for Myself

Bert McGowan, who had been my partner as an Aide to CID at West End Central Police Station was also living in police married quarters at Beckenham in Kent. I discussed my ideas and desires with him and not surprisingly found that his feelings were very much the same as my own. We decided to look around.

I was friendly with a captain in the local Territorial Army unit stationed at Highwood Barracks, in Lordship Lane, Dulwich. He was the regimental surveyor and a building surveyor by trade. He had given me considerable advice and assistance in some of my building fraud investigations. I mentioned my thoughts and quest to him, more on the lines of 'did he know of a pair of war-damaged houses that Bert and I might buy and do up for ourselves?'

My friend laughed and boldly told me that I was aiming too low. Too low! I could not afford to buy a ready-to-occupy house at the prices that existed in those days; neither, I knew could Bert McGowan. 'George', as I shall call him, was not to be put off. 'Buy a nice piece of land, and build on it', was his reply. This seemed silly to me, for I was never one to remain comfortably in debt to anyone, and I told him so. 'Leave it to me,' was his reply. 'I am sure that I can point you in the right direction.' The matter was left at that. I heard nothing further for some months. Then on one of my visits to Highwood barracks, where I occasionally gave talks to new recruits on the action of the Bofos gun, 'George' came over to me. He said that he had found a plot of land that should interest me. It was in Wrights Road, South Norwood, only a few miles away, and he wanted me to go with him to look at it and consider his ideas on what could be done.

That weekend, Bert McGowan and I travelled with 'George' to Wrights Road. The site was truly a mess. We were not impressed. It consisted of half of the garden of a very large house in Ross Road, a turning off South Norwood Hill. The actual plot itself was about two hundred feet deep and had a frontage that would easily accommodate a pair of semi-detached houses. On the site, however, were two old stables in a most dilapidated state and the wooden fence facing Wrights Road was in a terribly broken-down condition. What on earth could I do there?

I found myself being subjected to the rather strange chuckle that my friend was well known for, a noise that he always seemed to emit when confronted with a difficulty or problem that he could just see through. 'John,' he said, 'the trouble with you is that you are a detective, and I am a surveyor, a building surveyor. I look at a site with a view to either building on it or repairing it, and I do know what is required. You only investigate something after it has happened. This, my friend, has not happened yet, but I know what is required, and I know it is something that you could do.' I had to listen on.

Pulling the fence to one side, the first thing that confronted me was a monstrous elm tree. I had seen it, of course, from the road, but it was not until we parted the fence that I appreciated the size of the trunk. This tree would have to be removed, but if it came down it would either fall on the stables and neighbouring houses or into the street. There was nowhere else for it to go. Then there were those dirty, dilapidated stables.

I was entirely in a new field. The tree was one problem, but the cost of getting the stables demolished and the rubbish removed was one that I could not even estimate. It was also work that I could not even pay for if I were to buy this useless piece of land. 'No problem,' said the bold 'George'. 'Firstly you demolish the stables and salvage the bricks.' As he said this he took a penknife from his pocket and scratched away at the cement between some of the bricks. 'Lime mortar,' he said, 'no problem, start at the top with the slates. We will use them for the damp course of the house. Clean the bricks and stack them up, then use them for the footings. They are old London Stocks and very valuable bricks indeed, as bricks go.' This made sense, for I had come across these very bricks in my war damage enquiries. 'George' was making sense, but the task that he was letting us in for seemed to me to be huge.

I explained my feelings. This sounded all very well, but how much did the owners want for the land? That had to be the first question. 'The asking price is £800, but I am sure that I will get that price down'. Already I was out of my league, knowing the finances of Bert and myself at the time. 'No problem,' he said once again. 'There is a war damage claim on the stables and the front fence, and if you buy the land, the claim goes with it if you make it good'. I was beginning to see a light, just a glimmer of light, at the end of this somewhat confused tunnel. I was still faced with the problem of having to find £400, however, which I did not have.

Now I am not entirely clear just how much the asking price was at the outset or, for that matter, just how much we finally managed to

Building a House for Myself   51

get the price down to. Suffice it to say that we did purchase this piece of land, thanks to the good offices of 'George', and with our finances down to zero, very soon commenced work in the little spare time we had, as demolition men.

Now to work. A hammer, a cold chisel and a chopper were all that we required at the outset, according to our mentor. We had the hammers and chisels, but my question was what did we want choppers for? 'George' produced the choppers, from Woolworth's store, cheap choppers that were ideal for chopping up kindling wood, but bricks? We were soon to learn. Removing a brick from the stable wall he showed us how easy it was to clean off the lime mortar with a chopper. A bricklayer, of course, would prefer to use the tool of his trade, his trowel, but we certainly found the choppers far easier to handle. The next implement that he produced was a slating iron. I had never seen such a tool before, but it took him only a couple of minutes to explain to us and show us how this implement worked. We were learning fast, and no doubt would be adding to our knowledge as time went by.

Over the following twelve months, in our spare time, before going to work when we were on late duty, and during the evenings when it was light, we slowly demolished the stables. Our combined efforts produced a large stack of very serviceable slates and some thirty-six thousand perfect London Stocks. There was also a very large heap of 'bats' – half bricks – and an even larger heap of rubble. The latter we both felt we should dispose of, but 'George' would not hear of it. 'You will need all that and probably a lot more before you've finished,' is all that he wanted to say on that subject.

In addition to our labouring work, there were other equally important matters in relation to our project that had to be attended to. Even before we removed the first brick we had to ensure that we had proper planning permission to erect two houses. We also had to employ an architect to draw up the plans, which in turn had to be accepted by the local council and building inspectors. Our greatest worry was the local building inspector. He turned up one afternoon when we were busily cleaning up bricks. There we were, dead scruffy, and dressed in jeans and overalls. He probably at first sight thought that we were a pair of thieves, hence his undoubtedly hostile approach. Once assured of our honest intentions, however, he became one of our greatest allies. His knowledge of the subject that we had stumbled into, and his acceptance of us as we were, was to assist us over the next two years.

Our personal efforts over this painful period had produced, as I have already mentioned, heaps of useful building materials of different types. Quite frankly, we were not at all sure just what our next step would be. I say painful, because although we had used old gloves during our brick-cleaning efforts and had worn out every pair that we could lay our hands on, neither of us had any resemblance of fingerprints left. This was something that was not a little embarrassing. The problem came to light when I was called upon to supply elimination prints after visiting the scene of a crime that I was investigating. Fortunately, the fingerprint officer was very experienced. With a smile, on seeing the prints on the official fingerprint form, he immediately accused me of 'moonlighting' and doing brickwork in my spare time. I explained to him just what I was in fact doing in my spare time and also that brick cleaning had caused my hands, particularly the tips of my fingers, to bleed at times. He laughed and commented that I had typical bricklayer's hands and then proceeded to match up the very little detail remaining on my fingers with the file copy of my fingerprints, kept on record. In my ignorance of this very specialised science, I ventured the offer that perhaps they should have a further copy of my prints as they were then, on record. He gave a very authoritative grin and assured me that the fingerprint detail on my tender hands would soon return to their normal state once I had completed the work that I was doing before having the house built.

The next problem was to get rid of the elm tree. I had ideas of cutting it down piece by piece, but it was a very large tree and this was clearly out of the question. 'It has got to come down next,' said 'George'. We therefore toured round to find a tree feller who would do the job at the right price. Here again, our education was advanced. All of the artisans whom we approached wanted to give us a price for cutting down the tree and taking it away. many of them, being local people, knew that there had been bomb damage near the site and said that the tree was useless because it would be full of shrapnel. In my ignorance I thought that they were being helpful. 'George', however, would not hear of it. 'Just get it cut down and leave it where it falls,' he said. 'I will tell you what to do next.'

Finally we did manage to find a contractor who would do as was asked. Even then, the men who did the job, which was carried out with surprising accuracy, could not understand our logic. The foreman insisted that he was in fact doing us a favour by offering to take it away, but having faith in our guide on the subject, we thanked him for the offer and turned it down. The foreman just scratched his head and looked at us as if we were mad, then turning to leave the site, he said, 'I'm damned if I know what you are going to do with it now. It will cost you enough to get it shifted.' The very clear indication was that he was prepared to take it away for no extra charge. I had to speak to 'George' again. He must have got it wrong somewhere, but we had not proved him wrong yet.

That evening I went over to see our guide and mentor. I explained to him what the contractor had said, with the accent on the fact that he was prepared to take it away for nothing. He did it again, he just chuckled. There was a pause, and I thought that perhaps he was wondering himself whether he had on this occasion made a mistake. 'John,' he said, 'I would not lead you astray. I am in the process of selling that damned tree for you. Elm is unusual wood. It does not rot in the sea. I have measured it and it is ideal for use as a pile, and I think I have someone who wants to buy it. There is very little shrapnel in it, I've checked that angle. Be patient, clean off all of the branches and burn them. All that is wanted is the trunk.'

Through the good offices of a friend I was able to borrow two large felling axes and a sharpening stone, and we set about cutting off the branches of the massive tree and burning them. This task took us six weeks of our spare time. We were very fortunate to have made friends with the neighbours, who made no complaint about the smoke. Quite out of the blue, whilst having my breakfast one morning, I received a telephone call. The man on the other end of the line said that he had been contracted to remove the elm trunk and pay us eighty pounds for it. This was good news indeed, but when would he collect it? 'I shall be over this Saturday morning. I've seen the tree, I will bring a pole, and there will be four of us. Can you be there?' Fortunately the coming Saturday was a day that I knew I could take as a leave day. I told the contractor that I would be on the site at 7. 30 a.m. and probably there all of that day. One word, however, was sticking in my mind as I gave my agreement to meet this man on the site. Just what was this 'pole' that he had mentioned? I wanted very much to ask him, but had no intention of exposing my ignorance. I had learned of so many tools, implements, gadgets and things that were new and completely unknown to me since I had become involved in this latest project.

That Saturday, I arrived at the site at 7. 30 a.m. and there was the 'pole' parked in the road. I had of course seen them before; a rather weird contraption; a tractor with a small crane, pulling two sets of wheels with a long bar between them, joining them together. It looked somewhat 'Heath Robinson', but it was most efficient. In what seemed no time at all, the massive trunk was hauled to the roadside and loaded on this peculiar-looking set of wheels. A cheque was handed over and our tree trunk moved off. As they were leaving, I said to the man in charge, 'Just out of interest, where is it going?' 'To the docks,' he replied, 'it is going to be used as pier pile somewhere in the Arabian Gulf.'

With the site now somewhat clear, we had reached a stage where I could not see the next step in our building project. We had managed so far without using up all of our meagre finances, but there was very little left. My faith was pinned firmly to 'George'. Plans for the house had been properly drawn up by the architect. These had been approved by Croydon Council, but one problem remained. We were on sloping ground and short of arming ourselves, just two of us, with shovels and digging out a large chunk of ground where the houses were to be built, I could not see what we as two somewhat ambitious amateurs could do.

This to 'George' was once again no problem. We had heard him say this so often. 'We will get contractors to come in and dig out what we don't want and take it away.' He was now talking about a subject that I did know something about, and when I cast my mind to the antics that of some of the contractors got up to, I shuddered a little.

I had 'carried the bag', as we used to call it, for Detective Chief Inspector Shelly Symes on what was fondly referred to as a 'muck away' job, some months earlier. Some schools were being built in north London on a very large site, which had first to be levelled out and cleared, then the foundations for the buildings excavated: a very interesting job indeed. In this case I worked on with Shelly Symes, the Yard had been called in by London County Council because the Council felt they were being defrauded over the charges they had received from contractors who had been called in to carry out ground preparation work. The enquiry took us many months to complete and certain very interesting and unusual points emerged, which perhaps could now assist me. I began to think back.

The system adopted by the contractors and the clerk of works at the site meant that the contractors' lorries were each carrying five cubic yards, of earth away from the site. They would drive to one or other of the diggers, which would load the lorries with five cubic yards of earth removed from the ground. The lorry driver would then drive his lorry to the office at the entrance of the site and there be given a conveyance note, indicating that he had removed that amount of earth. That conveyance note was in fact a valuable security, for which the contractor would receive so much per yard payment for the earth removed. Following this, the driver would drive his lorry to a tipping point previously arranged, dispose of his load and return to the site for further loads. All very nice and straightforward one would think!

In our investigation we needed to know just where the fraud had taken place, or if indeed there was fraud, and acquire evidence of it. We therefore gathered together the copies of all the conveyance notes for which payment had been made. This was an extremely time-consuming task, carried out during an era when we had neither computers nor an adding machine at our disposal. This initial exploration revealed that we had accounted for far more earth being removed than was needed just to clear the site, level it and dig the foundations for the schools. We had in fact accounted for the removal of earth to the extent that, had the schools it was intended to build been placed in the hole left, they would have been below street level. Something was wrong, very wrong indeed, and pointed to considerable fraud somewhere. All conveyance notes had been signed by the clerk of works or his representative on duty, yet they, strange to say, were trusted servants of the complainant. It was becoming very clear that we would need to know a lot more before we interrogated the clerk of works.

Now we separated the conveyance notes, vehicle by vehicle. It was indeed fortunate that one of the requirements had been that each conveyance note also bore the registration number of the vehicle that had removed the earth. At this point of the investigation a most peculiar point arose, which no person had hitherto noted. Selecting six vehicles on a particular day, which we knew were to dump their loads at a tipping site in Kilburn, we found that three of these lorries would have had to travel at speeds in excess of one hundred miles an hour to have carried out the tasks for which they had been paid. This in loaded contractors' vehicles in an area of heavy traffic, where to have averaged fifteen to twenty miles per hour would have been very good going.

To take the matter further, Shelly Symes and I paid visits to two local public houses. Here we learned that some of the loads had been dropped off at a building site nearer than Kilburn. This, however, did not worry us very much, the lorries would have still had to travel a lot faster than they were capable of to have completed the task that they had charged for. Over a few more pints, and not a little time, we learned about a loose part of the perimeter fence facing the site. This, it appeared, had received considerable attention from one of their customers, who would sit on a chair near this part of the damaged fence, reading a newspaper and smoking. A lorry would drive up, sound its horn and the man would pull back the fence. The lorry would then drive on to the site and the driver would hand the man something. The man would replace the fence in its original position and resume his seat. 'Were the vehicles loaded?' we asked. 'Oh yes,' we were told, 'the drivers often used to come in for a drink and leave their vehicles there.'

In the back of our minds we were in no doubt just what had been taking place. This was a means of getting a loaded vehicle back on to the site, for the purpose of obtaining a further conveyance note for the same load of earth. We began to ask ourselves how many times a day this had taken place, but of course could not come up with the answer. The conveyance notes themselves were giving us the answer, however, and we knew now that we were indeed getting warm.

In making our calculations, we of course took into account that compacted earth, when dug out of the ground, bulks by about one third when thrown or dropped on to the back of a lorry. We had therefore reduced our imaginary hole by one-third. We then reduced the size of the hole by the amount that the Council had been charged, but there was still a great deal to be accounted for. That investigation was successful. We had learned a lot about 'muck away' and the antics of those engaged in that particular trade. Those responsible were duly brought to book and dealt with in the courts. As for the Council, they also learned the lesson of foolhardiness in their own lack of supervision.

Bert McGowan and I discussed our next 'muck away' move and found that our diminishing finances, such as they were, were our biggest worry. Notwithstanding this, however, the site had to be cleared properly before any building work could take place. Then, after all, it was 'George's' idea, and he should know the order of our activity. Perhaps he knew such a haulage contractor, one who would wait a month for the cash? His reply was not prefaced by the usual chuckle, and, I found this a little worrying. 'I'll have to look around on this one,' he said, and we took the matter no further.

We were fast becoming aware that we would shortly need cash in the bank and, by our personal standards, quite a lot of money. We approached various building societies, including those with whom we held small deposits. We put our project to them in all of the detail we could muster, but to no avail. Our general feeling was that these companies, large as they were, were not prepared to lend us money. To them we were two rather young amateur builders, who had purchased a piece of land and wanted to build ourselves a home. The negative replies we received disheartened us more than any previous experience. 'No.' 'I'm sorry.' 'Perhaps if you put the matter in the hands of such and such a building company, we might consider it.' Furthermore, it was quite clear that it was out of the league of our friend 'George'.

Bert McGowan, however, had not been idle. He had taken the matter far further than I had. He had an uncle who was employed by a north country building society and to him he went for advice. 'Very difficult,' he was told. 'You have no collateral between you. You have a piece of land and you have no money. You occupy accommodation that does not belong to you. This means that if you do get into financial difficulties, you have nothing for which a creditor could sue you. Your furniture would be worth very little and in truth, all that you have between you is a piece of land and building permission.' Stark facts which neither of us could deny. The enquiry, however, was not entirely wasted. The relative was at least prepared to put the matter before his board of directors and give his recommendation. We just had to wait and perhaps pray a little!

A few weeks later, a strange man arrived at the site whilst we were working there. He was from a firm of surveyors in Dulwich Village. He had been asked to inspect the site and report to the building society, who were considering giving us a mortgage. This was indeed a pleasant surprise, but it was clear from some of the remarks of our visitor that he felt quite sure that we had bitten off a lot more than we could chew. Finally, and after taking numerous notes and measurements, he left. We tried to obtain some indication as to what his report would be, but he would not commit himself. We adjourned to the Moore Arms at Forest Hill, where we knew 'George' was to meet a client. We were in something of a mood of despair and were of a mind to ask our friend just how we were going to get out of this latest problem.

Mac and I were worried and 'George' could see that. Then, as I mentioned the unannounced arrival of the surveyor from the firm in Dulwich Village, out came that old familiar chuckle. The sound alone was most heartening, but we were far from happy. 'Listen, you two,' he said, 'if that building society from so far away has instructed Dulwich surveyors to look at the property and report back, I believe that you will get the money.' We both felt happier.

Sure enough, the mortgage was in fact offered, on a stage by stage basis. We first of all had to put in the foundations and oversite concrete base. That would give us the first grant. When we got to first-floor level we would get a second grant. The third payment would be made when we reached 'plate high'. It turned out to be the stage when all vertical brickwork was completed and we were ready to put on the roof. The final payment would be made when the council had passed the premises for occupation. We eagerly agreed to the terms and virtually signed over the plot of land to the building society, praying silently afterwards that we had done the right thing.

Now at last we were in a position to make contact with a 'muck away' contractor. This, of course, sounded easy, but there was one problem. We would get no money until we had put in the foundations and oversite. We needed credit. We had little or no money, and the land upon which we were going to build now in truth belonged to the building society that had agreed to back us. Once again 'George' came up with the answer. He introduced us to contractors who would carry out the excavations required and give us a month in which to pay. I was not very happy about this. 'We will never get to the stage of being able to ask the building society for the first grant in one month,' I said. He looked at me as if I was just plain stupid and frankly, I wish he had said so. I was mad, I knew we could not pay in a month, and now he was going to come out with another of his pearls of wisdom.'

'Sit down,' he said. 'You have got to realise that you are now in business, and business, successful business, is run on credit. So you get a bill expecting you to pay within a month. Normal procedure. You can't pay, you have no money. Nothing new in that. So, they send you a second bill, a reminder, just in case that last one was lost in the post, or elsewhere. During this time six weeks has passed, and I will be most surprised if by then you are not in a position to expect your first payment. Don't panic. This is business.' This of course was sound logic, to the businessman, that is. The trouble was that both Mac and I had been brought up to pay our bills as they came in, and the explanation given, logical as it may have been, was quite foreign to us.

Our civil engineering contractor, the 'muck away' specialist, duly arrived on the site with his bulldozer and lorries, and we were both truly surprised just how quickly his men managed to remove the required earth. Two days work, and we were ready to mark out the ground prior to digging out the foundations. Unfortunately, I now found that my official duty got in the way. I was unable to get to the site because I found myself in the middle of a very time-consuming investigation at the Yard. In something of a panic I telephoned 'George' once again. 'No problem,' he replied. He had a jobbing bricklayer 'between jobs' who would help. He was a good friend and providing that he got his beer money, he would wait until the oversite was laid for his full payment. As to the marking out of the ground, 'George' and the architect were going to do that anyway.

Needless to say, Bert McGowan and I were in something of a 'muck sweat' during the period that followed. Our principal worry was that if we failed to reach the oversite level in time to get that first financial payment from the building society, we could be taken to court for the money. The Commissioner of Police for the metropolis would not look kindly on us for that. Furthermore, it could cost us our jobs, and we both really enjoyed our vocation as detectives.

The ground was marked out very shortly afterwards. Then Pat Murphy and a mate arrived to dig out the foundations and put in the first brickwork. Mac and I assisted, and it was here that I realised just how unfit I had grown in recent years since leaving the army. I had dug more trenches than I care to recount during the war and had rarely tired, but this was indeed damned hard work. Nevertheless, we did give certain small assistance with the task in hand.

Whilst the digging was going on, we were reminded that we would need building materials, sand, cement and bricks. We had enough bricks, but we were looking for a builders merchant with whom we could open up an account. We needed at least to let the supplier know that we would be getting all of our supplies from him. We were put in touch with a firm called E. R. Burtt, builders' merchants in Albany Road, Walworth. We were welcomed as new customers and on the question of credit asked to settle by the month and within the month. I had heard it all before. I was perhaps getting a little weak as a businessman. I am basically honest and felt obliged to tell the manager just what we were doing. He listened intently and was quite obviously turning everything over in his mind very carefully. 'OK,' he said, 'but first I want to see the site, I only live a half mile away from you. If it looks viable, I will give you a month's credit.' I left virtually silent and perhaps in prayer. I still had an unpaid bill from the civil engineers to pay for levelling the site. Now I was undoubtedly getting deeper in debt.

E. R. Burtt came up trumps. The manager inspected the site whilst Pat Murphy was digging away. He noted that we had plenty of bricks to hand and agreed to supply us with sand, cement and ballast. He also indicated that, although he expected to be paid within the month, as this was our first purchase, and providing that we were going to purchase our building materials from his company, he would be patient until we received our first payment from the building society. Our relief was such that I felt quite weak.

Pat Murphy was ready for the first delivery of materials within a few days. It arrived whilst I was on the site on my way to work, five yards of sand and ballast dumped in the road and one ton of cement to be placed under a tarpaulin which we had borrowed. Pat Murphy was not to be seen, and I was not a little worried because I had to get to work on time. I need not have fretted, for as I signed for the materials, he arrived, driving an old truck and towing an equally old cement mixer. Getting out of the truck, Pat rubbed his hands together and shouted 'Great! Give me a hand to shove this thing – the cement mixer – on to the site and leave the rest to me.' I was indeed relieved, and after doing as he bid, I made my way to the Yard.

It was in fact two months before we managed to get the oversite concrete work finished. The delay was due for the most part to a bout of shocking weather. Our civil engineering contractors, perhaps believing that they might be able to take over our building plot, went to extreme measures to force us to pay our bill to them. We had no money, not being in a position to claim that very important first payment, and consulted a friend in the legal profession. 'Don't worry,' we were told. 'Civil action in a case such as this could take quite a long while to get into the list, certainly not less than six months. Meanwhile, your money is virtually guaranteed. You will have done the work to justify your claim for the first payment from the building society. The building society, on the other hand, would want the ground work inspected by their people and this of course could delay matters, but only for a short while.' We were very much assured. Our friend felt quite satisfied that we would get our money within a short while. In the meanwhile, however, he warned us strongly to be very careful. He would write to these people, telling them that he was representing us, but under no circumstances should we speak to any of their representatives further than to refer them to him.

This was good sound legal advice, and I am happy to say that notwithstanding the fact that we were, through our legal friend, threatened to be reported to the Builders Merchants Supply Association, we were able to pay our bills on time and before receiving the threatened writ. The final warning came from our solicitor friend. 'Don't take lightly the threat about reporting you to the association. If you earn the name of being a 'knocker' – one who does not pay his bills – and you get reported to that association, you would have the greatest difficulty in obtaining credit from anyone thereafter.' The information was obviously very sound. Shortly after that discussion we paid off all our creditors and for the first time for some while actually had money in the bank.

Our friendly bricklayer, Pat Murphy, was paid off. In a way we were sorry to see him go, but that was how he always carried on. He would take on a bricklaying job on an expenses-only basis, to be paid in full when the job was done. He would collect all of the cash due in a lump sum and then go out on a king-sized binge, in an attempt to drink all of the public houses in south London dry. This would last until all of the money had gone. Then, when his latest hangover had gone, he would look round for another job. A very strange way to live. Despite all this Pat Murphy had done a grand job of work for us. He certainly was an expert bricklayer and had worked like the proverbial beaver. He knew only too well that he would not be able to carry on with the project that we had taken on, and his last words to us were, 'You have got to get a firm in now to finish the job.' Had he any ideas whom we should approach, we asked. 'No, but you had better have a word with 'Fingers', he said. 'Fingers,' I said,' who on earth is that?' 'Your mate George,' he replied. 'He has got his fingers into every aspect of the building business. He will know who to get hold of and he won't put you wrong.' I was a little relieved at the last explanation. 'Fingers' in underworld parlance could indicate any kind of crook, a crook who could not keep his fingers out of anything. I trusted 'George', and would have been most unhappy if after all this time, and the number of times that he had come to our assistance, he had turned out to be a doubtful character.

I did not have to consult 'George' on the subject of a building contractor. Bert McGowan by this time had transferred to Catford Police Station. His enquiries located one Reg White, who ran a very useful building business. We had a meeting, we discussed the work and the costing and were happy in our own minds as we left. Reg White could clearly do a good job for us, but we were not builders ourselves, we needed some form of confirmation from friend 'George'. He made his enquiries and confirmed our feelings about Reg White. He was a good builder; 'but,' added 'George', 'Don't give him the plumbing work and the wiring of the house. You would have no difficulty in getting that done privately and a lot cheaper than through a building contractor. Also if you are any good with a hammer, put down the floorboards yourself, and do some of the second fixings.' I had to ask just what these 'second fixings' were. 'Architraves, floorboards and skirting boards, as far as you are concerned. Don't get involved in door frames and door-hanging, that is a bit specialised. White's carpenter will put down the joists and set up the roof. He will also fix the door frames and later the doors.'

We returned to Reg White and agreed matters as suggested by our adviser. I can't say that I liked the nickname 'Fingers', but he certainly did have his fingers in many pies. His advice had cost us nothing and was, I felt, given out of the interest he had in our being prepared ourselves to see the project through. Reg White's men arrived within a few days and with their arrival came the first complaint. There was no water plumbed into the site further than the stand-pipe that we had earlier arranged for Pat Murphy. There was no drainage laid on to the site and no toilet.

I often wondered what we would have done without friend 'George'. 'You don't get paid for putting plumbing into a site at this stage. You don't get paid for connecting main sewers either. As for the toilet, they do have a point. Go out and purchase an Elsan toilet and set it up in the garden in a covered lean-to. You should be able to put one up yourself with all of the odds and ends you have on the site already.'

The bricklaying went well. To cut back on the time now being charged up, Mac and I would go to the site in the morning and evening, hod carrying and stacking up bricks for the bricklayers to use. As for the carpenter, he worked alone, said very little, demanding nothing, but he was a superb workman.

It was not long before I took on the job of floor-laying, cutting the tongues and grooved floorboards and secret-nailing them down. Then as the bricklayers got above first-floor level, our next search was for a plumber. For this purpose 'Nobby' Clarke from New Cross, whom I had known for a number of years, proved ideal.

Now, Nobby was a joker, a true Cockney and full of traditional Cockney wit. The great day came one Saturday morning when Nobby announced that he was going to turn the water on throughout the house. On hearing this, the bricklayers and the carpenter put down their tools and made for the outside of the house. The carpenter in all seriousness expressed the opinion that I should not allow the water to be turned on until I had inspected every joint that the Joker, as he called him, had made. I did not take this up, and the suggestion certainly did not deter the plumber.

As Nobby turned on the stopcock, we could hear the water tank in the loft filling up. 'Thaar she blows,' he shouted at the top of his voice. The bricklayers, not to be outdone, commented that the loft joists fitted by the carpenter were far too small for the weight of the tank when filled and would probably give way. The carpenter, however, just smiled. His attention was focused on the hallway. Then pointing in the direction of the hall, he shouted, 'If that is not a leak, someone has not been using the Elsan.'

We all went to the point of observation. Sure enough, water was dripping down from under the newly installed floorboards. Nobby was the first to rush to the point, after making a rather feeble attempt to direct attention elsewhere. There was not one leak, but many. Turning towards me, he said, 'I always knew that you should have been a musician, a fiddler, but I didn't know that you could play the flute.' At first I did not see the point of this remark, which was clearly meant to be a joke. On closer examination I fully realised what he was getting at. I was clearly the culprit. I had secret-hailed a run of floorboards at an angle through one of the water-pipes and into the floor joists. Nobby was relieved and the rest of the workers were delighted that for once they could have a go at me. I bowed to Nobby's suggestion that I should buy the beer that evening after knocking-off time.

The remaining work seemed to fit in like clockwork. We took on plasterers, an electrician, and even gave Reg White the main drainage work. We concreted up the driveway after hammering down literally tons of ballast and accumulated rubble. This left one item to be removed: the elm tree stump. 'Dig around it and pull it out with a block and tackle,' we were told. We tried this. It did not work. A friend came along with a breakdown lorry and hitched his two rope to it. All he managed to do was to make a dent in the road and cause my neighbour's drive to lift a little! We abandoned that angle. 'Get an auger, bore holes in it, fill the holes with saltpetre and burn it out.' It smouldered and smouldered and virtually stank out the street. When we realised what was happening, we had quite a job to put it out. Finally, when George had stopped laughing at our attempts, he said, 'There is only one way, but it will take time. Axes, wedges and your sledge hammer, split it up bit by bit.' This sounded too easy, but it was anything but easy. It was a hard task, and we were still nibbling away at it after we took up occupation.

Our house was finally completed and thankfully, the stage-by-stage payments came in on time. We ultimately moved in on 14th December 1956. This had been a task that both Bert McGowan and I had enjoyed, despite the difficulties encountered on the way. It was a challenge from start to finish, but I doubt whether we would ever want to do it again. Certainly, I would not.

PART TWO

MAKING MY WAY

7
Transfer to the Company Fraud Squad

I served in the Central Office at New Scotland Yard from 1949 until 1957, and for the last two years of that period I was attached to the Company Fraud Department. This was a period during which I learned a great deal on matters that tend to drift towards a grey area of criminal investigations, investigations that do not normally come the way of the CID officer.

Fraud Squad work was something different. The principal difficulty was that the particular job you were investigating could take a year to complete. The general office used by the Detective Constables was also referred to as 'the snake pit'. We were all posted to a particular detective superintendent's team and called upon to assist any one of our superiors as and when required. When you consider that as detective constables we were the lowest form of life in the Criminal Investigations Department, perhaps the origin of the nickname of our office is explained.

The element of frustration continued even more strongly now. I was rarely involved in completing the report or in the resulting arrest. Furthermore, whatever evidence I might be required to give only reflected the very minor part that I had taken in the case. My burning desire was to be able to see a job through from start to finish, not to be restricted to doing what in truth was just odd jobs and giving very minor assistance to the investigating officer. Looking back now, there is little doubt that this desire was backed up by the fact that in my spare time I had built up a very useful network of informants. These efforts had resulted in my arresting a number of wanted criminals and others and seeing these arrests through to the final reckoning when they were dealt with at court.

A TRIP TO WREXHAM

The one job in which I did manage to get fully involved came upon me as a complete surprise. In January 1955 Detective Superintendent Eddie McKechnie asked me to go with him to the offices of the National Coal Board. A shortage had unfolded of an extremely large quantity of pit-props and lids (the planks, rafters, or sleepers that rest on top of the pit-props when they are installed). This was an entirely new ball game for me. The only point I came away with was that a vast stock of these strange items was credited to Black Park Colliery, near Wrexham, in North Wales. A stock check had been made and had revealed that there was nothing like the number of items held as the book entries indicated there should be.

That night I went off home to pack my bag for a trip to Wrexham. The following day with Mr McKechnie we headed for Paddington railway station and a journey to Wales. On that journey, sitting in the restaurant car and feeling truly like the proverbial lord, I listened to the Detective Superintendent as he outlined to me the full details of the problem. He also informed me that we would get every possible assistance from the local Welsh police. This was nice to know, but the thought that kept bubbling up in my mind, and which I just had to put forward, was – why send a broad Scot and a London lad to Wales? Don't worry about that, I was told. Policemen the world over speak the same language. We have a job to do and we are going to do it. My doubts were gone, and his confidence made up for my temporary lack of it.

We were met at Wrexham railway station and taken to the local police station, where we were introduced to Detective Sergeant Berwyn Jones. He assured us that whatever we wanted, we had but to ask. First of all, however, the Chief Constable, Phillip Tompkins wanted to meet us. This was my first meeting with anyone in such a high position in the service, and I was not at all sure just how I would be received as a lowly detective constable. I need not have worried, however, for what a thorough gentleman he turned out to be; indeed, the reception and kindness we received was so good that I began to feel quite sure there must be a catch somewhere.

Wrexham police had looked into this matter when it first arose, but had been unable to find a satisfactory answer to the problem. They had checked the books and invoices, but all appeared to be in order. To check the stock of pit-props stacked in an area of about fifty acres, however, was a task that would have taken a battalion of Royal Engineers a long time indeed to carry out. Certainly, Wrexham police did not have the numbers of men that would be required to carry out such a task. They had therefore called in the Yard. Now Scotland Yard has a reputation world-wide. I knew it, and no doubt our Welsh friends knew that also, but I was beginning to wonder just what I had got myself involved in. I had never been down a coal mine and had little idea just what a mining area looked like. I knew miners to be proud people, who kept themselves very much to themselves. Then I found myself attempting to speculate just how they would react to our presence. I was soon to learn.

Checking the bookwork was no problem, though time-consuming and very boring. No way, however, could we find a leakage of stock. We accepted, of course, that the shortage put forward by the National Coal Board auditors was correct, but on our own we, two officers, with perhaps a little help from our Welsh friends, had no way of checking that figure against fifty acres of stock.

We spent approximately one month going through everything that was available. We worked late into the night, but with very little result at all. We also found in Wrexham a certain hostility amongst local inhabitants when we did venture into a local public house for a pint of beer. We were of course strangers. We accepted that. We were police officers. Everyone in the area knew that. We were doing an investigation into the books and stock at the local mine. That they knew quite well. Why then the hostility? It was a mystery to us, because knowing all those points, the locals would also know that we were looking towards the people in charge, rather than the actual workers. Notwithstanding all of this, however, it was quite noticeable that when we did enter a public house, those talking in English would immediately revert to the Welsh language. It was most uncomfortable.

We had been in the area just over a month and were a little frustrated at our own inability to come to some probable conclusion that might have led us to the ultimate solving of our problem. We decided to treat ourselves to a good meal at a quiet hotel outside Wrexham, near the town of Chirk. It was not just for the meal and comfort, it was more to have a quiet chat between ourselves about the progress or lack of it. Outside it was as cold as charity, but in the restaurant a beautiful fire was blazing away. Furthermore, the service and food were excellent.

With the meal over, we sat back for a quiet smoke and drink. Not sleeping, mind you, but deep in thought, turning over in our minds just what our next move should be, occasionally making suggestions, with me jotting down little points of interest as they arose. The fire was going down, but that did not worry us. The hotel, however, was not the type of establishment that would ever permit a fire to go out when guests were sitting nearby.

A waiter brought in a large box containing logs. He built up the fire and left the box containing more logs close to the fireplace. Logs! What beautiful logs! Every one was as near as dammit identical. Frankly they looked as if they had been machine cut by an engineer. Even the saw cut was perfectly square to the sides. We may not have uncovered our shortage, but this just had to be a box full of cut-up pit-props.

A quick telephone call to Detective Sergeant Berwyn Jones at his home, inviting him to join us, soon produced the answer. The hotel regularly purchased a lorry load of 'logs' from Mr 'X'. Furthermore, the same Mr 'X' served many other people in the area at their homes. This did not make much sense to me, because most of the people in the area were permitted to purchase a lorry-load of coal at a price that would seem to us to be a lot cheaper than the cost of logs as we knew it. Now at last we had a positive line of enquiry to follow.

We had during our travels in the area seen many heaps of coal outside miners' cottages. We had even seen lorries with their drivers shovelling off coal outside some of them, but we were not interested in coal, until we learned that most people had plenty of coal to burn, yet tended to leave it to one side. They preferred to burn logs and sit by a log fire. When you consider that point of view, you have to admit there is a lot to be said for the beauty of a log fire.

Our new line of enquiry took everyone completely by surprise. Within a few days those enquiries led us to arrest two people responsible for the disposal of a considerable proportion of the missing pit-props and lids.

To us this was a very satisfactory ending to our investigation. It has to be said, however, that we would never have envisaged how that shortage had arisen had we not decided to drop our work on that particular evening and go out and have a meal and a bottle of wine at the hotel near Chirk. Luck? No. We just went to the hotel to relax, but the job was still foremost in our minds all of the time, even when we sat back to relax after the meal. Then there was the sight of those beautiful, precision-cut logs that triggered off our reasoning and immediately registered in our minds a probable solution to our problem.

Experience was now in the making for me. In due course our prisoners appeared at Ruthin Assizes, where they were found not guilty and discharged. The result surprised me somewhat, for the evidence that we had produced had satisfied the Director of Public Prosecutions, and I knew that my detective superintendent had left no stone unturned once we had found this very unusual leakage. I expressed my personal dissatisfaction with the result to Eddie McKechnie, thinking that he would go along with my feelings. To my surprise he informed me that it was our job to produce the evidence and present it at court, and that was all. Thereafter it was for the court to decide upon the result, not us as officers of the law. We had done our job correctly. We had been complimented by the Chief Constable at Wrexham. The Director of Public Prosecutions had been pleased with our work and satisfied that we had produced sufficient evidence for him to put the case forward. Whatever happened thereafter was a matter for the judge and jury, not us as police officers.

THE HAMILTON TERRACE FLAT FRAUD

During those years immediately following the Second World War some pretty heartless frauds were perpetrated upon those seeking a new home. War-damaged property was being worked upon, repaired and rebuilt. Large houses were being converted into flats and apartments, and a few new houses were being built. The housing shortage was being felt by many unfortunate home seekers, and the price of property was continually rising. The Fraud Squad soon became aware that the appetites of a certain class of scoundrel were such that they would soon take advantage of the obvious situation then presented to them. The pickings available were too good to miss, and there was no doubt in our minds that we would soon be facing quite a problem.

Arriving at the office early one morning in May 1955, I was surprised to receive a telephone call from Detective Superintendent Shelly Symes, who wanted to see me in his office. My immediate thought was, what was he doing in his office so early? We had, however, worked together successfully before, and now that we were both attached to the Company Fraud Department it was perhaps not surprising that he should ask me to give him a hand with an enquiry that had been passed to him.

Our enquiries on this occasion were directed towards one Neil Gerstein Taylor, who was in business as an estate agent under the name Regent Flats Ltd., at 502 Edgware Road, in the Paddington area of West London. Information in our possession suggested that through the medium of newspapers and other reputable estate agents this man was circulating details of premises available to rent, furnished or unfurnished apartments, with a lease available for purchase. The information also suggested that Taylor and his partner, Peter St John White, were accepting numerous deposits for the premises under their control by false pretences.

Many of the apartments offered by Taylor were in Hamilton Terrace, a fashionable road in the St Johns Wood area of London, and very close to the offices of Regent Flats Ltd. It is a road that runs parallel with the Edgware Road and has a number of quite large houses built at the turn of the century. Some of these had been refurbished or were in the process of being rebuilt, decorated and turned into self-contained flats or apartments. These were quite correctly described in the advertisement circulated as desirable properties.

The story that unfolded during the many months of our enquiry was one of truly downright heartless fraud. Numerous deposits were being taken for the same apartment. Applicants were being told that such and such a flat, which they were interested in, was in fact the property of Haile Selassie's younger son or some other well-known person. The stories were for the most part completely false, but the purchaser, or would-be purchasers, cared little. All they wanted was to be actually able to purchase an apartment. They were only too pleased to listen attentively to whatever story they were told and part with their money. An indication of the extent to which these two characters were prepared to go was the use of telephones in the office. There were five or six telephones in various parts of Regent Flats general office, and also an impressive telephone switchboard. These, however, for the most part proved to be dummies, placed in prominent positions purely to impress clients calling at the premises.

Our enquiries revealed that Taylor had purchased four large properties, three in Hamilton Terrace and one in Eccleston Square in the

Transfer to the Company Fraud Squad 73

Victoria area of London. There was evidence that Taylor, together with his negotiators on behalf of Regent Flats Ltd., had taken deposits on ninety-nine occasions from ninety-nine different people, in relation to twenty-four apartments which he had for disposal in the four properties mentioned. Not one of these people had been supplied with a flat or apartment and none of the deposits had been refunded. The first deposit had to our knowledge been taken in September 1954 and the last in September 1955. Taylor had taken deposits from many other prospective purchasers, but these had apparently been returned. The chaotic state of the books and records which Taylor and his staff had attempted to keep made it impossible to compile a list of those affected. But the money kept pouring in.

In the words of Peter White, 'Every day was like a flag day. The money just rolled in. I could see the crash coming.' The day of reckoning came for both Taylor and White when they appeared at the Old Bailey on Friday, 11th May 1956, before the then Recorder of London, Sir Gerald Dobson. For, as Sir Gerald put it, 'building luxury flats in the air', Taylor was jailed for three years, and for assisting Taylor to talk people into parting with their money, White was sentenced to two years' imprisonment.

8
Detective Sergeant in the Flying Squad

In December 1957 I was promoted to the rank of detective sergeant, second class, and posted to 'M' Division in the Kennington area of south-east London. Within weeks, and before I had settle down to this new style of work, I was posted once more, this time to Leman Street Police Station in the East End of London.

I had very mixed feelings about this second posting. I had the strange feeling of coming home after a long while away, almost as I felt when I returned to Norbury after leaving the army back in 1946. This station covered Myrdle Street, where I had been born in August 1920. But, I found some difficulty in actually getting to work. I was expected to be in the office by 8.30 a.m. I lived some eighteen miles away and whichever route I took, I had to leave home at about 6.30, in the morning and probably not arrive home until nearly midnight.

My worries were short-lived, however. A surprise transfer in January 1958 to the élite Flying Squad at New Scotland Yard, gave me, if I dare say it, a new lease on life. The Flying Squad in those days was divided into a number of small squads each with approximately ten men under the command of a detective inspector. I was posted to Number Five Squad under the command of Detective Inspector Tommy Butler. My interview with Mr Butler was quite short and very much to the point. What surprised me most was that without doubt he knew more about me than I felt I knew myself. He was pleased to have me on his squad, he said. This was followed by a handshake coupled with a fatherly smile, and the information that early duty was from 9 a.m. to 5 p.m. 'But we usually book off at ten o'clock.' This did not surprise me very much, for in those days CID officers were generally expected to work ten or twelve hours each day. The next point rather shook me, however. 'Late duty is from 2 p.m. to 10 p.m. You can have a lay-in on those days, you don't have to get here until 9 a.m.' This was a bit much, but I could not say anything. Don't ask me why, but I laughed. The pleasantly hawk-like face of Tommy Butler suddenly became fierce and almost frightening. He continued: 'If you think that's a joke, try coming in a few minutes late. Detective Sergeant Barney Gay is your partner. Now get out and do something useful.'

I left Mr Butler's office very much aware that I had put my foot in it. I just hoped that I could redeem myself, for this was a department where my father had served with some success, when I was a lad. Furthermore, I believed that it was the target of almost every active CID officer and of many older members of the Criminal Investigation Department.

In the outer office I met up with Barney Gay and told him what had taken place. 'Let's go and have a coffee,' was his reply. Our next step, as opposed to going to Johnny's café in Derby Gate just outside the entrance gates to the yard, was to get into a squad car and make our way south of the river to Bermondsey. Nothing was said once in the car, not even to the driver to give him instructions or directions. We travelled over Westminster Bridge, due south, then in an easterly direction, and pulled up outside the Anchor Tap public house, opposite Courages Brewery, on the south side of the river near Tower Bridge.

As we walked into the bar nothing was said again, but the barman pulled up two pints of Courages Best Bitter in pewter tankards and placed them on the counter. 'Morning, Barney,' said the barman. 'How's business?' 'Up and down, like Tower Bridge,' replied Barney. Then turning to me, he said 'Meet John Swain. He's with me now.'

Now I never was much of a midday drinker and I began to feel a little worried. I don't think this was really my day. Firstly I had fallen out with my boss Tommy Butler, and now it looked as if I was going to fall out with the man I had been posted to work with, and Barney Gay had a hell of a reputation for catching thieves. Summing up my courage, I told my partner that I would really have preferred coffee at eleven o'clock in the morning. He laughed and replied that you don't catch thieves drinking coffee. He probably had a point but I was not too sure about the midday drinking bit. My initiation into the Flying Squad was not going too well. First the brush with Tommy Butler, now this. My thoughts were that without doubt I would at least to start with, have to go along with Barney's ideas, whatever they were.

To put the record straight, I have to say that during the following twelve months I learned more about villains in the general London area than I ever put together in any period of my later service. My contribution to Barney Gay was to give him an insight into Soho and Mayfair, an area about which he had very little knowledge before we met.

It soon became apparent to me that the strength of every good detective lay in the number of reliable informants he could call upon. These were not necessarily people who would tell you what was going to happen or had happened. These could be people who were just plain friendly, knew the areas where thieves lived and were prepared to have a social drink and chat with you. The fact that you were prepared to stand just a little more than your own round of drinks was soon known. It is that starting point so many fail to locate. These are the people who impart those 'pearls of wisdom' on matters you are interested in, without ever realising that they have passed to you that one small part missing from the puzzle. I very soon learned that if you are not prepared to go into the less reputable public houses and have a drink with friends and associates of your future 'customers', you can hardly be, or ever hope to be, in a position to learn about their activities.

Thus, on reflection my first period on the Flying Squad was spent in learning from my partner and other experienced detectives the art of developing those all-important informants. I sought advice from those older and wiser than myself on this very important subject. The advice was forthcoming, but accompanied by heavily laden words of warning. 'Develop them! Yes. Buy them drinks! Yes. Talk to them freely on the subject of their choice! Yes, so long as you keep them to something like fishing, football or dog racing. Be a good listener and coax them to talk quite freely with you, but don't get involved with them in their activities. Always remember that you may have to arrest them if they decide in their doubtful wisdom to commit a crime. For the fact that they 'may' assist you does not give them a licence to commit crime of any description. Above all, keep in the forefront of your mind the fact that the majority of police officers who get into trouble find themselves in that invidious position through misjudging their informants, or through failing to remember these words of warning.'

With the advice of the masters still in my mind, I decided that I would now set out to develop my own informants, but try as I might, I found myself in some considerable difficulty. I was working with a senior and experienced detective, a man of great knowledge and many informants, but I found it virtually impossible to develop my own sources of information. I enjoyed working with him, but that feeling of utter frustration was building up inside me once again.

I reached a point where I could contain my feelings no longer. I decided to express my misgivings on this ticklish subject to Barney Gay. Looking back, his answer should have been obvious to me had I sat and thought the matter out. He pointed out that when he was working as young man with the current boss, Tommy Butler, and Peter Vibart, one of the senior members of our squad, he had had the same feeling of frustration that he was getting nowhere on his own. He quoted Tommy Butler's words of advice on the very subject. 'Study my informants. Study their friends. Get to know them by sight and you will be surprised how what you learn now will come in very handy in the future'. He had to be right.

As it turned out, however, my frustration was relieved by a chance remark which I overheard in the Globe public house in Merrow Street, Walworth, shortly after this discussion. I have to admit that I did not realise it at the time, but the remark opened up an entirely new horizon in the field of detection for me.

CHARLIE FINCH, 'VAN DRAGGER'

Barney and I were experiencing a most unusual short period of exasperating inactivity. My informants, such as they were in those days, were not producing the much needed 'pearls of wisdom'. Furthermore, my partner was acting in a very strange manner. Barney was a man who possessed a bump of humour that had always carried those working with him through frustrating periods of inactivity. On this particular occasion, however, he seemed quite unable to blurt out those infections quotations and jocular remarks for which he was so well known. The most he could suggest was that we sought inspiration over a few pints of beer. Those of course were not his exact words! To be precise, his answer to our problem went something like this – 'Sod it John. Let's call in on the Grapes and get pissed.'

We both stood at the bar in The Grapes slowly consuming a pint of Courage best bitter ale, discussing personal and private matters, far removed from police work. It was shortly after midday, and the lunch time customers were arriving in the bar. Two characters who had just come in struck up a conversation in quite a loud and jocular manner which could not fail to attract our attention. The conversation went something like this:

'How about that Ginger?'
'That's the funniest thing I have ever heard.'
'He's about the best van dragger in the business, yet he does that.'
'Yes, but now he's got it slaughtered, I'm buggered if I know what he is going to do with it.'
'I shouldn't worry about that. He knows the game, that Ginger. He'll get rid of it alright.'
'Yes. That's alright, providing the bloody stuff don't melt.'

With that they erupted into peals of hearty laughter.

As for my partner and I, our conversation about nothing in particular came to a very abrupt end. There was a job here somewhere, and we were hungry for work. The trouble was that we needed to know more, a whole lot more. We quietly left the bar, and waited close by to see just what our two talkative locals got up to next. As we waited, we discussed just what we had overhead. It was not very much, but it had to be interesting. We had a name – 'Ginger'. Apart from the fact that the fellow probably had red hair, the name alone did not mean much. According to our talkative duo, 'Ginger' was a 'van dragger' and not just an ordinary 'van dragger', but the best in the business! In underworld parlance a van dragger is one who steals from vans and lorries loaded with saleable goods. It is an activity undertaken by many not very expert thieves. The man referred to, however, had been mentioned respectfully as 'the best in the business', and that suggested he was both expert and successful in his activity. Against that, our talkative pair seemed convinced that he would have difficulty in getting rid of his stolen load. Then there was the remark that 'Ginger' had got it 'slaughtered'. This really made it interesting. The very word slaughtered indicated in the language of the underworld that, whatever it was, it had been hidden in a safe place ready to be moved by or to a prospective purchaser. Given the area we were in, this would be a disused railway arch, garage or warehouse, and there were many such places in Walworth.

Detective Sergeant in the Flying Squad 79

We got no further in our discussion, for our talkative pair were seen to emerge from the Grapes. We stopped them for a 'friendly chat'. For want of a better excuse they answered the description of two men who were on the wanted list. Both men thought this was quite a joke, but at the same time were most anxious to convince us that they were hard-working members of the local community. They succeeded in satisfying us on this point, and after taking a few particulars, we parted on the friendliest of terms.

John Beresford was a market trader, or barrow boy, from East Street Market, in Walworth. He had lived in Walworth all his life, and although he had appeared in courts on various occasions for different offences, he could hardly come into the class of the suspect Ginger. Pat Marshall, on the other hand, was a little more interesting. He was in fact unemployed. 'Between jobs at the moment' were his exact words. The name rang a bell for both Barney and me. This man was a driver of some repute. He had in the past been involved in some fairly hairy car chases, where he had, according to police jargon, 'come second', that is to the police who caught him and arrested him.

We had no intention of wasting time. We wanted to know more about the activities of these two and we knew exactly where to go to find the answers. The archives at New Scotland Yard may have been antiquated in those days, but notwithstanding, they were efficient and effective for our purpose. Pat Marshall had been arrested after one of the car chases mentioned and was then suspected of being a close associate of one Charlie Finch, known as 'Ginger' Finch. Finch had one conviction for assault and one for theft of a vehicle contents – van dragging. Furthermore, Finch, it seemed, lived in one of the tower blocks of flats off Albany Road, Walworth. He was certainly going to receive our very close attention that day.

It was late afternoon by the time we completed our researches. We knew exactly what Finch looked like and we now had his last known address. At the moment all we intended was to confirm that our suspect still lived in the tower block mentioned. After that it was a matter of going home early in order to be up with the lark in the morning, for we intended to crack this case before breakfast if at all possible.

We were in Albany Road at 5 a.m. the next morning and quietly waited for Finch to leave his home. Our patience was rewarded at 8 a.m. when he emerged from his flat in an obviously jaunty manner.

From Albany Road he made his way to Brandon Street. There, at some double gates leading to a lock-up garage or shed, he stopped. Turning round, he looked up and down the road, and we wondered if he had realised that we were following. We had kept our distance, as far as was possible without losing sight of our man, and just silently prayed that he had not seen us. After what was probably not a minute, but seemed like an age, our target put his hand in his pocket and drew out some keys. He unlocked the padlock on the gate, placed the padlock in his pocket and disappeared from view, closing the gates behind him.

Very interesting. Very interesting indeed. The question was, however, 'What do we do now?' This was a time for decisions and a time when it is all too easy to make the wrong decision. Do we await developments, or as we used to say 'just steam in'? As the very question was passing between us, a large covered van stopped outside the gates. As it did so, the double gates were opened by Finch and the driver backed his van through the gateway. The feeling we now had was that whatever was inside the garage or shed was going to be loaded on to the van. As far as we were concerned we were going to give them a few minutes and step in whilst the loading was going on.

From our position of observation, we could not see what was actually going on. All we could spot was the front of a Bedford van. That vehicle, however, told us all that we needed to know. Periodic jerking movements of the vehicle indicated that something heavy was either being loaded or unloaded. We had seen enough. We moved into the space behind the gates. Charlie Finch and the driver of the van were in the process of loading drums of butter, which were stacked up inside the garage, on to the van.

'OK Ginger, this is the end of the line for you two,' said Barney Gay. Now the opening remark when police come upon an incident, such as this, is most important. We have to assess the opposition, for there is no saying what they will do. In this instance, the two men could not get out into the street without getting past us, and that would mean a fight. We were prepared for this, but we were not prepared for what actually happened. Finch sat down on one of the drums and roared with laughter, putting his arm round the shoulders of his mate Bates, who sat down beside him. I was more alert than ever. This surely was just a ploy to get us off our guard, and I certainly was ready for whatever surprise the two villains might have had up their sleeve. Suddenly, Finch stopped laughing and at the top of his voice shouted, 'Jesus, I go out after a lorry load of "snout" – cigarettes – and land up with this bloody butter that nobody wants. We get together to dump the damned stuff before it goes off. Now you walk in, and we're nicked.' Strange to say, his laughter continued even after we had told both of them that they would be arrested, and placed them in our squad car.

We had recovered one ton of butter in drums, property which had been stolen three days earlier form a vehicle parked in Jamaica Road, Bermondsey, less than a mile away. The vehicle concerned had been dumped some fifteen miles away after the contents had been off-loaded. Our prisoners were duly charged with the theft, and under normal circumstances, all that was left was for us to formulate the report and give our evidence in court when required.

Most reports on prisoners, strange to say, seem to fall into an almost set pattern. In the case of Finch, however, the pattern that emerged was most unusual. He had volunteered for the army the week war was declared in September 1939. He had joined an infantry regiment and subsequently volunteered for the commandos, where he served with distinction until demobilised from the services in 1946. Many of the prisoners I had dealt with had served their country well during the war years, and there was nothing really new in this style of information coming form Finch. What was new to me, however, was the fact that Finch was so insistent that I did not mention his army service in court. He told me that the period when he was in the army was the proudest time of his life and he had no intention of permitting me or anyone else to bring disgrace upon his service years. He stated that he had no intention of denying the charge against him and that after making such a fool of himself by stealing butter, when he thought it was cigarettes, he was finished with crime for good.

I had heard it all before, and this plea must beat the lot. The words of the garrulous pair in the Grapes public house were still fresh in my mind: 'Ginger is the best in the business'. I should say so! Hardly the type who would suddenly finish with crime for good. My personal feeling when I had finished the interview with Finch was that not only was he an accomplished thief, he was also quite a con man.

The hearing at Lambeth Magistrates Court some three weeks later brought out even more surprises. Both prisoners pleaded guilty to the charge of theft and were represented by eminent and greatly respected counsel, who excelled themselves in their efforts to convince the court that their clients were finished with crime for good and were sorry for whatever trouble that they may have caused. Then to my surprise, counsel for Finch brought out his army service in line with what I already had in my possession. In addition, however, he said that he had located his commanding officer who was prepared to attend court that day if so required and give evidence of his excellent wartime service.

Surely now I had heard everything, but there was more to come. As counsel resumed his seat, the magistrate remained silent for what seemed an age. Then leaning forward, with a touch of menace in his voice, he said, 'I have listened intently to the evidence and the words of wisdom spoken on your behalf by learned counsel'. He seemed to hesitate, as if not sure of what to say next. I was convinced that his next words would be a sentence of imprisonment for both prisoners. This was not to be, however. Both Finch and Bates were discharged conditionally for a period of two years, on the undertaking that if they broke the law during that period, they would be brought back to Lambeth Magistrates Court and sentenced to a term of imprisonment for the offence for which they were currently charged.

Outside the court, Finch was standing alone. 'Mr Swain,' he said 'I want you to know that I appreciate the way in which you dealt with us. I also want you to know that I have finished with crime for good.' With that he turned and walked away. I said walked away: in fact he was clearly marching away, and his military bearing was very obvious. I did not know that I would shortly be hearing a lot more from Charlie Finch; neither did I know then that he would never again get into trouble with the law and that we would remain good friends for many years.

THE 'BLOWING' BUSINESS

At about this time there was a spate of crimes committed with the use of gelignite, in the main safe blowing. The bulk of these offences seemed to be directed towards railway stations after they had closed. Thieves would break into the station by night, blow the safe in the ticket office, take out the cash inside and depart. Our squad had been nominated 'the blowing squad' and two of us had to visit the scene of every blowing as it was reported. Many may ask, 'Why us?' The answer was simple. Both Barney Gay and I, together with other members of our squad, had considerable army experience with explosives. Barney had been in the commandos during the war and during that time my experience in the Royal Electrical and Mechanical Engineers had involved a certain knowledge of explosives. At the outset this task became something of a bore, with too much time travelling from one place to another. It was not unusual to go to a blowing in Harrow in Middlesex, in the far north of the Metropolitan Police District, and whilst there receive a call to go to Orpington, in Kent in the south-east. Such enquiries as we were able to carry out were small in number, but the safety of the public was the paramount factor that directed our actions. Gelignite is a very unstable substance.

The villains broke into premises, prepared the safe for detonation, then stood back out of harm's way and set it off. There would be a loud bang in the very early hours of the morning. This could well raise the alarm, but rarely did. Then with the safe open, the thieves would grab whatever cash they could and hasten from the scene before someone was drawn to the premises by the noise or had telephoned the police to report the matter. Detonators and gelignite were often left behind, and in the hands of innocent and inexperienced people, unaware of just what damage these items can do, serious injury, the loss of a limb or even death could result. We consequently took our task in hand very seriously.

By these regular visits, we managed to build up quite a file of 'blowings', with the various jobs grouped according to the particular *modus operandi* used. Patterns emerged which resulted in our being able to arrest a number of people specialising in this type of activity, and the numbers decreased substantially. We then found that we were left with one group specialising in railway booking office safes, where entry to the premises had always been effected either from the railway line area or with no sign of forcible entry or exit. Under this heading we also found a number of cases where, although there had been no sign of a forcible entry, there was the sign of an unauthorised exit, where a previously locked door had been left open after the event. From these paper exercises we were left with one group whose method of operation was always the same. We arranged numerous watches at various railway stations, but came up with nothing until one railway worker found some explosives and detonators on a railway line near Vauxhall in south London.

Our first thought was that these were explosives used by railway workers for some legitimate purpose. Our enquiries with the British Railway Police, however, soon put this theory to one side. The items discovered were not of the type used by British Rail. They had been found between Vauxhall and Lambeth. There had been no 'blowings' at Clapham Junction railway station or Vauxhall station, and it was unlikely that the thieves would attempt to open a safe at Waterloo railway station. Right in the centre of the particular area, however, lived a family known to be particularly expert in the use of explosives. Their residence was in a block of apartments backing on to the railway line.

The particular find of explosives had put us on the right track. We decided to pay the family now in our sights a visit and were fortunate in that we managed to obtain sufficient evidence to arrest and charge two members of this family.

The Poole family's method of work was simply to use the railway line to go from one place to another, as we would use the roads. They had travelled quite long distances around London, on foot, by night, to the station of their choice. They would then blow open the safe and return home, usually on foot, to the railway embankment at the rear of their apartment block. Their cache of explosives would be left in a convenient hiding place somewhere along the railway line, ready for use on the next criminal expedition. Then, when the coast was clear, they would climb down the railway embankment and stroll into their apartment block. An almost foolproof system, with little or no chance of being stopped by police and searched for their loot.

The case ended at the Old Bailey, where the two men concerned were convicted. At the completion of the case, the wife of one of the prisoners went over to Barney Gay, when we were standing outside the courtroom, putting our papers into our briefcases, apparently to thank him for the way we had dealt with her husband. She put out her hand to shake hands with the sergeant and I heard her say something like 'No hard feelings, Mr Gay.' He took her hand, but before he could say anything, she stubbed out a cigarette, which she had been smoking and had been in her left hand behind her back, on the back of his right hand. The sergeant's remarks were unprintable. As for Rosie Poole, she quietly made a hurried exit with a smile of satisfaction on her face.

STEALING AND RECEIVING

The passage of stolen property is not unlike the passage of leaves that fall from a tree in a storm. Rarely would it be possible to find all of the leaves that flutter down. Mother nature in the form of the wind distributes those leaves into strange places. Passing vehicles assist in their scattering. Birds and animals dispose of them in varying ways that they alone understand. In a similar way, stolen property is hurriedly disposed of by the thieves through their many and various sources, in an effort to complete that disposal before they are caught with the goods in their possession. Rarely is every item of property stolen from one location ever recovered completely.

During the night of 21st and 22nd May 1958, furs and jewellery to the value of £1,000 were stolen from a flat in Rodney House, Dolphin Square, in Pimlico in London, on the banks of the river Thames. The loser was the singer Shirley Bassey. The matter was reported to Gerald Road Police Station, but despite exhaustive enquiries by the local police, the many items of stolen property seemed to have disappeared into thin air, perhaps in a similar manner to those leaves.

On 30th July 1959 I received a most unusual telephone call. Charlie Finch wanted to see me. Would I meet him in Brandon Street, Walworth, in half an hour? 'Where is Brandon Street?' I asked. 'Where we last met,' said Finch. With that he put the telephone down. I had never forgotten my first meeting with Charlie Finch, some twelve months earlier. His name had never since been mentioned, and I had good reason to believe that perhaps he had kept his word and was leaving his life of crime behind him.

In Brandon Street an old Mercedes diesel saloon motor car was parked outside the garage gates that had figured in the arrest of Finch and Bates. As I approached the car, the passenger door was opened and from inside Finch called out 'Jump in, John.'

The conversation that followed was of itself something of an education. Firstly, Finch wanted me to know that he had kept his word and had put aside his life of crime since appearing at Lambeth Magistrates Court. He assured me that it had not been an easy promise to keep, but he was determined to continue to keep out of trouble. Furthermore, he wanted to express his thanks to me for the manner in which he had been dealt with after I had arrested him.

I did not know just how to take this remark. What had he in mind? All manner of thoughts were passing through mine. I had to say something, but what? 'Express your thanks. How do you propose doing that?' I asked. Finch hesitated, and I found myself silently praying that he was not going to attempt any form of bribery. His next remark came as a surprise of similar magnitude to the many surprises that had been sprung on me when I had arrested him previously. 'Shirley Bassey's jewellery,' he said. 'I think I can point you in the right direction for that job.'

There had been a lot of talk about the theft of Miss Bassey's property. At the time, she was singing at The Prince of Wales Theatre in Coventry Street, about a hundred yards from Piccadilly Circus. Shirley Bassey was indeed very popular, and I believe that her popularity inspired more policemen to attempt to get to the bottom of her particular case than any I had previously come across. Many on the Flying Squad, including myself, had attempted to produce some evidence or information that might lead us to either the thief or the property, but none had succeeded.

I could hardly believe my ears. 'OK,' I said. 'Point me in the right direction. I'm very interested in this one.' Ginger then described a bracelet to me. 'Does that mean anything to you?' he asked. It was without doubt one of the items on the list of stolen property taken from Dolphin Square. 'Well,' he said, 'I think that bracelet is in the window of old Lou Beck's shop in Soho. Go and see for yourself.'

My next visit was to the premises of L.P. Beck, jeweller, of 6 Newport Court, Soho. Sure enough the bracelet was on display, and as I walked into the shop, my worry was whether Ginger had been involved in the theft himself. According to Lou Beck, whom I had known since I had been stationed in the West End, he had purchased the bracelet from Sydney Weldon, a jewellery dealer, for £45. The description of the item was properly entered in Beck's goods inward book, and as far as I could see, this had been a straightforward deal. Nevertheless, the bracelet was identical with the one stolen, and we therefore took possession of it for further enquiries.

Mr Weldon lived or worked out of Kenton Street, in the Bloomsbury area of London. He had no difficulty in recalling the bracelet and produced his records to show that he had purchased it for £30 on 23 July 1959 from the jewellers J. & A. Lasky, of Theobalds Road, Holborn. At Lasky's, one of the principals readily recalled the bracelet.

Detective Sergeant in the Flying Squad 87

It had been one of a parcel of jewellery that his company had purchased from one David Gilmour on 27th May 1959. To back up this statement, he produced a letter signed by Gilmour, stating that the property had belonged to his late mother and that he was seeking an offer for the purchase. Mr Lasky offered £17 and obtained from Gilmour the declaration mentioned. The document also gave his current address in St George's Square, a very short distance from the scene of the actual theft. The interesting point was that it was to this address that Lasky's had sent the cheque in payment on 29 May 1959.

Other items included in this parcel of jewellery had been sold over the counter; some, however, remained and were retained in Lasky's safe. We were quite clearly on the track of the missing Shirley Bassey jewellery, but who was this Gilmour character? The information about the item in Lou Beck's window had been so accurate that I began to wonder whether I was going to find that Gilmour was in fact 'Ginger'.

On 1st August 1959 Detective Constable John George and I went to 91 St George's Square, Pimlico. The occupier was, sure enough, one David Gilmour. We could not identify him with anyone who had come into our hands in the past or who had been suspected of house-breaking or theft of any description. Our thoughts as we entered the address were that perhaps we were now going to meet a thief who had just started up in business. On the other hand, was our informant, who had been honest with us so far, wrong on this occasion? David Gilmour was in and greeted us at the door. Our first impression was that this was certainly not a thief, but we had learned long since not to be over influenced by those first impressions.

Gilmour at first denied any knowledge of the bracelet. It was very obvious he was lying. He was told that he would be charged with receiving stolen property, knowing it to have been stolen, and that his apartment would be searched. His attitude immediately changed completely. There had been a decided note of arrogance in his denials. Now he appeared completely deflated. He sat down and looked as if he was going to break down in tears.

The search revealed a white metal ring with a red stone set into it. Gilmour admitted that this was the property of his employer, Shirley Bassey. We then took Gilmour to Lasky's in Theobalds Road, where he picked out a gold and silver purple-stoned ring, a gold-filled bracelet and another ring. All had been the property of his employer.

From Theobalds Road, we took Gilmour to Gerald Road Police Station. There he made a statement under caution to the effect that an unknown man had asked him when Miss Bassey would be out of her flat. This request was apparently made together with the promise that the unknown man would 'see him alright'. He told this person, he continued, that Miss Bassey would be out on the evening of 21st February 1959 and would not return until the early hours of the morning of the 22nd.

Gilmour insisted that he did not know the man, could not make contact with him and had never seen him before. We, of course, had considerable doubt as to the veracity of this story, but as matters stood, could take the matter no further. According to Gilmour, he later learned that a number of articles had been stolen from Miss Bassey's apartment during this particular period. He said nothing, of course, but about a week later received a parcel at his flat containing the articles that he had taken to Lasky's; also, a white fox fur stole, which he sold to a furrier in South Molton Street, Mayfair, after claiming that it had belonged to his late mother. The company offered £15 for the article.

Gilmour was charged with receiving the articles that we could prove had passed through his hands, knowing them to have been stolen. He subsequently appeared at Bow Street magistrates Court on 31st August 1959, where he pleaded 'Guilty' to the charge and was given a conditional discharge. The most heartening loyalty of an employer for her employee came to the surface here. Miss Bassey sat in court throughout the hearing, and counsel for Gilmour pointed out that notwithstanding what had taken place, Miss Bassey believed Gilmour to be a man of honesty and integrity. He also pointed out that in the past Gilmour had handled considerable sums of money for Miss Bassey, and suggested that he must have been under considerable stress at the time, or this offence would never have been committed.

We had at least recovered some of the 'leaves that fell during that storm'. None of the further items of property stolen ever came to light. I had made a point of personally thanking Ginger for the accuracy of his information, shortly after we had arrested Gilmour. I also asked him if he knew who the thief was. His reply was that he thought that we had arrested the person who carried out the theft. My next question was probably expected. 'How did you arrive at the idea of directing me to old Lou Beck's shop?' 'Simple,' he replied, 'I just happened to be passing when that fellow was looking in the window and he seemed very agitated. I had seen him with Shirley a few weeks earlier when I was with Shani Wallis. Then I had been told that he was Shirley's secretary. The rest was an educated guess, but it paid off.' His replies put my mind entirely at rest, because I had originally been very worried about Ginger's probable involvement in the theft. I did know at that time that he was himself working with Shani Wallis, the singer and actress.

I thoroughly enjoyed my first attachment to the Flying Squad. This was what I had joined the Metropolitan Police to do. It was an exciting period of successful action against numerous very active criminals; and was also a period of many changes within the Service generally, and the Flying Squad in particular.

Behind all of these changes were many moves afoot to procure more efficient equipment. Our radios were heavy, cumbersome and at times in London grossly inefficient. Our vehicles, although not the finest on the road, were at least adequate for their purpose. At the same time, however, we did have our doubts about some of them on the new motorways that were being built in the Metropolitan Police District. We should, moreover, at least have two good motor cycles that could keep up with or catch any normal vehicle. I had proved my point with my motor cycle when I had followed the American PX truck from Staines to Edmonton, and this had clearly been noted. (The ironical fact was that although I had been told that I had done a good job of work, I was also told that I was not allowed under any circumstances to use my own vehicle or motor cycle on duty.)

We found that we were being reminded, when we asked for something different in the way of equipment, that we already had nondescript vans fitted with radio equipment. These of course were ideal for observation purposes and quite useful at times for following another vehicle, but they had their limitations, particularly at speed. We knew that criminals were ever on the lookout for more efficient means to thwart their sworn enemies, the police.

THE EMPTY BOTTLE RACKET

The education of the criminal mind was brought home to me quite vividly one morning. Barney Gay and I had been detailed to come on duty at 6 a.m., watch a block of apartments in Burntwood Lane, Wandsworth and follow a suspect to see what he got up to during the day. The suspect was a brewery lorry driver. The company security officer, Albert Wells, who was well known to us, told us that this man was spending more money than he could ever earn with the brewery, 'spending it like water'.

At 6.30 that morning, our suspect came out of the apartment block where he lived and got into a Ford Thunderbird motor car. Not bad for a lorry driver! He then drove slowly round the roads surrounding the apartments for about a quarter of an hour. Then quite suddenly, as he turned once more into Burntwood Lane, he put his foot down and took off at a fast rate. During his circular tours he had passed us on three occasions, and we were therefore very much aware that immediately we attempted to follow him, he would realise that all was not well. We had to give the Thunderbird a few cars' start before we got in behind him, and that in London traffic is clearly not on. Our surprise, however, was at the speed of the vehicle in Burntwood Lane. It passed two cars at a speed that must have been well in excess of 70 miles an hour.

We pulled out and attempted to follow, but this was a lost cause. We could not lessen the gap between us, and our target simply disappeared from view. We broke off the chase, and Barney's language was foul. The driver, Glyn Powell, tried to make efforts to convince us that it was not his fault. We knew that, of course, and I tried to calm them both down. I had an idea.

For the purpose of travelling to and from work, I had purchased a Lambretta motor scooter. It was not particularly fast, but it gave me good service. I had followed the American PX truck a few years earlier with my motor cycle. Let me try my Lambretta out on this character? The suggestion was agreed to. We also agreed not to discuss internal regulations, for at that hour in the morning I could, after all, be on my way to work. So the following morning was decided upon. We knew his car, and I could wait for him a short distance away near to the nearby normal traffic build-up.

As arranged, I went to Burntwood Lane at 6 a.m. the following morning. My colleagues were at Tower Bridge Police Station, waiting for a telephone call from me. Our suspect came out at 6.30 a.m., got into his Thunderbird and once again did a couple of circular tours around his apartment block. I drove slowly up Burntwood Lane and

Detective Sergeant in the Flying Squad 91

was passed by the suspect a few minutes later. I did, however, manage to follow our man all of the way to the Courage Brewery in Horsley Down, behind Tower Bridge Police Station.

Once again, his speed up Burntwood Lane was very fast indeed. Once he arrived at the traffic lights at the junction with Trinity Road, however, he joined in with the normal speed of commuter traffic, and I had no difficulty in keeping him in sight. There were no strange moves by the suspect, and I was therefore able to join up with my colleagues, to await the time when he drove off with the brewery lorry.

We did not have to wait long. Within a very few minutes, we saw our suspect and his crew driving a Courage lorry out of the brewery compound. This appeared to be a normal delivery run, so we followed.

It did not take a genius to realise, after two turns into various streets, that the driver's eyes were glued to his rear view mirror. This was no good. We had, however, driven out of Tower Bridge Police Station yard, so decided to return to the station. Within a few minutes, our friend Albert Wells was able to tell us the names and addresses of the public houses which the lorry was making deliveries to. I therefore set out to the location of the third named hostelry. After waiting in the vicinity for about twenty minutes, the lorry arrived and delivered part of the load.

The next stop was to a public house in Peckham. In this instance, a crew member got out of the lorry and rang the front door bell of the premises. When the door was opened, he handed the occupier a piece of paper. The door was shut and the next thing that happened was that the cellar flaps on the pavement near to where the lorry was parked were flung open. Barrels and crates of beer were taken from the lorry and passed down into the cellar. This was followed by the passing out of crates of empty beer bottles from the cellar to the lorry crew, who placed them on the back of their lorry. Everything seemed in order, and I was beginning to wonder just what I was watching for.

I followed the lorry to three further public houses and in each instance everything seemed in order The seventh stop, however, was different. The lorry stopped as before, near the cellar flaps. The crew member got down, but instead of going to the door to ring the bell, he went over to the cellar flaps and stamped on them twice. He then stood back. Almost immediately the cellar flaps opened and by this time the driver and his mate were at the back of the vehicle, taking down crates of bottles that must have been empty by the way they were being handled. These were all passed down into the cellar in very quick time. The cellar flap then closed and the brewery lorry drove off. No paperwork was handed over, there was no ringing of the front door bell, no apparent checking of the crates as they came off the lorry. In any event, what was the reason for passing empty beer crates into the cellar? This public house was not on the list that we had been given. Something was going on, but what?

I had no time to contact my colleagues, because the lorry was driven off almost immediately. Once again I was following as before. Within a quarter of a mile, the vehicle stopped outside another public house and the procedure was repeated almost to the letter. The drayman got down and stamped on the cellar flap. The driver and his mate started unloading crates of empty beer bottles, which were passed down into the cellar. The cellar flap then closed. As this was being done on this occasion, I noticed that something was handed up to one of the crew members from below. Whatever it was, it was immediately placed in his trousers' pocket. As before, whatever they were up to, was completed in about two minutes or perhaps even less, and they drove off.

The lorry was by now making its way back to the brewery, by the direction it was taking, and I was beginning to get a little worried because I had had no time to contact my colleagues. Fate, however, must have understood my predicament and came to the rescue. The lorry stopped at a café in Asylum Road, Peckham, and whilst the crew were enjoying their tea and sandwiches, I was able to ring up Tower Bridge Police Station and talk to Barney Gay. A reception committee was arranged for the vehicle and crew when they returned to the brewery, and I could relax for a few moments at least.

With the brewery security officer we visited the public houses where I had noticed the suspicious crates being passed down by the draymen. 'A couple of empty crates' was the gist of the general reply by the publicans. Then on asking, 'Why crates of empty bottles?' We were told of the numbers of bottles that were broken or taken by customers, for which they, the publicans, were charged by the brewery. The explanation sounded quite reasonable, but these licensees were receiving stolen property and knew it.

The three-men crew of the brewery lorry were all arrested,

following our enquiries, and charged with stealing crates of empty beer bottles from the brewery. This of itself does not sound like a very serious matter. It did, however, prove that our friend Albert Wells, the brewery security officer, was right in his assumption that the suspect now arrested was up to no good. It went considerably further than that, however. It transpired that there had been little or no check at that time on empty bottles returned to the brewery, despite the fact that they were aware there was a shortage amounting to many thousands of pounds in the empty bottle accounts. Needless to say, our action not only cut off this popular form of pilferage, but it brought home to those in charge certain accountancy failings. The brewery was delighted and took immediate steps to put their accounting system in order.

9
Posted to Brixton

My first period of work on the Flying Squad came to an end in early December 1959. I had thoroughly enjoyed myself in that very special department. The work was interesting and varied to the extent that when you came on duty you never knew whether the day was going to end in an exciting car chase through London; a dull observation stuck in one of our mobile hothouses – observation vans; or finding yourself in the middle of an East End rough house. Excitement of some kind would always arise. Of course it was not always physcial excitement. The majority of cases which we became involved in resulted in the arrest of highly efficient thieves, who made plenty of money from their escapades and could afford the best of counsel, counsel who knew far more about the activities of their clients than I at first gave them credit for.

With a little sadness I found myself posted to Brixton Police Station in south London just before Christmas 1959. This was going to be boring, of that I was convinced. No more car chases and fights, but worst of all, very little chance to knock the rough edges of my ability to give evidence and deal with expert cross-examination at the Old Bailey. That was what I thought. I was very wrong indeed.

Jock Marr was the detective superintendent. He was a one-time Flying Squad officer himself, with a vast experience of catching thieves. He knew exactly what I was thinking about my posting and went to a lot of trouble to tell me that most people only remain on the Flying Squad for two years. I did not entirely believe this line, for many I knew had remained there much longer than that. I think he saw my doubts and went on to tell me of the number of cases that were dealt with at Brixton by his officers. Then to cap it all, he pointed out that if I wanted to go back to the Yard, I would have to make a name for myself on his division first. Those words rang very true, and I decided there and then that once again my personal target was going to be to get back on the Squad.

I took a walk round my new area and very soon found that there was a lot happening on it that should attract my attention and with luck would assist me in fulfiling my ambition. The Brixton sub-division covers quite a large area, and right in the centre are to be found Somerleyton Road and Geneva Road, almost entirely occupied by people from Jamaica. I found myself extremely glad of my short but educational stay at Leman Street in the East End of London.

I had been told that black people were not entirely popular and were certainly not co-operative towards police. I am afraid, however, that I could not accept that at face value. I had been able to work up a useful form of co-operation with the Maltese and black people during the short time I was serving at Leman Street. Why should I not do just that at Brixton?

My first quest was to find someone who was trusted by the black population, someone who commanded their respect and had no fear of them. You had to prove yourself to them before they would be open with you. In those days few public houses encouraged blacks, on the grounds that they loved to haggle over prices, even over bar prices in a public house. This, as you will probably appreciate, did not endear them as customers.

My search, however, was not in vain. One of the Aides to CID, John Bland, who was always in trouble with the detective inspector, Harry Pugh, could well be my man. He seemed to bring in a lot of prisoners, both white and black; yet he gave me the impression of being something of a tough nut to crack. I certainly appreciated his efforts and his efficiency, but Harry Pugh very rarely acknowledged this. John Bland was indeed a very rugged young man, quite small by usual standards for a police officer, with a strong midland to North Country accent. He was scruffy in his dress, but he was scared of no man. He was, however, very worried about Harry Pugh's attitude towards him and confided in me to this effect. Then one evening, when things were a little slack in the CID office, John Bland told me that he was going to apply to be returned to uniformed duty, because of the attitude of the detective inspector. He was a very respected member of the Metropolitan Police rugby team. He was going to play more rugby and enjoy life away from the inspector, who, for a reason that he could not account for, had taken a dislike to him.

My thoughts went back to the day that Harry Stuttard had come to my rescue, when George Chesney was taking it out of me to the extent that I could willingly have left the police force and gone back into the army.

I took John Bland to the Volunteer public house, which lay in the back streets behind Brixton police station. John was very disturbed about some of the inspector's recent remarks to him and clearly needed consoling. As we walked into the saloon bar, Freddie Sykes, a character whom I had had past dealings with, acknowledged us in a manner that was intended to lower whatever prestige I might think I had in the area. His remarks, however, had quite the reverse effect on those present and on John Bland. It showed that I was known and respected as a detective in other areas of London. This was not the effect Sykes had in mind.

During the course of our conversation, I induced John Bland to come for a walk with me around the area principally inhabited by the blacks. In those days this was Railton Road, Somerleyton Road and Geneva Road. In Railton Road he introduced me to Ebun Davis and his wife Babu. Ebun was Nigerian, whilst Babu had come over from Jamaica. They were anxious to put over the fact that they were honoured that John should bring me to see them. There was no doubt in my mind but that John Bland had a very interesting way with black people. I needed to see more and learn from his approach, which I could see paid dividends in the obvious respect that he had earned.

Our next call was to 21 Somerleyton Road, the home of a huge man known as Tommy Farr. We walked down the basement steps and into the large room at the front, where about twenty black men were playing cards, dice and dominoes. They certainly accepted John Bland, but I could see from their frowns, as they all stopped playing, that they were not too sure about me. 'Where's Tommy?' shouted John. One of those present left the room. he returned with a man I had previously met in east London named Seaford Allen. 'Hello, Seaford,' I exclaimed, 'what are you doing over this side of the water?' 'What do you want here, Mr Swain?' he asked in a somewhat guarded manner. 'You are on the wrong side of the water, not me.' 'I've been posted to Brixton and have been for a walk round with John Bland here,' I replied. His response surprised me, but also satisfied me that my judgement of John Bland had been correct from the outset: 'If you're a friend of Blandy, then you are OK.' He extended his huge hand and we shook on it. With this, the various games that had stopped during this interlude started up again. Clearly, if Tommy Farr accepted me, then I must be also accepted by those present. I was also accepted by John Bland. Thereafter, although our personal temperaments were entirely different, we worked together successfully at varying times during our respective careers.

TWO YOUNG SMART DRESSERS

The sudden change in the style of work I was now doing was brought home to me quite soon after joining my new appointment at Brixton. On 7th January 1960 the Detective Inspector called us all together in the CID office, for what he termed a conference about the latest spate of housebreakings in the area. It was called a conference, but in point of fact we were all getting well and truly told that our efforts as investigators were falling far short of what was expected of us.

There had been some thirty cases of entry being effected into houses during the month, when gas meters had been forced and the cash contents stolen. Few of the cases amounted to more than ten pounds, but the statistics reflected an extremely large number of 'unlawful entries into dwelling houses', each of which was helping to push the number of undetected crimes far above the norm. The detective superintendent was clearly having pressure brought to bear on him from above, which of necessity was passed on by him to his staff. We, on the other hand, as members of his staff, were only too well aware of this sudden increase in the numbers of this type of housebreaking. Unfortunately, we were getting nowhere in rooting out the cause. There had been no violence and nobody had seen or heard anything unusual taking place before discovering that the small lock on the gas meter had been forced. To make matters even worse the occupiers of the premises were held responsible for the missing cash. This was a comparatively poor area, where people could rarely afford the loss.

The detective inspector's tirade of abuse over, Gordon Harris, one of the detective constables, and I went through the Crime Book, itemising and assessing the numerous thefts from gas meters that had recently taken place on our ground. No jemmy or other tool had been used to break open a door or window. Entry in each case had been gained through an open window or door. The only point our analysis picked up in some of the cases was that local enquiries had noted that one or two black boys had been seen near the vicinity. Closer examination of these Crime Book entries indicated on three occasions that young black boys had been seen in the area during the time in question. As much as was ever said about these two lads was that they were smartly dressed, not a common sight in this particular area.

As Gordon and I chewed over the most recent cases, I stood by the window of our first-floor office, looking out over part of the main Brixton shopping centre. Our attention was drawn to two quite small black boys aged between ten and twelve years, who walked across the station parking area. They were smartly dressed and wearing what were described in those days as Robin Hood-style trilby hats.

As they walked across the forecourt they looked up at our office on the first floor, laughed, apparently at us, waved and passed on their way. Were we really the joke?

There was no need to say anything to each other. We closed the Crime Book, walked out of the office and left the building together. These boys just had to be interesting. Our quarry stopped at the corner of nearby Overton Road and looked back. This could be good! I said 'looked back', but it was in a manner that I had seen so many times before when following adult criminals. In Overton Road, they stopped outside number 16. One walked up the steps and entered the open front door. He then returned and beckoned his friend to come inside. They disappeared from view. It was 11 a.m. Perhaps the little blighters lived in the house?

We waited. I was still thinking about that first searching but hesitant glance back at the junction of Overton Road and Angel Road. At 11.20 a.m. the two boys came out of the house. They appeared to be counting whatever it was they had in their hands. It could be sweets, but I wonder? They walked into Wiltshire Road, still engrossed in whatever it was that they were carrying. They seemed to be sharing something out. I know I had originally thought it could be sweets that were taking up their attention, but could these be the rascals who had caused our boss to give us all a hard time in the office that morning?

As the two boys entered Wiltshire Road, a man walked out of number 3. The two lads calmly walked into the house. It was 11.30 a.m. At 12.10 p.m. both left the house by the side entrance and walked into a nearby sweet shop.

We stopped the boys as they came out of the shop. They were not particularly worried that we were police officers. They had called at the last house to see a cousin and could not understand why we should be interested in them. They were calm, polite to the extreme and almost convinced us of their utter respectability; and they certainly looked respectable enough. Their pockets, however, revealed an entirely different story, quite an amount of shillings, far more than any ordinary person would carry, let alone two young boys. We were convinced that this money came from gas meters. They on the other hand insisted that they had saved it all up!

The attitude and answers of these very young boys were those of experienced and active thieves. Both of the houses which they had been seen to enter had had their gas meters forced and the contents stolen. The two had never been in trouble with the authorities before. Their parents were sent for and proved to be extremely decent and respectable people, deeply shocked at what confronted them in their sons. With their assistance we cleared up all of the outstanding gas meter jobs and the boys were charged with theft. Both were placed on probation at the Juvenile Court, and I am very pleased to be able to say that, although I remained at Brixton for a further three years, they never came to the notice of the police again.

In May 1960 I was delighted to find myself posted to the Divisional 'Q' Car. Back to Flying Squad work all over again, I thought! I was so wrong. We had an unmarked police car with a radio, driven by an officer from the uniformed branch in plain clothes. Myself as the detective sergeant was in charge, with a radio operator or observer, a detective constable or Aide to CID of my choice. I chose John Bland. My colleagues expected me to produce work of Flying Squad standard, and for my part I had no intention of letting myself down in their eyes. There was, however, little time to get down to investigations and observations. The radio would call us up and our next visit would be to a screaming domestic quarrel; a child with its head stuck between the railings of a park; a shoplifter handed over by a store detective; or a fight in a café, club or public house.

LOSING A PRISONER

Losing a prisoner is a subject rarely talked about. It is something that brings about the highest degree of frustration any police officer can possibly experience. Just stop a moment and think about this one. During December 1961 our safe-blowing friends the Poole family, from Vauxhall, came back into the frame once again. This time they were suspected of using explosives in our divisional area. Our enquiries to trace the family, however, proved that they were no longer living at the back of the railway line in Lambeth. For all we knew they could even be living abroad. Spain at that particular time was beginning to become the home of many of our missing customers.

Detective Sergeant Fred Lambert and Detective Constable Gordon Harris joined in the search for our missing links and came up with an address in Paddock Wood, Kent. As this was outside the jurisdiction of the Metropolitan Police, we made contact with the Kent police to go to the address with some of their officers. We duly met up with Detective Sergeant Seabourne of Kent Constabulary and went to a caravan parked at Willow Cottages, Willow Lane, Paddock Wood. Sergeant Seabourne knocked at the door and asked if the man who opened it was Poole. He was; we, of course, knew him by sight. The sergeant told him that we had a warrant to search his caravan and read the warrant over to him. Poole was not in the slightest surprised. He even said he was expecting the visit and politely invited us inside.

This was a very large caravan and took a lot of searching, for it had so many nooks and crannies. We searched everywhere: cupboards; cooking stove; fireplace; bookcase and even the stowaway bed, which was kindly pulled down by Poole himself. Having searched the bed, however, and found nothing, we told Poole that he could fold it back in position. This he declined to do, saying that it could stay as it was. This had to be interesting. Sergeant Lambert pushed the bed back into its original position and closely examined the retaining leg, which also acted as a newspaper rack. Inside a sock in the rack he found a tin marked 'Nobel Detonators'. When opened, the tin proved to contain a number of these items.

The atmosphere inside the caravan virtually erupted. Rosie Poole, who had been sitting peacefully near Sergeant Seabourne, asked what we had found. Poole replied, 'They've found the dets'. As he said this he tried to snatch the tin from the sergeant. Sergeant Lambert turned away from Poole just as Mrs Poole got up swiftly and attempted to snatch them from him. I reached over and took them from Fred Lambert and took them to the police car outside. As I left the caravan,

Poole came running out, chased by Fred Lambert and Gordon Harris. Poole stopped and threw brickbats at the officers and at the police car. At the same time he was shouting to Mrs Poole, 'Let out the dogs and get the gun.' A large Afghan hound and an Alsatian dog went for the officers, whilst Poole disappeared into the gathering fog.

We now had a tin of detonators and Rosie Poole, who in truth had done nothing more than try to assist her husband escape from us. Obstructing police, yes, but she was not charged. With red faces we returned to our respective police stations. Excuses we had none. We made out various reports and accepted the criticisms fired at us from every conceivable quarter, and indeed some that we had not thought about. Finally we circulated our man as 'Wanted'. He was, of course, duly arrested and dealt with, but quite a period had passed before he was brought to book.

RELUCTANT WITNESSES

In October 1962 I was called to interview Mrs Ethel Dawson, who had come to Brixton police station to complain that she had been assaulted. Not a very exciting prospect, just another interview, which would turn out to be a wasted half hour. Assaults were very common. The majority of complainants were referred to their civil remedy at the County Court or advised to take out a summons for common assault. On the other hand, when it came to serious assaults, although we heard about them through the grapevine, those assaulted were rarely prepared to give evidence before a magistrate against the person who had assaulted them.

In the witness room I was confronted by a woman aged about thirty-five years, who had two very inflamed black eyes, a face that was swollen in a most ghastly manner and a broken nose. I knew this woman, but could hardly recognise her. I was shocked, even though experience had taught me that it was most unwise to show my feelings. 'Christ, Ethel, what have you been up to?' I exclaimed. 'Not me, Mr Swain', she replied. 'It was that bloody John Henry and he has done my old man as well.' I immediately knew whom she was talking about, John Henry Woods, a local coalman and a giant of a man, whose strong arm tactics and activities in the area were almost legendary.

My first task was to induce Mrs Dawson to permit me to put into writing just what had taken place. She was quite prepared to tell me what had happened, but had no intention of making a written statement or allowing me to write one for her. 'Just some notes, Ethel, that's all'. She finally allowed me to write down her story, which I did take down in statement form. This revealed that her sister was married to John Henry Woods, a fact that I was not previously aware of. She had been in a mental home or hospital for some months, had discharged herself and without telling her husband, whom she was terrified of, came to live with the Dawsons. Woods had discovered this and called at the Dawson home in Mayall Road, Brixton. He was refused entry into the house, but forced his way in, struck Mrs Dawson a mighty blow in the face, which knocked her back along the passageway, and then knocked Mr Dawson out when he came to her assistance.

I had come to the point now, having written down everything that had been said, to ask the most important question, and I knew precisely what answer I was going to get. 'Would you give evidence and prosecute this man?' 'Oh no, not me, Mr Swain, he'd kill me,' was her timorous reply. 'What about your husband?' I asked. 'Not him,' she said, 'he doesn't want to get involved.' I had heard it all before. On so many occasions in the past I had been obliged to take no further action in such a matter for want of a witness who would actually go to court, stand up in the witness box and say, on oath, exactly what had taken place.

John Henry Woods was very well known to all the CID officers at Brixton. He was quite notorious for his violent behaviour and feared by a great many of the inhabitants of the area. Rarely, however, was he brought to justice for the simple reason that those whom he did assault, and he assaulted many, were frightened out of their wits to report the matter, let alone think of going to court and give evidence of what had taken place.

Somehow I had to even the score and end this round of terror by bringing the bold John Henry to book. I had just such an opportunity in my hands at that moment. All I had to do was to induce Mrs Dawson and her husband to co-operate with me. I wanted their statement in every detail and quietly set about the task, which had ended in failure and much wasted time on so many occasions in the past. I had to tread very carefully with my couple and had the strange feeling, as I progressed, of walking on thin ice.

I did manage to get signed statements from the Dawsons, thanks to the notes I had taken down when I first interviewed Ethel Dawson at the police station, also an undertaking that they would attend court and tell the magistrate what had taken place. I could not get the word 'evidence' over to them in any form. They were not going to speak against John Henry Woods. All they intended to do was to tell the magistrate what had happened! I could hardly ask for more. On my way home that night I knew I still had a problem on hand, to get this case to a satisfactory conclusion. I was comforted by one of the first phrases I had learned when I joined the police force as a constable, a phrase that kept coming to mind: 'The preservation of public tranquillity', one of the primary objects of an efficient police force. I knew quite well that the tranquillity of the public in Brixton had been seriously disturbed on a number of occasions by the unpredictable and violent outbursts of John Henry Woods. It was therefore my sworn duty to ensure that this man learned his lesson.

The following morning I attended Lambeth Magistrates Court and obtained a warrant to arrest Woods for 'assault occasioning actual bodily harm'. Returning to the office, I found myself turning over in my mind the best way of putting this into effect. I have to say that I am rarely frightened for my own safety, but on this occasion I knew that there was no way I would be able to arrest Woods alone. As I was thinking over this knotty problem, Peter Jones walked into the office. Peter was the smallest detective constable at Brixton, but lacked nothing in guts and determination. I knew quite well that I could rely on him in a tight corner.

'I've got a little job for you, Peter,' I said. 'Bring your stick' (truncheon). He looked a little surprised, for I was one of those known very rarely to carry my official issue truncheon. Peter did as he was bid and accompanied me in the police car to the coal wharf in Shakespeare Road, Brixton, where I knew Woods should be at that time in the morning.

John Henry Woods was there, and I would ask you to stop for a moment and meditate on his personal method of loading up his coal lorry; then try it yourself one day! The coal was stacked in one hundredweight sacks. Woods would walk over to one of the stacks, first swing one sack under one arm with one hand, then swing a second under the other arm. He would then, with apparently no effort, walk over to his lorry and without putting the sacks down, hoist first one sack then the other on to the back of the vehicle. Quite a man.

I had taken Peter Jones with me for a particular reason. I told him that I was going to walk slowly over to Woods, as casually as I could possibly manage under the circumstances, and tell him that he was arrested. Whilst I was doing this, I wanted Peter to stroll over and get behind him if at all possible, before I broke the bad news to him. I also told Peter to make sure that he had his truncheon handy and that if Woods struck out at me, to hit him as hard as he possibly could. Then dropping my voice a little I went on to tell him that if Woods should get violent, he would only have one chance to hit him and prevent a nasty scene. To my complete surprise, and not a little relief, Woods gave me no trouble. He came to Brixton Police Station with us and was charged with the assault on Mrs Dawson, as set out on the warrant.

My big worry from then on was to ensure that the Dawsons did what in law they were expected to do. Neither of them wanted to give evidence, to stand in the witness box, alone, to take the oath and give actual evidence. On the other hand, however, they had no disagreement with my request that they should come to Lambeth Magistrates Court, and 'tell' the magistrate exactly what had taken place. Very much to my relief, they came to court and accepted that they would have to say their piece in the prescribed manner, from the witness box and upon oath. Mrs Dawson in particular related just what had taken place on that very frightening evening. Woods pleaded 'Guilty' to assaulting both Mr and Mrs Dawson and occasioning them actual bodily harm. The only excuse that he attempted to put forward for his outburst of violence was that he had been receiving treatment from Alcoholics Anonymous. Describing him as 'a strange throw-back to the Stone Age' the magistrate sentenced him to twelve months' imprisonment.

FACING UP TO FEAR

One of the last cases I got myself involved in at Brixton, although simple of itself, was one that truly brought home to me the frailty of man and some facts about myself, which I had up to that time never even considered. I had always prided myself that I kept fitter than most people of my age. I had never been confronted with real fear that had obliged me to back down. Thus I always carried out whatever task confronted me with complete confidence, although sometimes with a little more thought than usual. I still had a great deal to learn.

In December 1962, we learned that there was stolen property lodged in a house in Brighton Terrace, Brixton. We had no idea what we were looking for, but the indication was that it was very valuable and we would not be disappointed. I knew the house in question. I also knew the occupants. What did surprise me, however, was that they should be involved in stealing or receiving stolen property of any kind. They were to my knowledge a respectable family in regular employment and I had never even heard the slightest suggestion of their being involved in matters criminal. Nonetheless, the information was there.

Our visit to the house produced a number of rolls of roofing felt, with a total value of £15. They belonged to a man whom I shall call 'Steve', the son of the owner of the house. Steve was working on the Post Office Tower in Maple Street, in London's West End. We had heard about this unusual structure and seen it at a distance as it was in the process of being built. We went to Maple Street and enquired at the site office for our man 'Steve'. The clerk of works smiled, then ushered us out of his office and pointing skyward said 'Up there', indicating the top of the building – the Post office Tower. He then returned, still smiling, to his office. We entered this building, such as it was, and found ourselves in what is best described as an extremely large chimney stack 620 feet high. It had a spiral staircase six to eight feet wide, which ascended almost as far as the eye could see finally disappearing into the darkness.

We looked at each other and shrugged our shoulders. We had started the enquiry and we had to see it through. We started our upward climb. The fact that the stairs jutted into the wall was some comfort, but every few feet we came to a gaping hole that looked down to the streets below. Worse still, there was no inner rail towards the centre. As we climbed higher, we found ourselves hugging the wall between the holes or window spaces. Furthermore, we were very much aware of the strong wind blowing through these gaps in the wall as we climbed higher. In due course we arrived at the top of the building. Six hundred and twenty feet does not sound much to those used to heights, but for my part I do love the feeling of *terra firma*. My legs felt like rubber, my knees were burning and I was somewhat out of breath. Then, bearing in mind how some of my 'customers' react when arrested, I knew that the last thing in the world I wanted was to become involved in an argument of any kind.

The workers, and there were a dozen or more of them engaged in the roof work, were sitting in a circle around a brazier, eating sandwiches and drinking tea. It was their lunch break, and our man 'Steve' was amongst them. He saw me first. 'Hello, Mr Swain,' he said. 'What are you doing up here?' 'I want a word with you, lad,' I said as I walked over towards him. We both left the party gathered round the brazier, and I told him that I had found some roofing felt in his house and suggested that he came back with us to Brixton and sorted the matter out. There was no argument. He clearly knew what we were talking about. 'OK,' he said and picking up his coat, he accompanied us back to Brixton.

Relief! Both Ken Chittock and I breathed a very deep sigh as we made our way very carefully back down the shallow steps towards the ground, which never seemed to get nearer. We said very little during our descent. For my part, I was having to accept that I had been barely able to reconcile myself to the height when ultimately at the top of that building. I had been frightened, damned scared, in fact, not through fear of violence from those present but through fear of my inability to control my personal actions in a manner to which I was accustomed at ground level. My knees were still shaking and I really wanted to cling to the wall, especially as we passed those draughty openings for the intended windows. One thing was for certain: I was never cut out to be a steeplejack.

'Steve' insisted that he had not stolen the property which we had recovered. His story was that he had accepted it from a workmate to assist him in a job he was about to commence in his own home. He had no intention of indicating who that workmate was, and we for our part had our doubts as to whether he ever existed. The following day, he appeared at Lambeth Magistrates Court and was fined £25 for his efforts in receiving the roofing felt, knowing it to have been stolen. It had in fact come from his employers and was in due course returned to them. 'Steve' was a man whom I never encountered again, although I saw him on a number of occasions in passing. I like to think that he kept away from the temptation of 'borrowing' other people's property after that incident.

Posted to Brixton

Studying for promotion whilst at Brixton was always in my mind, but it was difficult. Somehow, I never seemed to have sufficient time to relax and study. I had built up a number of very useful and trusted contacts during my stay in the area, but this had allowed me little time to get down to those books that held my future inside their covers. I began to realise that I had missed the first and most important run of early promotions, which some of my colleagues had earned. I had to make the necessary effort and set to that task. Happily, and notwithstanding my preoccupation with my work, I did finally manage to obtain the necessary pass marks to qualify for advancement.

10
Return to the Flying Squad

On 8th February 1963 I was posted back to the Flying Squad, as a detective sergeant first class. When I reported for duty I found I was posted to Detective Inspector Fred Byers' team, on what was then referred to as Number Seven Squad. 'Big Fred', as he was fondly called, was a veritable giant of a man. He had a heart of gold, but suffered no nonsense from anyone. My first squad boss, Tommy Butler, was now in charge of the whole Flying Squad. To cap all this, John Bland, my one-time partner at Brixton, was also a member of this team and had been posted to work with me. Quite clearly, someone had done their homework on the pair of us! Life was once again taking on an increasingly interesting outlook, and the activity that I knew so well was going to get its full attention from me. Behind all this was the variation of the work, which truly drew me to the Flying Squad.

Our attention was always directed towards the more serious crimes, but we never knew from what angle they would appear. There were often times when the apparently innocent and cheeky replies from young suspects would nearly drive us to distraction. Then we were grateful that the training we had received had taught us to listen to what was said in reply to our questioning and never to lose our temper. Happily, I have never suffered from a quick temper, but I have to say that many of the answers received during the course of an investigation or interrogation invited me to do just that. The following is just such a case.

THE JOKING THIEVES

On 8th March 1963 John Bland and I were travelling along the

Fulham Road in south-west London, on the look-out as usual for suspects, when a Talbot motor car attracted my attention. I had once owned a similar vehicle myself. The occupants, two young men and a girl, did not fit in with the vehicle. We decided to stop it and find out who they were and what they were doing. This may sound all very routine. It was. I must say, however, that when a member of the Flying Squad stops either the driver of a vehicle or a person and tells them that he is a Flying Squad officer, they generally know that the matter is serious and act accordingly.

I said to the driver of the vehicle, a lad named Gunning, 'Is this your vehicle?' 'No,' he replied, 'I borrowed it from a friend.' I asked him if he knew the registration number of the vehicle, but he did not. I asked him if he had anything with him that proved that he was in lawful possession of the vehicle and he replied, 'No.'

John Bland went to the girl sitting beside the driver and asked who she was. She replied, 'I'm his girl friend,' indicating Gunning. I have had that old feeling so many times, and I knew that once again we were in business. I asked the other male passenger, 'Who are you?' He replied, 'I'm a friend of theirs,' indicating the other two occupants, 'but they've just picked me up.'

I need hardly say that these were not the sort of replies that I could easily reconcile myself to. I could feel the hairs on the back of my neck tingling, but the last thing I intended doing was to lose my temper with these cheeky youngsters. They had something to hide, of that there was no doubt. I intended searching the vehicle, but not in the street. These were the type of young jokers who could get a crowd around in no time at all, a crowd, which in this particular area could well be very hostile to us.

I told the trio that they would have to accompany us to Chelsea Police Station, where further enquiries would be made. The driver, Gunning, had no objection to this and said so. Once in the station yard, I told them that we were going to search their vehicle in their presence and commenced to do so. Gunning, however, took a poor view of this action and insisted that we had no right to do so. I carried on.

Behind the driver's seat was a sack, which contained an old violin and bow. As John Bland picked up the sack, Gunning said, 'I don't want you to touch that, it's personal.' Taking the violin out of the sack, I asked 'Whose is this?' He replied, 'It's mine, I'm a bit of a fiddler.' This comment drew loud peals of laughter from his partners.

On the back seat of the car was a suitcase. This was opened and proved to contain a number of furs. I asked Gunning whom they belonged to. He replied, 'A friend of mine has asked me to move them from "A" to "B"'. I pressed him further over the ownership of the property, to which he said 'Come off it, but I'll tell you this. The other two don't know anything about it, because I've only just picked them up.'

The young woman, Winter, insisted that she knew nothing about the property in the car. When told that Gunning had said that he had been asked to move the property from 'A' to 'B', she just shrugged her shoulders, laughed and said, 'Oh no, you can't catch me with that one.' To her the whole matter was a joke to be enjoyed to the full. There was, however, no doubt in my mind that the property was stolen and recently stolen at that.

I had heard enough. I told all three that they would be charged with receiving stolen property, knowing it to have been stolen. The two lads said nothing. Winter, however, joker to the last, laughed and said, 'That's right, I'm the ringleader.'

These were quite presentable youngsters, not in the normal run of housebreakers; but the property seemed to indicate very strongly that it had been stolen from someone's home. At the same time, considering their age, the fact that the trio were making such a joke out of this obviously serious matter, made us stop and think a little. Looking at them inside the police station, I was saying to myself, 'Who could possibly believe they were the type who would steal anything?' In fact, John Bland and I were beginning to wonder just what we had got ourselves involved in.

The third passenger in the car, a lad named Moore, was just as innocent in his replies. He knew nothing about the property. It just happened to be beside him, on the back seat of the car when his friends stopped to give him a lift. When he realised that we were serious in our intention to charge all three with receiving the articles, knowing them to have been stolen, his attitude changed. 'Come off it. If I was going to mess about, it would be for something a lot bigger than that.' He too clearly wanted us to know that he also felt that our accusation was a joke to be enjoyed by all.

It was quite a relief to both John Bland and me when we found that the violin was an extremely valuable item, believed to be a Stradivarius, and that the property found in the suitcase was the proceeds of housebreaking. All three appeared before the magistrate at West London Magistrates Court and were found guilty as charged. In fact, the pretty young girl admitted stealing the valuable violin whilst staying at the house of the owner.

In this instance we found just how easy it is to be 'conned' and confused in our own judgement of a situation. It was a relief to us when we ourselves uncovered the truth of the matter. The jocular answers this trio had given us, although they created certain titters in the public gallery when repeated in court, did not fool the learned magistrate for one instant. At the same time, on hearing the full details of the case, he decided in his wisdom that this was a situation, serious as it was, that could be dealt with by way of a fine and a severe warning as to their future conduct. I never came across this trio again and sincerely hope they took the words directed at them at West London Magistrates Court to heart.

A DRIVE ABOUT TOWN

One part of London that had always drawn me was the Isle of Dogs, an area in a deep double bend of the River Thames on the north bank of the river between Rotherhithe Tunnel and Blackwall Tunnel. It covers Millwall and Cubitt Town. I can understand how it became known as an island, because this was one of the busiest of the dockland areas, with dock entrances to the east and west. I have never, however, worked out why it should be so commonly referred to as the Isle of Dogs. No doubt it goes back to a period well before my time.

The public houses in this area were well known for good food at lunch time, at the right price. It was, therefore, to the Isle of Dogs that I often went for my midday meal, between other jobs when in the East End. The Robert Burns public house in West Ferry Road was one of my favourite eating houses, and it was to this hostelry that John Bland and I went for a midday meal on 5 April 1963.

It was 12.45 p.m. and on entering the saloon bar, I noticed two young men sitting together talking in the corner of the bar. I did not take a lot of notice of them, I just noticed them out of habit, while habitually glancing round to take in the faces of those present. At this particular time I was more interested in what food the house had to offer that day, in ordering a meal and a pint of beer.

As I ordered I could see the two young men in the reflection of the mirror behind the bar. They were talking urgently together and undoubtedly talking about John Bland and myself. There was nothing unusual about that, it often happened, and we were sufficiently thick-skinned to ignore it. The unusual point in this instance was that they ended their short discussion about us quite abruptly, got up and left the public house, leaving their drinks on the table. They were undoubtedly in the type of hurry that had to be explained.

The hairs on the back of my neck began to twinge. We just had to be on to 'something'. Perhaps they were wanted men. Two young men abandoning their drinks on the table and leaving a public house without a word: something was wrong. I went over to the window and looked out. They had got into a black Ford Thames van and were driving north up West Ferry Road. I decided to follow.

Now, to cancel an order for dinner in this particular area does not make you the most popular person amongst publicans, but with apologies, and not waiting for a reply, we left. The van was by now almost out of sight, but thankfully this road, West Ferry Road, is quite long, and certainly in those days had very few turnings running out of it. We caught up with the van at the traffic lights at West India Dock Road. It turned left, then shortly afterwards turned right into Salmon lane. Continuing onwards it stopped outside a betting shop in White Horse Road. Here the passenger got out and went into the betting shop, leaving the driver in the vehicle. This could mean anything. Could it be a robbery? Betting shop robberies were fast becoming popular amongst the criminal fraternity. Quite honestly this pair did not look like robbers, and the passenger had not appeared to be taking anything into the premises that could have looked like a weapon. We waited.

At 1.30 p.m. the passenger returned from the betting shop and got into the van. There was no sign of the engine being started, and we were still trying to work out just what was going on. Something was undoubtedly afoot, but what? Five minutes later a blue Ford Thames van arrived and stopped behind the vehicle we were watching. The driver got out and stood beside the black van, talking to the occupants. Whatever the connection between the two parties was, we had no idea. The main point was that I could not shake off that old feeling that we must surely be in business and that patience was the order of the day.

Whilst trying to decide whether or not we were wasting our time, the man got back into the second vehicle and drove off. At the same time the original vehicle we had tailed started up and followed close behind. We followed at something of a safe distance. The two vans were being driven at a modest pace, but to the onlooker they could have been glued together. We began to believe that we had been 'tumbled', but that feeling had proved false on many occasions before. The two vehicles did something of a circular tour of the area. Right into Ashton Street, right again into Maroon Street, then into Salmon Lane, and round the block again. We were fairly certain now that they had seen us, for they stopped once again in White Horse Road.

At this stage, things became a little complicated. The passenger of the first van got out, walked up White Horse Road and turned into Maroon Street. The two vans followed very slowly. In Maroon Street there was now a Bedford van, which had obviously arrived since we had passed a few minutes earlier. The two vans stopped. The passenger from the first van got out, climbed into the driving seat of the Bedford van and drove off slowly. The man from the blue Thames van got into the black van and drove off after the Bedford, leaving the blue Ford Thames van behind. We followed once again.

I think that John Bland and I had got well past presumption of the innocence of any of the people involved here. We were now faced with the problem that we would have to stop two vehicles and question three men. Not a clever prospect with only one vehicle ourselves. We needed assistance. We called up Detective Inspector Fred Byers, our squad boss, on the radio. He was somewhere in the Notting Hill Gate area of West London and immediately turned round to stream over towards us as fast as he could to assist us. In the meantime, we were able to pass on to him a running commentary of our progress, in order that he could meet up with us somewhere!

From Limehouse, through Poplar, to Whitechapel and into the City of London. Fortunately for all concerned, our quarry was not in a particular hurry and quite obviously did not want to offend the law and become involved in any traffic violations. Fortunately for John Bland and me, the inspector had arrived by this time. We managed to stop both vehicles in Fenchurch Street.It was about 2.15 p.m. and we were most relieved at the prompt arrival of Fred Byers and his crew. We did, however, cause considerable traffic congestion in this extremely busy part of the City of London. I went with the detective inspector to the Ford Thames van. John Bland and other officers went to the other vehicle, the Bedford. It was full of radios of varying types, and from the packaging they were quite obviously recently stolen. I said to Saunders, the driver of the Ford van, 'What are you doing in this vehicle?' He replied, 'A mate of mine asked me to drive it for him.' 'Who is this man?' I asked. 'Mind your own business' was his belligerent reply. There was no point at that stage in asking any more questions. We had seen enough and therefore took him to Limehouse Police Station together with his empty van.

In the station yard, I saw Saunders again. This time he was with Bailey, obviously his partner, by the Bedford van and the radios. All Bailey would say was that he was taking the radios to a man over the river. When asked who the man was, he would only say that he would tell the judge. Clearly he had no intention of telling us whom he had got the property from or the identity of that person, if he ever existed. Watson, the driver of the Bedford van, was even less communicative. He just did not know what we were talking about. He knew nothing about anything. When told that he would be detained whilst further enquiries were made, his only reply was a very resigned 'Suit yourself.'

We now had three prisoners and quite a large quantity of radios. That of itself would have been enough to justify charging the three with receiving stolen property. The whole performance we had observed earlier would provide evidence that they knew the property to have been stolen. But we still needed to know more. Enquiries very soon revealed that the radios had been stolen from a warehouse in Kentish Town, in north London, on 8th March that year by robbery. Those involuntary feelings had not let me down. I told them that they would be taken to Kentish Town Police Station and charged with the original offence. Bailey, the only one to answer, said, 'I don't suppose it makes a lot of difference.' They were probably right. It did make no difference. There was no attempt at denial of complicity in the offence or offer of an alibi. They were taken to Kentish Town Police Station, charged with the original offence and were subsequently dealt with in the courts.

The important point to be remembered in this case is that these arrests only took place because John Bland and I had decided to pay a call at the Robert Burns public house on the isle of Dogs, for a midday meal, a quiet meal, out of the way, where we believed we were not known. We were not expecting to become involved in anything, but a police officer is never truly off duty.

Just for the record, we did return to the Robert Burns public house for a meal on a number of occasions after that incident. The licensee in due time was told what had taken place, and we remained good friends for many years. As I understand it, he himself later retired and returned to his beloved Ireland, to take in the beauties of the Emerald Isle, far from the Isle of Dogs.

LIGHT-FINGERED LADIES

On a sunny day in June of the same year, John Bland and I were travelling past the Plough public house at the side of Clapham Common, when we saw three very interesting people. They were engaged in quite a heated conversation, and if we had not known just who they were and their particular trade or calling, we would have taken no notice of them. The trio consisted of Kitty Lloyd, Rose Costello and Dora Lane; three quite famous shoplifters. To be more accurate, I should say three notorious shoplifters. Each one had been convicted more times than most. Each one had spent quite a considerable part of her life in prison, but none of them had ever learned her lesson.

We had no idea what the conversation was about, but of one thing we were certain, if they did not break up the chatter and make their way to their respective homes, someone was going to be very sorry. This had the makings of a well-organised shoplifting raid. Someone, somewhere, was going to lose a lot of stock from their shop. These were truly professional shoplifters.It was just after 3 p.m. and the Plough public house had obviously just closed. We waited and watched the trio for some twenty minutes. There was no doubt that they had just come out of the pub. It was a moment when their courage would be well fired up, when they would be determined to get back some of the cash they had no doubt just spent in drink, during a midday drinking session.

Finally Dora Lane walked away and left the company. Perhaps we were wrong. Kitty Lloyd and Rose Costello stood together talking, but we were beginning to believe that they too would soon split up. Then they walked towards a bus stop and boarded a bus going to Putney. They were travelling in opposite directions to where they both lived, for Kitty Lloyd lived in Brixton and Rose Costello in

Dulwich. On the bus they sat together talking earnestly to each other, very deep in conversation. My bet was that they were at that moment planning their next escapade. I could feel it in my bones, that old feeling I knew so well.

In Putney High Street the two women got off the bus and wandered apparently aimlessly in and out of various shops. We could not follow them into these premises or get too close to them, for they both knew John Bland and me well from our previous service at Brixton, which was their usual haunt. We waited as near to each shop they visited as was reasonable and watched their coming and going. These were clever shoplifters, and even if we had gone into any of these shops as perfect strangers to them, it would be very doubtful that we would actually see them steal anything. We did know what to look for, however. Their shopping bags. Don't make any mistake about this. Their shopping bags looked as if they were full, but they always did. Inside the bags would be 'padding' of some kind, screwed-up newspaper, old rags or even old discarded clothing. There were also the women themselves. We knew their statistics as if they were fashion models, although believe me, they bore no resemblance to such people. We did know, however, that both of them were quite capable of enlarging on their basic statistics by putting on another dress, or two, or more under their coats. They might even put on another coat or costume under their coats. In addition, we knew of their ability to 'clout' items. This is typical shoplifter's jargon for wearing a strong pair of drawers or knickers, with firm elastic around the waist and legs, into which they might stuff smaller items that took their fancy.

There was not the slightest indication in Putney that anything untoward had taken place. The statistics seemed the same. The bags may have altered in shape slightly, but they seemed to be about the same weight and size as they were when we first saw them.

From Putney High Street, our quarry made their way to Wandsworth High Street. Here once again, we followed them from one shop to another. here we could see that without doubt the bags had gained weight. As they came out of the Dolcis shoe shop, there was no doubt but that we had been spotted by them, although there was no direct indication of this. We just presumed it was so, because instead of their usual casual meandering from one shop to another, they hastened their pace and made for a nearby car park. Then as they passed a parked VW van, they put their bags down and continued on empty handed.

We stopped them both. John Bland picked up the two bags and brought them over to where we stood. I said to them. 'You know who we are. What have you got in these bags?' Rose Costello, noted for her quick wit and temper, came back immediately with 'We've got no fucking bags.' I reached over for one of the bags and said, 'These bags.' Rose was a little deflated. her first attempted verbal volley had been completely ignored. All she could now think of was, 'Give us a chance.' Kitty Lloyd, however, insisted that she had purchased the costume that was in the bag now produced.

Both women were taken to Wandsworth Common Police Station, where the saga of the afternoon slowly began to unfold in a somewhat complicated way. Kitty Lloyd decided upon her line of approach immediately she sat down in the charge-room. 'Ain't it nice,' she said. 'I've only just met Rosie and she asked me to carry her bag.' Rose Costello, on the other hand, was going to play the complete innocent. Her approach was 'We ain't done nothing wrong.' She then sat with her legs crossed in a feeble effort to look defiant. These acts were far from new to us, they were to be expected, and if they only knew it, they fooled nobody. In fact, quite the opposite, for as she crossed her legs, the bottom of one shoe came to immediate notice. It was clean and shiny, in fact, brand new. I said 'You were seen leaving the Dolcis shoe shop in Wandsworth High Street, and those shoes you are wearing look new to me.' Kitty Lloyd decided in her wisdom to answer. 'Dolcis. No.' Costello laughed and said, 'You've made a big mistake there. I've had them for months.'

In Costello's bag we found a pair of old shoes. We gave them to her and told her to put them on. They were hers without doubt and fitted her perfectly. Also in her bag were two woollen cardigans with the shop labels still fixed on them and twelve pairs of men's socks with the labels still intact. The shoes that Costello was wearing had been stolen from the Dolcis shoe shop, as were the men's socks. In Lloyd's bag we found a suede costume and four pairs of men's socks, similarly with the labels still intact.

In due time, both women appeared at the County of London Sessions, where their activities of 14th June, coupled with their past history, qualified them each for a term of imprisonment of some eighteen months. A quite harsh sentence, one may feel, but in truth only one that would put them out of harm's way and away from the public for a short period of time. On their release, have no doubt about it, they would revert to the only calling they were expert in — shoplifting.

The growth in my knowledge of the underworld was assisted by my frequent visits to magistrates courts, even when I had no case at the time at the particular court. I might, however, learn that a certain very active criminal, who had evaded capture although wanted for some time, was appearing at such and such a court. My object, in these instances, was to take a good look at the friends, relatives and associates who would be lining up in the public gallery at the rear of the court. In the service, we used to refer to these onlookers as the 'Oohs and the Aahs'. Without doubt these characters would have loved to give full-blooded, vociferous support to their prisoner friend. As far as they generally got, however, was to utter the odd 'Ooh' as the evidence against their friend came out, or 'Aah' when their friend or his advocate scored a point in his favour or against the police.

A waste of time? You might think so, but not a bit of it. These visits were most important. Our attention may have been focused for a while on the man now in the dock. We never overlooked, however, the fact that there were hitherto unknown associates to be accounted for. To me there was always something to be learned.

I made such a visit to Lambeth Magistrates Court a few days before Christmas 1963. There I sat in court, paying more attention to those at the rear of the court, standing in the public gallery, than to the actual proceedings. My thoughts, however, were suddenly directed to the court proceedings. There was Dora Lane, the old shoplifter whom I had last seen talking to Rose Costello and Kitty Lloyd near the Plough public house at Clapham, before they left to go on their abortive 'hoisting' spree in Putney and Wandsworth. I had to listen to this one. Dora to my knowledge had a pedigree of previous convictions which had earned her considerable respect and admiration from her criminal friends and associates around London. This was going to be interesting.

A young CID officer from Carter Street Police Station climbed into the witness box and commenced to give evidence. He had walked into Woolworths store in the Walworth Road to make a purchase. Whilst at the counter being served, he had noticed Dora Lane take an article from a nearby display and put it into her bag. He decided to follow her and as a result saw her make her way round the store, helping herself to whatever took her fancy. When she left the store he arrested her. I had heard, it all before. A straightforward arrest of a person caught red-handed, or as the villains themselves would say, 'Bang to Rights'.

Dora Lane, of course, denied the charge and allegations, insisting that she had paid for everything in her possession. She further insisted that the young man was telling 'awful' lies. A brave try on her part, but she was fooling nobody. The learned magistrate had heard it all before and in an apparently tired manner enquired of the officer, 'Is there anything known?' The young detective stepped into the witness box and proceeded to give out the catalogue of Dora Lane's previous convictions, which brought the magistrate to the edge of his seat. The result was obvious. She was sentenced to a term of six months' imprisonment and received the sternest of warnings that, regardless of her age, if she ever appeared before his court again, he would commit her to a higher court where she would receive a far more severe sentence.

A very obvious conclusion but it was far from over. As the magistrate stopped talking, and before he could wave to the gaoler to take her to the cells, Dora Lane shouted, 'I'm innocent. I want to appeal.' The magistrate commented that this was her privilege and she would be told how to go about it in the gaoler's office. With that she was taken from the courtroom. According to the court list, the case that I was interested in would not come on for a while. I therefore decided to go to the gaoler's office and see just what Dora lane was up to. In the office the young detective was talking to Dora as she was filling out a form for her appeal. 'Dora,' he said, 'You must be bloody mad. You'll get two years from the Appeal Court and that's for sure.' Dora laughed and put her pen down. 'Listen, son,' she said, 'I've never let my Arthur down at Christmas yet and I'm not going to now. We'll have our Christmas dinner. We'll have a bloody good drink and I expect we will have a good row. When it's all over, I'll go and knock on the door of Holloway Nick and abandon my appeal and do my time.'

This was a new angle, which I had never previously considered. I knew from my enquiries that Dora's husband, Arthur, was a labourer, in fact a hod carrier. He was totally honest, had never been in trouble with the police and was very rarely out of work. He did not associate with his wife's criminal friends and from enquiries I had made in the past was regularly described as an extremely nice fellow. Now, it seemed, Dora Lane's loyalty was being demonstrated in a most admirable way. Early in the new year, I made a few enquiries in a spare half hour. The Lanes had had their usual brand of Christmas: good food – plenty of it, drink in large quantities and a very noisy party, followed by a domestic row. Then a few days after Christmas, she had done exactly as she had indicated to the detective constable at Lambeth Magistrates Court. She had, true to her word, made her way to Holloway Prison, abandoned her appeal and was then serving the sentence she had received at Lambeth Magistrates Court.

I did not even try to suppress the feeling of admiration I had for this habitual and indeed incorrigible rogue and for her loyalty to her husband, the man she loved, who himself was quite incapable of a criminal act of any kind. Life truly is full of surprises.

PART THREE

PROMOTION

11
Promotion to Detective Inspector

My return to the Flying Squad in 1963 had been most welcome. My informants were now producing plenty of work and my knowledge of the underworld was increasing. Notwithstanding this, I was rarely happy with the standard of work I was producing. Thieves, receivers of stolen property and drug addicts satisfied my superiors, statistically, so in truth I had no worries. As far as I was personally concerned, however, I had that strange feeling of frustration I had previously experienced, nagging away at me and driving me to produce better results. The only trouble with that was that the search for a better class of work would be time consuming, to the extent that it would prevent me from producing the quota of work that would satisfy those whose eyes were fixed on a target governed by statistics. I was indeed on the proverbial horns of a dilemma.

Nonetheless, I kept pace with the desires of my superiors and continued producing miscreants of the types I have mentioned in sufficient numbers to satisfy them. In addition, I was also fortunate in being able to bring to book some extremely active and dangerous criminals. I knew that a selection board for detective inspectors was due and hoped that my efforts had been noted and that I would be directed to appear before the board.

I was fortunate. On 8th February 1965, I duly appeared before a selection board and was successful. Then, shortly afterwards, in April of that year, I found myself retained on the Flying Squad with the rank of detective inspector and of all teams, put in charge of Number Five Squad. What a strange turn of fate. I was now in charge of the team I had joined back in 1957. Furthermore, the current head of the Flying Squad was Commander Tommy Butler, who had been the detective inspector in charge of Number Five Squad when I had joined it eight years earlier. I had a lot to live up to now!

Very shortly after taking over my new team, Commander Tom Butler sent for me. As I walked towards his office I was turning over in my mind his words of advice on booking on duty when I had joined him back in 1957. I was therefore wondering what 'pearl of wisdom' he was going to come up with on this occasion. Before I knew it I was knocking on his office door and being politely invited in.

The Commander wanted to tell me that there was a vacancy on my team for a detective sergeant. I knew this and was waiting the replacement to be posted to me in the usual way. Past experience had taught me that when there was a vacancy, the new boy just appeared on the scene. It was accepted that the last person to know who that person would be was the detective inspector. So, why tell me? It must be obvious to him, for he was only telling me something I was fully aware of. The next question, however, really took the wind out of my sails. Was there anyone in particular whom I would like to bring on to my squad? The fact that I had actually been asked by the Commander just whom I wanted took me completely by surprise.

I was momentarily lost for words. To me the question posed was something of a compliment. 'Well?' said the Commander, somewhat frostily. My reply was instantaneous. 'Give me a pink-faced young man who really wants to learn, who will do what he is told and does not argue with my decisions. I don't want a 'wide boy' who thinks he knows it all.' Tommy Butler leaned way back in his chair and laughed out aloud, and that of itself was something most unusual. 'I might have just the chap for you,' he said as his laughter subsided. He then waved me out of his office. Detective Sergeant Mike McAdam joined me about a fortnight after this interview. We had never met before and I knew nothing about him. He was, however, everything that I had asked for and a lot more. Although I did not realise it at the time, he turned out to be one of the finest detective investigators I have ever met. We are now both retired and are still close friends.

ROBBERS AND JURY NOBBLING

I think that the first job we saw through from start to finish was a

Promotion to Detective Inspector 125

conspiracy to rob Lloyds Bank in Lombard Street, in the City of London. Our original information was sparse to the point of vagueness. We needed, and were most grateful to receive, the full co-operation of the City of London Police.

We inspected the bank form the outside, and this worried us a little. The bank was in one of the busiest and narrowest streets in the City of London and whatever was going to happen could hardly take place in broad daylight. We would have to set up an observation. To do this without being discovered seemed to be the most difficult part of the operation. It did not look like a very promising project and was going to need a great deal of thought. It was, however, the type of work that I had always been determined to get involved in. I had to make sure that our efforts were successful.

As was usual we checked out our equipment. The step was purely routine, but something that I always insisted on. Others would constantly tell me that I was wasting my time, but I had always done it and had no intention of changing now. On this occasion, things were different. The first thing we found was that the Metropolitan Police radios were virtually useless in Lombard Street, a very narrow road with high buildings on each side. Fortunately for us, our City of London Police friends had obviously experienced this difficulty and, with their well-known thoroughness, had taken the necessary steps to overcome the difficulties. The discovery was of itself something of a slap in the face for the Flying Squad. Traditionally it had always been accepted that we had the best equipment, but this time we had to admit that the City of London Police were one up on us. We needed help, but we did not even have to ask, help and co-operation was given us on a plate and we were indeed grateful.

After analysing every small item of information we could lay our hands on, we found ourselves faced with an observation which would have to commence at about six o' clock in the morning. Our enquiries had indicated that between 6 a.m. and 7 a.m. the waste paper from the premises was placed at a nearby collecting point, to be picked up at those early hours by the waste paper contractor. Furthermore our informant had suggested that whatever was going to take place would happen on a Saturday morning, when the City of London is comparatively quiet. Here many probabilities came to mind. Traffic would be light and the likelihood of a traffic jam minimal, making it easier for the thieves to spot any police officers on the scene and far easier for those villains to get away if they suspected there were police in the vicinity.

All of these points went to confirm that Saturday morning could well be the day and time chosen by the thieves. Our information was that the villains were going to rob the bank. On a Saturday morning very few members of staff were in attendance. Indeed, the banks were not open for business. The thieves would therefore have to break in and carry out the robbery. Then one of my team came up with a point that had evaded us all. 'Don't forget, Guvnor, these bank lads love their cricket, football, squash and all of the other games that get played on a Saturday. I know many of them bring their gear in with them on a Saturday.' What a point! If someone in the bank was involved, and it seemed highly likely, anything could happen. Anything could be carried into the premises on the pretext that the holdall or case contained sports equipment.

I was very much aware of the amount of research that thieves put into their planning of an operation. They plan in order to eliminate any probability of getting caught. We as police officers, on the other hand, plan to catch the opposition before the offence had been committed – if that is at all possible. We plan to catch them in the act, but that is difficult indeed, for they have a good head start on us in most cases.

We had so many confusing points to consider. Was this going to be a hold-up? A shot gun job? Of all days, Saturday morning seemed to be obvious. If this was so, how were the villains going to get into the bank? Had they a point of entry already planned? Were they going to work over the weekend and sneak out on Sunday, when all was quiet? This latter option seemed most likely, but of itself it presented one big problem. How were they going to get into the bank? How were they going to get in without being seen by someone? Or, and this was the big question, which seemed a little unlikely, were they going to just burst in, hold up everyone in the premises and rob the staff at gun point?

The questions kept coming to mind, and the more that cropped up the more confusing it became. Finally the obvious kept coming to light. There just had to be an inside man. The trouble was that the more we thought about it, the less likely it seemed that anyone in the actual headquarters of Lloyds Bank, a nationally respected house, could possibly be involved in such an escapade.

Having worked ourselves into the confused state of mind that rejected the possibility of involvement of any bank personnel, I realised that our train of thought had become more in line with that of ordinary people. We were not ordinary people, we were police officers. It was not up to us to disregard any line of possibility, no matter how improbable it might seem. There must be an inside man.

The movement of the waste paper was the one point that rather fascinated me. The waste paper was being taken out early in the morning by a member of the staff. What a wonderful opportunity for the villains to kidnap that person and replace him with another! The villain could then walk calmly into the bank and let in his associate or associates at will. Thereafter, they could do whatever they wished at their leisure. The inside man, maybe an employee or one substituted by the conspirators, had to be the key to the whole situation, and the movement of the waste paper on the coming Saturday morning had to be the answer to many of our questions.

The more we considered this waste paper movement, the more worried about it we became. What if this was a blackmailed employee, who was bringing out a sackful of money for the thieves to just pick up from some point in a quiet city street early on a Saturday morning at a time when there would be very few people around? We were certainly going to keep a very close watch on the coming Saturday.

To keep close observation on a bank without letting that bank know or without being discovered by members of the bank or the public generally, is, as you must appreciate, extremely difficult, and in this instance particularly so, because we would need quite a few men to carry out the operation successfully. We were also faced with the disturbing thought that we ourselves did not know who else might be watching the bank. Our avowed intention therefore, was not to disturb the opposition under any circumstances until we arrested them.

The manager of Coutts Bank on the opposite side of Lombard Street to our target, Lloyds Bank, was sympathetic to our cause. Very thankfully he permitted us to keep watch from a suitable position on his premises.

On Saturday, 6th November 1965 we were in position well before 6 a.m. With me was Detective Sergeant Meyrick, one of my officers, and Detective Constable Squires of the City of London Police.

At 6.15 a.m. a man in his sixties Richard Barton – obviously bank staff, dressed in overalls, came out of the side door of the bank in Change Alley, which led into Lombard Street. He went to some waste paper bins opposite his door, then returned back through the side entrance of the bank and away from sight. At 6.20 a.m. the same man came out and stood at the end of Change Alley, looking up and down Lombard Street. He then returned to the bank. At 6.27 a.m. the same man appeared once again from the side entrance of the bank. This time he put some waste paper on the waste paper heap outside the door. He then went to the end of Change Alley and again looked up and down Lombard Street.

From our position as watchers, we were beginning to become extremely interested and alert. If this man's actions had been put on as a play of acting suspiciously it would have earned public acclaim. To us, tired after being out late the previous night, tidying up our plans, and then obliged to get up far earlier than was normal, the man's actions were a tonic that money could not buy. We were, once again, 'in business', of that there could be no doubt.

At 6.40 a.m. a tall man in a mackintosh entered through the side entrance of the bank. His arrival, to us, was as sudden as was his disappearance inside the premises. Who was he? Should we go after him? What if he had a gun? Questions, questions, questions bombarded my mind. I had to put the brake on my thoughts and think clearly. The decision was mine alone and I must not cloud the issue.

My state of mental confusion was brought to an abrupt standstill a few minutes later by the appearance of another member of staff coming from the side entrance of the bank Obviously things were going quite normally inside the premises. This man – Frederick John Williams – was about forty-five years old and was wearing a similar overall to the first man seen. He walked into Lombard Street, turned right and disappeared from view towards King William Street.

At about this time, my colleagues, watching from another vantage point in King William Street, saw three men, Dunlop, Clarke and Curtis, drive up to the entrance of Post Office Court and deposit two heavy sacks from a vehicle. Their demeanour was very much out of the ordinary. Whatever was in those sacks was not waste paper, yet this was the assembly point for waste paper to be collected by the locally accepted and appointed contractor.

The three men bore no resemblance to other workers in the area, who had been seen placing sacks in Post Office Court, for most of these had been dressed in overalls of one sort or another. In addition, other sacks dropped at this location had from their appearance, although fairly large, not been so obviously heavy. These men were followed away from the scene, for something was going to happen and whatever it was we did not want to alert whoever it may be over London Bridge, into Borough High Street, down to the Elephant and Castle roundabout, then into Kennington Lane, where they were stopped, arrested and taken to Cloak Lane Police Station.

At 7.7 a.m. Williams, who had in all probability seen the two men in the car drop off their sacks, returned to the bank. At 7.10 a.m. Williams came out of the side entrance once again. He stopped at the end of Change Alley, looked up and down Lombard Street, looked at his watch, then crossed Change Alley to the dust bins, where he appeared to straighten some cartons of waste paper. He then walked back up Change Alley, lifted the lid of one of the dust bins, replaced it, and returned into the bank. This man was quite clearly agitated, but we had no idea why. Everything seemed to be going right for the opposition, we were glad to be able to say. The three men now detained and on their way to Cloak Lane Police Station could not raise an alarm. I contented myself with the thought that whatever had been dumped at the waste paper collection point was no doubt the root of the agitation. Furthermore, the three men who put those sacks there were not going to return that morning.

The big question that I now began to ask myself, was, were they supposed to return, and if they did not, what evidence did I have against them? I resigned myself to the thought that whatever was in those sacks would either be collected by the contractor as waste, or perhaps taken inside the bank by one or both of these very agitated men, Barton and Williams.

At 7.30 a.m. both Williams and Barton came out of the side entrance of the bank. From Change Alley, they turned right into Lombard Street and then made their way to Post Office Court. There they examined some of the sacks and picked out the two that had been left by the occupants of the motor car.

My feelings of frustration departed, and the spirit of the chase was now taking over. The two men made their way back to the bank. Williams, who was leading, was carrying a very heavy sack, which he hugged to the front of him. The white top of what looked like an oxygen bottle protruded from the top of the sack and it was clearly very heavy for the man carrying it. Barton was virtually staggering under the weight of whatever was in the very bulky sack that he was bearing. Both took their sacks into the bank.

I collected my men together, including the City of London Police officers who were assisting us. Then to my surprise, and dare I say it gratitude, Williams came out of the side entrance of the bank again and stood at the entrance of Change Alley and Lombard Street. My assumption was that he was waiting to escort the men who had left the sacks at Post Office Court, into the bank, and I was very happy in the certain knowledge that this was not going to happen. I was, however, delighted that Williams had decided to come out into the open again, for I knew only too well that we would have had an almost impossible task in locating him, had he remained inside this very large building.

We stopped Williams and told him that we were police officers and had reason to believe that he and others intended stealing a large sum of money from the bank. Then just to add a little strength to that suggestion, we told him that we had seen him taking what we felt must be cutting equipment into the premises to enable others to get into the vaults. I also told him that I wanted to see the grey-haired man who was obviously working with him. Williams expressed his shock. His act of innocence was most convincing, but I knew only too well what I had seen and I was certainly not going to rest until we had examined the sacks we had seen taken in.

Williams insisted that all that he had taken in were sacks of waste paper. Nevertheless, he took us to the basement office where he worked. To our delight and satisfaction Barton was there. He too insisted that all that was brought in were sacks of paper and that the contents of those sacks had been put into a larger one and sewn up: a very convincing story to someone who had not observed their actions earlier. These two men were very convincing liars and the more they lied, the happier I became.

On searching Williams, we found three skeleton keys. Now we were even more satisfied that we were on to something good. Notwithstanding the evidence now in our hands, Williams still insisted that these were bank keys and that he had signed for them. We certainly could not believe this. We then searched Barton. He was of a different calibre to Williams and I had a very distinct feeling that he was in all probability something of an innocent party in this very ingenious plan. Innocent party he may have been, but he had still brought 'something' into the bank and was therefore still part of the conspiracy.

I hardly need to enlarge on the fact that searching a bank is somewhat different to searching a house, shop or even a warehouse. Here there would be too many locked doors for our liking, and what were the skeleton keys for? There were also many valuable items, which quite frankly we would not even want to touch. We needed the presence of a very senior bank official to accompany us on our quest for whatever had been brought into the premises. I knew full well that finding such an official on Saturday morning was not going to be easy. The trouble was that in the back of my mind I was worried in case explosives had been brought in, in those sacks. To make matters easy for everyone, I attempted to induce the two men to show me the sacks we had seen them carrying. I was not going to settle for bags of waste paper. Whatever was in those sacks that these men had brought into the bank was heavy, and I could not forget the top of the oxygen bottle I had seen.

At 9.25 a.m., after we had made contact through Scotland Yard, a bank official arrived. At the outset, he was more than a little disturbed to find that we were actually in the basement of his bank. He listened, however, to our explanation with increasing interest. The skeleton keys we had found in Williams' possession proved to operate in pairs and opened every vault grill except the internal strong room grill. Was this the reason for the cutting equipment – the oxygen bottle seen – or had explosives already been brought in? There was little doubt that we were into a conspiracy to relieve Lloyds Bank of a very valuable consignment of something.

Very shortly after this, a shout from Detective Sergeant Gwyn Waters drew me to a temporary storage cupboard, where there were two sacks. These contained two cylinders of gas and various items of cutting equipment, which we took charge of and removed to Cloak Lane Police Station. Nothing further was found, and we finally took our property and the two prisoners, Williams and Barton, to that police station at 10.30 a.m.

Later, the three men detained earlier, together with the two men from the bank, were charged with conspiracy to steal from Lloyds Bank. Neither of them wished to offer any explanation for what we had seen and found. This did not worry us. We had seen enough and what we had discovered inside the bank was evidence sufficient to place before the court. All that was left for myself and my colleagues to do now was to put together the mountain of paperwork that was unfortunately necessary to enable me to lay a case of this magnitude before a judge and jury.

This case, needless to say, caused quite a stir at the preliminary hearing at the Mansion House Magistrates Court. Four of the prisoners were committed for trial in custody, with Barton alone being allowed bail. Subsequently, at the Central Criminal Court, the Old Bailey, there were complications. Two trials in fact took place, the first before Judge Rogers. Then after a few days it became known that the wife of one of the prisoners had approached, or attempted to approach, two jurors. That jury was therefore discharged. The second trial started before the Common Sergeant, Judge Mervyn Griffith-Jones. Here, from the dock, one of the prisoners challenged seven jurors, another challenged four, whilst Williams challenged five. This was something very new to me and very obviously surprised the court officials. To challenge a juror is every prisoner's right, but this was clearly an extension of the conspiracy with which these prisoners were charged. It was also quite obvious that those being challenged were the jurors who by appearance alone looked as if they were the more intelligent. Finally, after all of the challenges had been dealt with and a jury satisfactory to the prisoners empanelled, the trial got under way.

A few days later, counsel reported that one of the jurors had been seen talking to a man with a known long criminal record and that the particular juror had been offered money. That juror was discharged from service in the trial. The following day it was disclosed that another juror had been offered £600 to say 'Not Guilty' at the end of the trial. He reported this to the police. Certain counsel then made application to the judge to discharge the jury. The judge, however, a man of vast experience, would not permit this to happen. Then followed the reporting by yet another juror of the fact that he had been offered £100 to say 'Not Guilty' when the time came. Again there were applications for the jury to be discharged. Once again the judge refused the application.

After these many delays we were ultimately able to get on with the trial. It was quite obvious, however, that it was going to be beset with many difficulties, even though we were quite satisfied that our

Promotion to Detective Inspector 133

evidence was conclusive in indicating the guilt of all concerned. Cross-examination by defence counsel was stringent, but we had little to worry about. Our evidence was perfect and despite their efforts, counsel was unable to destroy any part of it.

On the eleventh day of the trial came a further incident of a kind I had not met before. As I recall it, it was on a Monday morning after the weekend recess. John Dunlop refused to come up from the cells and take his place in the dock, insisting that he was going to remain below. This caused not a little concern. The judge called the counsel to his chambers to discuss the issue. I and my colleagues could only sit in court and wonder what was going to happen next. I had never come across such a strange affair in court before and neither had any of my colleagues.

After some while, the judge and counsel returned to the court and recalled the jury. Addressing them, the judge said: 'Dunlop has indicated to me that he does not propose to sit in the court and listen to any more of the proceedings.' He then indicated to the court that he was entitled, with the charge involved, to continue with the trial in Dunlop's absence and that was what he proposed to do. Turning to the jury, he pointed out that they had already listened to the prosecution evidence; they had heard Dunlop's evidence; they had also heard witnesses called for his defence; therefore Dunlop had no further active part to play in the case. Then addressing Dunlop's counsel, he said, 'If your client feels at any time that he would like to occupy a seat in the dock, he is entitled to do so.'

The evidence in this case slowly came to an end, followed by speeches by various counsel involved and the judge's summing-up of the case. The jury then retired, leaving myself and my colleagues waiting for them to come to their conclusion, which to us, after all these strange and unusual incidents, seemed obvious. With the strength of our evidence and all of the antics behind the scenes, how could a jury ever find any other verdict but 'Guilty' for all concerned?

Then we found ourselves with time on our hands. We found ourselves examining everything that had taken place in relation to the jurors who had reported certain irregular behaviour. We knew and trusted our jury system, it had proved its worth over the years. We were most grateful for the fact that honest jurors had come forward. Now we found ourselves worried about the remaining jurors. Had we missed something? Any small detail? Had there been further approaches to the jury that we did not know about? We were worried, very worried, and that last question was the one that worried us the most. Had there been further approaches?

After what seemed an age, the jury returned to the court to say that they could not agree. Our fears grew. We must have missed something, but what? The jury was given a further direction by the judge and again they retired to consider the words of wisdom that had been put to them. This time it did not take them long to make up their minds. After twenty minutes they returned to the court with 'Not Guilty' against four of the accused, finding Williams alone 'Guilty'. He was sentenced to five years' imprisonment.

Williams lodged an appeal against this sentence, which was heard later at the Court of Criminal Appeal by Lord Parker, the Lord Chief Justice. Here, as was expected, the wisdom of the Law Lords was amply demonstrated. Commenting on the fact that four of the five persons accused of conspiring to raid the bank had been acquitted after several attempts had been made to bribe jurors, he said that the case left a very nasty feeling in one's mind. Then addressing counsel who appeared on behalf of Williams, he said, 'I rather sympathise with your client, I think he was the "inside" employee who the jury had no hesitation in convicting. One has the impression that the others got off because one of those bribery attempts succeeded. Think of the strength of the case against the four who were acquitted.' The appeal was refused and the sentence of five years' imprisonment was upheld.

We were, of course, most disappointed in losing such an important case as this one. We were, however, happy in our mind that we had done everything true to the book, and there was no doubt in the minds of our superiors about our action. we criticised the jury system amongst ourselves, but we were officers of the law. Our duty was to produce the evidence to the satisfaction of our legal authorities, who would in turn present it to the court. Thereafter the matter was out of our hands.

Our personal and unpublicised opinions were also in the minds of others. They were echoed in a number of newspapers that had not let the matter pass. In fact, I was most happy to open the Daily Mail of 4th March 1966 and read headlines that indicated there was now a move to foil 'jury nobblers'. There was even a suggestion that the jury system must, or would be, drastically overhauled. The article quoted incidents that had happened during the trial of our Lloyds Bank conspirators.

The newspaper also pointed out the irony that under the then law jurymen were fully protected from approaches by police officers and court officials, but there was little that the authorities could do to keep 'jury nobblers' away from jurymen. It also quoted from the last annual report of Justice that the British section of the International Commission of Jurists had said of the jury system: 'It may be unwise to underestimate the ingenuity and corrupting powers of the criminal forces at work in society today'. It further quoted a member of Justice as saying: 'That still applies. Our jury system needs a long hard look'. The most heartening point in the articles was the information that the Home Office had indicated that new legislation, including such matters as the accessibility of jury lists, was being prepared.

Once back at the Yard, I found that other colleagues had read the particular article that I mentioned and also that other newspapers were latching on to the angle that a much-needed change should, and would, take place in the not too distant future. The change did come and it did not take very long. Dunlop and company may well have got away with their case by criminal cunning, but those actions prevented many future criminals from evading justice by adopting the same methods, methods which I am quite sure had been used for many years but had gone by undetected, because they had not been seen to be as open and blatant in the actual courtroom. For my part, I would like to think that it was my efforts and that of my team that did much to bring about the change in the jury system from the once unanimous verdict to the majority verdict of the jury that is accepted today.

THE VALUE OF GOOD INFORMATION

It has been said that a good investigator is only as good as the information he is able to obtain through his contacts and sources. Believe me, however, there is a lot more to it than that.

As a young investigator, I had often found myself quite elated when I had picked up some snippet of information, which to me looked promising. I would generally go to my partner or immediate superior officer and discuss the next step with him. My requests for guidance were always accepted, and from the many officers I had gone to over the years I gained knowledge that assisted my own successes as I climbed through the ranks of the Criminal Investigation Department.

As an officer in charge of a Flying Squad team it was only on matters of dire necessity or urgency that I sought advice from my boss. Furthermore, if I did go to him for advice or guidance, I did not tell my team of officers. I needed above all their loyalty, trust and obedience.

Such a series of events occupied my mind on 14 September 1966. One of my trusted informants had come to me to indicate that Tony Baldesarre, who lived in a block of flats in Vauxhall in south-west London, was going to carry out a robbery the following day. 'Where?' I asked my informant. 'Somewhere in London. South of the river. Definitely on your patch, and I think it is going to be a wages job. A security van.' Try as I might, however, I could not pin my man down to even a district where the crime was to be committed. I had to satisfy myself in the knowledge that the criminal whom I knew as Tony Baldesarre was very capable of effecting such a robbery. I knew where he lived, at Tidbury House in Nine Elms, near Vauxhall, so we did at least have a start point. The prospect of following such an expert criminal as this in London traffic and on his way to carry out a robbery, however, was not a proposition that I rejoiced in, for I knew quite well that I would soon be discovered.

London is a very expansive city and my 'patch', as quoted by my informant, was the whole of the Metropolitan Police District. Just consider it: the whole of the County of Middlesex, parts of the Counties of Essex, Kent, Surrey, Buckinghamshire and Hertfordshire. Right in the middle of all that is the City of London, an area little over a square mile, covering many large banks, business houses and the Stock Exchange and with its own police force. Quite a 'patch'. Many square miles of densely populated areas and wide open spaces. I badly needed a crystal ball! I could see no useful purpose in going to my superiors for advice on this 'pearl of wisdom'. This was one I would have to sort out myself. Alternatively, of course, I could keep the information to myself in the hopes that no robbery took place. But that, however, was never my style.

When I sat down to analyse this piece of information, it was soon very clear that the only positive pointer was that Tony Baldessare was in on the robbery. Quite obviously he would not carry this one out on his own. According to our Method Index he was not a 'loner' and always worked with others. My estimation was that this case would need not less than three, probably four, associates and they would more than likely start out from their own addresses in various parts of London. There was the unfortunate point that Baldessare was very much respected by his friends, associates and partners in crime, and he had many. Thus we were resigned to the fact that we would have to start with Baldessare and his home at Nine Elms.

I sent Detective Sergeant Lampard and his partner to Tidbury House early the following morning to watch number 38, where Baldessare lived. With the remainder of my team I remained in the squad office at New Scotland Yard, not a little frustrated, but at least hopeful: frustrated that I could not work out where the robbery would be likely to take place, hopeful that my informant would ring me up with further information, hopeful that a robbery might be reported with the description of a man that would fit Baldessare, above all, hoping that Tony Lampard would see something that would get the operation moving.

That morning a robbery was reported in Mitcham. Details at that stage were vague, but those details, such as they were, were sufficient to get us all on the move to Vauxhall. On the way we listened intently to our radio for further particulars of what had taken place. Then we heard that it had only been an attempted robbery, and Baldesarre was not given to mere attempts. Whatever he started he generally finished. The geographical location of Mitcham to Vauxhall, however, was enough. It was also south of the river Thames, as my informant had indicated to me. Yes, this could well be the one that Baldesarre was on. It was decision time and I was the only one who could make the decision.

I decided to take my team to the area of Tidbury House, wait for Baldesarre and his mates to return and take the matter from there. Somehow I felt quite sure that they would return to Tidbury House, despite having no evidence that they had ever left that address that morning.

On our way southwards from New Scotland Yard, Tony Lampard called up to say that Baldesarre and three men had arrived at his location. They had entered the lift, travelled to the seventh floor and entered Flat No. 38. I breathed a sigh of relief as the tingle of the hairs on the back of my neck gave me the telltale sign that I knew so well and respected. This just had to be the team of robbers who had attempted to hold up and rob a vehicle belonging to the cash carrying company Armour Speed, the name we had earlier heard over our radio.

Experience teaches us many lessons. I had learned over the years never to rush in. Always size up a situation, no matter how simple it may seem, before taking immediate action, even if confronted with need for immediate action. In this instance we had a large block of flats served by a lift, with a number of flats on each floor. Each flat opened on to a balcony, which had a comparatively low wall overlooking the courtyard below. I was not happy with that balcony wall. It may well have complied with Council regulations, but it was not the most exciting area in which to have to arrest violent men, particularly seven floors up.

We were faced with, or perhaps I should say I was faced with, two alternatives. Firstly, charge up to the seventh floor, force our way into flat 38 and arrest the occupants. That may sound easy to the uninitiated, but we did not truly know that these were the men who had attempted to hold up the security van. In any case, if they were, they would be armed and we certainly were not. The second option had to be the one to follow. Wait until they come out. There were four of them and eight of us. We will play the waiting game.

As my mind was made up, the door of number 38 opened and three men came out. Now we had to move. Surprise had to be the order of the day. We saw the three disappear in the direction of the elevator and rushed across the courtyard to wait by the lift. Then, as the lift doors opened, we stepped inside. For my part, I had quite a shock, although happily we had the important advantage of surprise, for the occupants had no warning of our arrival.

The three men who confronted us were well known to me. John McVicar, an extremely dangerous man, well educated, a physical fitness fanatic and a confirmed robber; George Nash, the youngest member of the notorious Nash family, probably a little out of his class in this instance; the third man was David Bailey, a man of known violence and another confirmed robber, suspected of involvement in a serious London robbery that had taken place a short while earlier, where firearms had been used.

This was the type of opposition that under no circumstances could be underestimated. Knowing the opposition, however, was a wonderful advantage. We had them at that particular moment safely cooped up in a lift, but we had to get them out. Furthermore, there was still Baldesarre upstairs in his flat and we did not like the thought that he could turn up any minute, perhaps armed.

I was not unduly worried about young George Nash and therefore directed Detective Sergeant Lampard to take him to his car. Before having another removed, I made sure that he had got him safely to the waiting police vehicle. Detective Sergeant David Dixon and his partner escorted David Bailey to one of the cars. This left John McVicar, who, I knew only too well, had to be handled with great care. The task of escorting him to one of our vehicles was given to Detective Sergeant Nick Birch and Detective Constable Playle. The wisdom of my choice of the escorting officers was soon apparent. McVicar, the escape artist, did not know it, but he was in the presence of Alan Playle, an Olympic sprinter of some note. He would no doubt have assessed Nick Birch, the smallest man in my group, as easy meat. Here again, he did not know Birch, a man of extremely sharp reflexes. The son of a clergyman, Nick Birch was scared of nothing and he was certainly not scared of McVicar.

Whilst all of this was going on, I had a man watching the entrance of number 38. He would signal me if anyone else were to leave the premises. My gaze was therefore now in two directions, towards my watcher and also to the two men now escorting McVicar to their vehicle. I did not have to wait long.

After a few steps, McVicar produced the power that we had heard spoken of with considerable awe in the past. He was being taken to the car with one officer, Detective Sergeant Birch, holding on to his left arm and Detective Constable Playle holding his right arm. Suddenly, he raised his left arm with apparently no difficulty at all, lifting Nick Birch high in the air. He then hurled him to the ground. With his left arm free, he struck Alan Playle and knocked him to the ground. With that McVicar was off like the proverbial hare, across the courtyard. Strange to say, I was not particularly worried. He could never outrun Playle, and Nick Birch was not going to take kindly to being hurled to the ground in such a manner. Alan Playle caught up with McVicar within a few paces and grasping one wrist, swung him round. By this time, Birch had caught up with them and with little difficulty subdued McVicar.

Our next move was to flat number 38. Baldesarre fortunately had not seen what had taken place at the lift or in the downstairs courtyard. He claimed that he had been in his flat all morning, something that we knew to be false. Having taken the precaution of obtaining a search warrant before leaving the Yard that morning, we searched the flat and found a quantity of guns of various types, together with the necessary ammunition to go with them. We were happy. This confirmed our gut feeling that we had arrested the right men. Our prisoners were subsequently charged at Mitcham Police Station, and in due course dealt with at the Central Criminal Court, where they were all found guilty of the attempted robbery of the Armour Speed vehicle and sentenced to varying terms of imprisonment.

The value of informants and of the information they can supply was once again amply demonstrated. The interpretation of the information, however, is a matter for the individual officer in charge. He has to make the decision, then stand by that decision. If that decision is correct, the probability is that no one will say anything. If he is wrong, however, then he will find himself in considerable trouble from his superiors. The difficulties, however, do not stop there, for having made a wrong decision, he will also lose the respect of his men, and that respect is the most important point of all.

12
Upwards to Detective Chief Inspector

On 18th September 1967 I was promoted to the rank of detective chief inspector and posted back to 'C' Division, with my office at West End Central Police Station, the station where I had commenced duty as a uniformed constable way back in 1946. My activities were now confined to Soho, Mayfair and the Covent Garden and Tottenham Court Road areas of London. I felt somewhat restricted after my many years of freedom within the Metropolitan Police District, working from various departments at New Scotland Yard. With promotion, however, one is obliged to accept such situations as they are presented to you.

Over the years I had built up certain very useful connections and sources of information in London's West End, probably because it was what is best described as my birthplace as a policeman. I was therefore quite confident that I could put those sources to good use for the benefit of both the public and the service; but I was soon reminded that my work in my now elevated rank was going to keep me so heavily involved in matters of administration and supervision, that I would have very little time to exercise those outside sources. As to visiting the more 'interesting' lower-class clubs and public houses, where I knew that I could glean useful information, I was told quite firmly that this would be frowned upon.

This was frustrating advice to say the least and I was not at all happy in the thought that I now was to become something of an 'office wallah'. I had begun to enjoy being a detective investigator.

Fortunately for me many of my worries were put to an end within a few days of commencing work at West End Central. Whilst I was still mulling over the restrictions placed upon me in my new role, an incident occurred on 23th September 1967, which brought me back to the work that I loved so much.

An American Embassy official and two young CID Officers had been seriously assaulted in the the Stork Club in Swallow Street only a few yards from Piccadilly Circus. This was one that I would certainly investigate myself and I found myself praying fervently that I would have some success.

The two young officers, whom I shall call Detective Sergeant 'Eric' and Detective Constable 'George', had been working with the American, 'Garry', on a matter that I do not propose to discuss. Suffice it to say, it was a matter with high ranking and official backing. The American had no intimate knowledge of the West End of London, but aware that the two officers knew their way around the area, had asked them to take him to some of the more interesting places.

Now there is an unwritten law amongst CID officers in London that many to their detriment take all too lightly, and I am afraid that it was the case in this instance. This unwritten law goes something like this: 'When off duty, get out of the West End by eleven o'clock at night'. Whether this sound advice had got to these officers or not, I have no idea. Their misfortune, however, proved the wisdom of those warning words.

Having finished their enquiries on 22nd September, the officers booked off duty at Vine Street Police Station at 11 p.m and then took 'Garry' for a walk round Soho. The American was fascinated with this little tour, and as they made their way back to their motor car, parked near Vine Street, he asked the officers if they could take him to a cabaret show.

The Stork Room, or Stork Club, in Swallow Street can only be less than fifty yards from Vine Street Police Station. It was well known to the officers as a licensed club, but after a couple of drinks, and finding the service to be exceptionally slow, they decided to leave and go back to 'Garry's' apartment for a meal.

Outside the club, in Swallow Street, they met Bill Offner, the manager of the club who was at that moment returning to the premises. He was a respected club owner and knew the officers. He asked them why they were leaving and had not remained to see the cabaret. He was told that they were going for a meal elsewhere. Bill Offner, however, persuaded the trio to return to the club and placed them at a table close to where three other men were sitting.

Upwards to Detective Chief Inspector 143

Everything went on quite normally until about 1.45 a m just before the cabaret show came on. Thereafter there was some confusion amongst the various stories put forward. The impression I gained during my investigation was that one of the trio, probably the American, pushed his chair back in order to have a better view of the stage and bumped into one of the three men on the next table. Apologies for the inconvenience caused were no doubt forthcoming, but were clearly not accepted. Of one point, however, there was no doubt. One of the three men got up and set about 'Eric', 'George' and 'Garry' in a most violent manner before they could get to their feet and defend themselves. 'Garry' was knocked almost unconscious and could hardly stand up, whilst the two officers were subjected to a succession of blows which made them realise very quickly that they would be quite unable to subdue the aggressor.

Sensibly, and having no desire to make a heroic attempt to bring about the detention of the villain on their own, they left the club. In their minds there was no doubt the feeling that they should get to the nearest telephone and call for assistance. Perhaps, however, it was that unwritten law in the back of their minds that prevented them from doing so. They decided to make their way to 'Garry's' apartment in St John's Wood, patch themselves up and perhaps have a good meal as had been their original intention. This, however, was not to be. The injuries and bruising were sufficiently serious to require medical attention and resulted in the three being taken to Paddington General Hospital for treatment, particularly necessary in the case of 'Garry.'

The trouble with investigating a serious crime in a club, particularly a West End club, is that nobody wants to tell you the truth about what has taken place. The clientele, staff and hostesses are always very much aware of the unwritten laws of the underworld, never to be a witness and when questioned, never to have seen anything. My experience over the years had taught me to expect nothing more, even in a serious shooting, than to be told by an obvious eye-witness, that he or she had only heard a bang and looked round. The fact that you could actually put them at the scene of the shooting and even place them within a few feet of the incident had little bearing on the case as far as they were concerned. They, purely by coincidence, were always looking the other way when the fatal incident occurred and heard nothing, or had heard something, and looked round, but saw nothing!

In this instance there was no shooting or loud staccato bang. There was plenty of shouting, loud shouting. The man had suddenly stood up, shouted something in a very loud voice and rained a hail of blows on to the nearby customers. This must have been seen by many, and there just had to be a witness or witnesses. Unfortunately, the only person or persons who would gain anything from our investigation would be those responsible, for the grapevine would soon carry our anger and interest back to them.

Fortunately, this is the time when true experience comes into its own, and my past experience was to stand me in very good stead. I had no intention of 'beating the drum' in my attempts to track down all those who were present at the time of the assaults in the Stork Room that night. I knew there was only one way to solve this matter and I had to act quickly and silently.

There are few West End clubs that do not have their own pet photographer, and when I say 'pet' photographer, I refer to one whom the club owner and management can trust. Such club photographers are a very specialised group, expert in their particular trade and highly trusted by those who employ them. They in turn are very much aware of the value of the photographs they take: husbands with their girlfriends, wives with their lovers and villains with their partners in crime. Then, of course, there are the decent people out on the odd visit, such as the victims in this case, who only pay a call to these places for the experience. Thus you can well understand that the last thing that they would ever want is to lose face, or their clients' trust in them, particularly by letting it be known, even in the vaguest way, that they do not treat the photographs they take with the utmost confidentiality.

I was very much aware that by interviewing those present in the Stork Room that night, word would soon get back to the photographer. I knew what his immediate reaction would be: those photographs would be promptly lost or destroyed. I had to silently find that photographer, and my efforts to trace him, whoever he was, had to be carried out in such a manner that he would not be forewarned of my interest in him.

It was not long before my well-tried sources of information in the West End came up with the answer. The photographer's identity, his address and details of his studio were soon known to me. He was assured by my contact that his identity was safe in my hands, providing that he co-operated with me. The result was that I was very soon browsing through the negatives of photographs he had taken that night. Armed with photographs of groups of men who were in the Stork Room during the night in question, I soon had one of the assailants identified by one of those assaulted. We were now, shall I say, halfway home with the investigation.

Now it is all very well being able to say: 'That is the man who caused my injuries' by looking at photographs. It is a different matter to trace him. He was not known by my usually helpful contacts, but a man who was capable of exploding into a fit of violence such as that experienced by those assaulted just had to be known by police somewhere. Easy, you may think, but I also knew that by hawking the photographs around those present in the club that night, word would soon get back to those responsible and they would fade away into the background and never be traced for some while. I was determined to ensure that this did not happen.

Within a few days, photographs of the three men at the adjoining table to those assaulted were circulated through police circles in an attempt to identify whoever was responsible. One of them, Kenneth Charles Palmer, was soon recognised and named. The next move was to trace his whereabouts, but this was not half as easy as it sounds. To this end, my time spent on the Flying Squad paid dividends. Detective Sergeant Nick Birch, who had served for a number of years with me in that department, was the first name that came to mind. I put him in the picture as to what had taken place and within a few days he had arrested Palmer.

Palmer's initial reaction was a categorical denial of any involvement in this matter. This, however, he very soon retracted. He admitted assaulting the three men, 'Eric', 'George' and 'Garry', but was quite unable to give any explanation for his violent outburst. He was duly charged with the assaults, and appeared before the Bow Street Magistrate. To say he was surprised at the speed with which he had been identified and arrested, would be putting it mildly. He was obviously shocked, being quite convinced that the unwritten law of the West End underworld would come to his assistance and that he would never be identified following his outburst. Of one thing I was quite sure: he was clearly amazed at the positive manner in which he had been arrested and identified.

For my part, my efforts in this case were quite surprisingly appreciated by my superiors, to the extent that they placed no restriction on my visiting those very 'interesting' clubs and public houses where I was able to continue my activities in building up further contacts who were prepared to assist me in future investigations.

My success in the Stork Room affair and the very complimentary remarks that followed, lulled me into a false sense of satisfaction and security. My boss, Detective Chief Superintendent Arthur Butler, was himself a superb investigator. In addition to being my superior officer, he was older than me and considerably more experienced. Thus, when a job did come along calling for an investigation that would have to be carried out by a senior CID officer, he would take it over. This resulted in my spending the most part of the following twelve months carrying out supervisory and guidance tasks.

Such work was very necessary for the good of the service and very important for the instruction of younger officers. It was, however, terribly frustrating for me as a detective who thrived on difficult investigations. I can truthfully say that the only satisfaction I gained during this particular period was from the value of the contacts whose trust I had been able to build up over the years. On a number of occasions I was able to produce information from my various sources, which helped many of my junior officers to bring their cases to a satisfactory conclusion.

TRANSFER TO 'M' DIVISION

On 6th January 1969 I was transferred to 'M' Division in south London, with headquarters at Southwark. This division is a most interesting wedge in the Metropolitan Police District. It stretches from Waterloo almost to Deptford along the south bank of the Thames, then comes to a point at Crystal Palace, ten miles south. This was an area that I knew extremely well, far better than most of my colleagues. At that time I lived only a mile from the southernmost boundary at Crystal Palace and my journey to work was far easier than before.

Here at Southwark, I was again the second in command of the Divisional CID, under successive detective chief superintendents. Again the accent was on supervision, but I found that the frustrating and apparently time-wasting period spent in the West End of London involved in supervision stood me in very good stead. There, I had disciplined myself in my new role as a supervising officer. Now I

Upwards to Detective Chief Inspector

intended to impress my superiors with my efficiency, if I could I was still seeking advancement in the service and had a long way to go yet on the promotion ladder. It was at this juncture that I was reminded in a quiet and serious manner that I was forty-nine years old.

'You are unlikely to gain promotion further at your age. After all, you will be retiring in five years,' I was told. What rubbish! What utter poppycock! I could not find the right words; even if I had I would have had to suppress them. I put forward the argument that in any career job, and being a police officer is certainly a career, what makes the work so interesting and satisfying is that you are adding to your expertise and learning each day. I pointed out furthermore that I passed much of my accumulated knowledge to my junior officers and thus made them more efficient as they made their way through the service. I fully realised that I had only five years to go, but had much to give by way of experience. It just did not make sense that I should call it a day and quietly coast along until I was pensioned off at the age of fifty-five.

Charles Renshaw was the Commander of 'M' Division in those days. He was quietly known as 'Boom'. When he was annoyed everybody knew and heard him. He could be a quite frightening man, but I found him to be a perfect gentleman. I did manage to earn his blessing, at least, and also an extremely fine recommendation for promotion.

With the Promotion Board coming up in April of that year I was determined to ensure that I projected myself to best advantage. Remembering all the past times when I had stood before such a Board, I was determined to have something to talk about. The Board has a limited time in which to interview you. Keep their interest to the subject of your choice, not theirs, give them no time to throw in those absolutely destructive questions. My preparation for the forthcoming event had to be thorough. I recalled my earlier success on 'C' Division, when I had effected the arrest of Palmer for the Stork Room assaults, a few weeks after joining that division. A job like that was just what I could do with, and with that thought foremost in my mind, I paid particular attention to the happenings on 'M' Division.

I did not have to wait long. As I recall it, it was on 12th February 1969, a Wednesday. There had been an attempt to rob a rent collector at Cadsby House, in Jamaica Road, Bermondsey, on the Tower Bridge section. Two police officers called to the scene had been threatened with a shotgun by the robbers. Roy Hilder, a man whom I knew, had been brought in for questioning, and I was certainly going to look into this case.

At Tower Bridge Police Station I was met by Tony Lampard, the detective inspector. We were old friends. Tony was no fool and was delighted to hear that I had dropped in to give him a hand, and not just in my role as a supervising officer. We interviewed Hilder and told him he would be charged with conspiracy to rob and possessing an offensive weapon, the sawn-off shotgun produced to him. He was then asked if he wanted to make a statement about the matter. His reply was almost complimentary to those who had arrested him. 'No,' he said, 'You've already got enough to hang me.' The prospects of hanging did not come into it, though the offence he was going to be charged with was of a most serious nature.

Hilder's accomplice had made good his escape from the scene of the attempted robbery. I was very anxious to learn his identity. Clearly, however, Hilder had no intention of telling us who the missing conspirator was and indicated this to us in his answer to our question. 'Mr Swain, it would be more than my life is worth. I'm no grass.'

We required information. We needed help, someone to point the finger in the right direction. Informants were the answer, and I knew that I had plenty of these in this particular area of London. Then with my mind on the forthcoming Promotion Board, I silently prayed that one of those contacts would come up with the answer to my quest. If ever I needed assistance, I needed it right now and not in a month's time.

I left Southwark Police Station early that evening and virtually went to ground. I looked up every informant I could find and put my question to him or her. I assured them that this was a matter to which I would appreciate an answer in double quick time. No questions would be asked. We wanted a name, an address if this was possible, and we would take it from there. Police officers had been threatened with a sawn-off shotgun. It was very well known that I personally do not permit that on my 'manor'. The message was well received, and although it cost me a lot more in drink than I could ever claim back in incidental expenses, I went home satisfied in my own mind that I had done all that I could. I was also fairly confident that I would have an answer very soon.

On 14 February, to my relief, a message had been received, and

Tony Lampard called me over to Tower Bridge Police Station. David Frank Fraser was awaiting my pleasure. Again with the detective inspector, I carried out the interview, this time directing my attention to Fraser. His denials were truly professional and his attitude almost gentlemanly. He was in fact, adopting the copybook stance of an accomplished crook. I knew, as I had so often felt in the past, that we were once again undoubtedly 'in business'.

The almost convincing air of innocence Fraser gave off confirmed my own gut feelings immediately I spoke to him. I said, 'You know why you are here? The casual reply, 'Yes, something about a robbery,' gave me all the confidence that I required. This was not the attitude of an innocent man who had been woken up rather early in the morning. Such a man would surely have been enraged at having to accompany police officers to a police station on a matter he knew nothing about.

His next statement confirmed my feelings. I told him that Roy Hilder had already been charged with conspiracy to rob a rent collector at Cadsby House, Jamaica Road, two days earlier and that he was also wanted in relation to that offence. His reply was, 'You'd better prove it, then. I'm saying nothing.' This could hardly be the reply of an outraged citizen. It was the very calm challenge that we had no evidence against him, by a very obviously guilty man. In truth, at that stage we did have no evidence, but I was sure that our investigation would soon prove his guilt.

We had witnesses to this incident, and my next step was to ensure that an identification parade was arranged as soon as possible. I told Fraser of my intention and asked him if he was prepared to stand on such a parade. His reply again confirmed our original feelings. 'Yes, but not until I have seen my 'brief'. Get my old man to get in touch with Sampsons, and if they say it is alright, I'll stand.'

The request was his right as a citizen, and we lost no time in relaying it. Shortly afterwards Sidney Rae, one of Sampsons' managing clerks, arrived at Tower Bridge Police Station to represent and advise Fraser. It was 11.45 a.m. and after a short consultation, Fraser agreed to stand on the identification parade providing that Mr Rae was present. He was identified by two witnesses, both police officers, who had no doubt it was he who had threatened them with a shotgun before making good his escape from the scene. He was charged with conspiracy to rob and possession of the shotgun. Both Fraser and

Hilder were in due course committed to stand trial at the Central Criminal Court.

On 24th April 1969, having been so recommended, I duly attended New Scotland Yard and appeared before a Promotion Board for selection to the rank of detective chief superintendent. The Board consisted of the Commissioner, the Assistant Commissioner for Crime and Commander Millan. I entered the room full of confidence. The attitude of the Board was truly amiable and the questions most trivial. My answers, I knew, were perfect. I did not have to draw on my recent success at Tower Bridge Police Station with Hilder and Fraser and was indeed very happy.

The interview over, I left with a spring in my step. It was not raining, and I decided to walk the mile back to Southwark. On my way I examined the questions that had been put to me. The lowliest sergeant could have answered them. The extremely pleasant manner in which the questions had been put to me seemed somewhat out of place. In fact, the nearer I came to Southwark, the more worried and confused I found myself. The eager manner in which my answers had been accepted was all wrong. I recalled previous Promotion Boards I had attended. As far as I could recall, where I had passed and been selected for advancement, I had had quite a hard time convincing members of the Board that my answers were correct. On only one occasion previously had I had such an easy interview with my peers. That was in 1962, when I had appeared before them for interview for promotion to first class sergeant, and on that occasion I had been passed over.

My step was a little heavier when I arrived at Southwark Police Station. 'How did it go?' was the popular question. 'Fine,' was my repeated answer. Only to Commander Renshaw did I voice my doubts. 'Rubbish,' came his booming reply. 'You had as good a recommendation as anyone else and a great deal better than most.' I believed him, he was not a man to lie on such matters, but I still had little confidence in the outcome. Thus, it came as no surprise to me when I was told only a few days later that I had failed to pass.

Now I do not give up easily, and although the odds were against me somewhere, I had no intention of sitting on my backside and letting the next few years float by quietly. I was going to justify my personal claim for consideration for promotion, even if I did not get it, and had no intention of retiring in five years' time with a king-sized chip on my shoulders.It was at about this time that a new department at Scotland Yard called A10 was formed, a department to handle complaints against police and carry out investigations into such complaints. Not a bad idea. As far as I was concerned, this was something that should have been done many years before. Complaints were coming in thick and fast as the result of the misguided manner in which the launching of this department had been publicised. In fact, so many complaints arrived at the Yard that the staff of this new-found department could not handle them all. Many were passed out to unfortunate senior officers like myself to investigate.

In my personal estimation, at least half of these complaints were spurious allegations made by convicted villains or their relatives in an attempt to discredit the officers who had effected their arrest. Then, of course, allegations began to arrive against officers who had effected arrests many years beforehand. Believe me, I hold no brief for the crooked police officer, but I do wish that more thought, and less publicity, had been given to this very necessary department. I am quite convinced that had it been quietly formed, more crooked policemen would have been accounted for and positively dealt with.

During the period of time that I am discussing, almost every senior officer had a number of serious allegations against police officers to investigate. A very large proportion of these allegations were either withdrawn during the course of the investigation, or were proved by the investigation to be spurious. Normal allegations of crime, because of this sudden influx of complaints, were now being passed over to be investigated by comparatively junior officers, or by our uniformed colleagues, hitherto rarely involved in the investigation of crime. I have to say, however, that our uniformed colleagues became progressively more engaged in this aspect of police work and nothing but good could come from that.

13
The Stanley Butcher Murder

On 3rd February 1971 I was able to put aside my enquiries into complaints against police for a short while. At about 7 p.m. that evening, Stanley Butcher, a clerk employed by the bookmaker Sidney Read, was found shot dead and laying in a pool of blood in the Sidney Read Betting Office at no. 10 Lower Road, Rotherhithe. I was called from my home shortly after this. I visited the scene at 10 p.m. and took over the enquiry.

As far as could be made out, the murder must have taken place at about 6.15 p.m. that evening. Mr Butcher had been shot dead with a small-calibre pistol, probably a ·22. This man had been employed by the Read family for some thirty years. He was a faithful and highly trusted member of staff. His usual practice was known and virtually automatic. Unfortunately, he would check his money before 6.30 p.m., lock it in the office safe, then take the betting slips to the second Sidney Read office at 233 Lower Road, Rotherhithe. Again by general practice, he would arrive at that office between 6. 45 p.m. and 7 p.m. There he would hand the slips over to John Albert Paver, who was on duty at that office.

On the fateful 3rd February Stanley Butcher had not arrived by 7. 15 p.m. Because of his unfailing regularity, Paver became worried and telephoned the office at 10 Lower Road. He received no reply and at 7. 25 closed the office at 233 Lower Road and drove to No. 10. There to his amazement he found the front door ajar, and to his horror then found the unfortunate Stanley Butcher, lying face down in a pool of blood. Paver immediately telephoned the police.

Upon receiving this report, Detective Sergeant Nick Blake, on duty at Rotherhithe Police Station, immediately went to 10 Lower

Road, arriving there at 7. 45 p.m. He at once alerted his detective inspector, the photographer, the fingerprint officer, the divisional surgeon and Dr Cameron, the Home Office pathologist. I was similarly notified and arrived shortly afterwards.

Post-mortem examination revealed that Stanley Butcher had been shot with a ·22 calibre firearm. The bullet was removed and submitted for forensic examination immediately. Door-to-door enquiries in the immediate vicinity of the scene were launched, with the occupiers being questioned in an effort to obtain the smallest piece of information that might assist our investigation. Passers-by were stopped in the surrounding streets in an attempt to trace witnesses who might have seen or heard anything unusual in the vicinity of the betting shop. From these enquiries it appeared that Mr Butcher must have been shot at about 6. 10 p.m.

The betting shop at 10 Lower Road is situated on the first floor of Leader House. It is immediately above a derelict shop and on what is best described as an island in the one-way system immediately opposite Rotherhithe tunnel. In this extremely busy area the sound of a shot would undoubtedly be taken for the backfiring of a vehicle in the traffic-crowded roads at the time in question. Moreover, the majority of persons passing at the vital time would have been driving home, probably more intent on road safety than on paying attention to people on the pavement or unusual traffic noises.

The probability in this case of a late punter seeing strange people loitering in or near the betting shop was our principal hope at the start of the investigation. Betting slips for the week prior to the murder were seized and enquiries concentrated from the last bet taken in an effort to obtain the slightest piece of useful information. Here we found a further stumbling block. Rarely do punters use their full or correct name when placing a bet. More often than not they used a nickname or just one of their Christian names. Some three hundred people using the betting shop were traced, but of these only one gave any information at all. It was a very time-consuming operation.

The till roll was examined with the co-operation of Mr Edward Read, who had taken over the business from his father after he had died. This showed that the last bet had been taken at 6. 10 p.m. The interesting point here was that the entries numbered 539 and 540 were blank. Furthermore, that number, 540, appeared four times. This did not make sense. The accounts were checked and it was found that there should have been £137. 1. 7d in the till. This was missing.

The last timed bet was at 6.10 p.m. It had been made by a Mr Louis Dick, a timber porter who lived in nearby Jamaica Road. He was seen and recalled that after placing his bet, he had gone to the men's toilet situated in the middle of the road opposite Rotherhithe tunnel. He then returned to collect his cycle, which he had placed against the kerbstones immediately outside the betting shop. Before going to the toilet, at a stage upon which he was not at all clear, Mr Dick had noticed three men leaving the betting shop premises.

To make matters just a little more confusing at this stage, Mr Dick mentioned that when he got on his cycle, he noticed someone walking from behind him who went into the betting shop and closed the door behind him. The description given of this caller to the premises was very vague indeed, but fortunately for us we took down every minute detail given. You will hear of this man later as the story unfolds.

Detectives investigating every serious crime take down every snippet of information they obtain, no matter how trivial or apparently useless it may seem. The truth is that you never really know what is useful and what is not. The description given in this instance by Mr Dick, was of a man who, he thought, was aged 'fortyish', who walked with a slight 'wobble'. He insisted that when the office was open, no person ever closed the door when they entered.

Our local enquiries were stepped up, with over thirty officers of the Special Patrol Group searching the area on 4th and 5th February for a trace of the weapon. In addition, Southwark Borough Council co-operated in our search for the murder weapon by emptying and checking all drains in the area. The results were, unfortunately, all abortive. I produced five hundred notices, which were circulated to shops, public houses and betting shops, to be prominently displayed for everyone to see. Still no information came forward, despite the continued and concentrated enquiries in the area. The co-operation of the local residents in this case was wonderful. Stanley Butcher was highly respected locally.

On Wednesday, 10th February, a week after the murder, we still had no information as to those responsible. Five thousand further leaflets were obtained. The scene was floodlit from 5 p.m. to 7 p.m. and all pedestrians, bus passengers and drivers of vehicles passing were handed a leaflet and questioned. Everything gathered was carefully studied and investigated. Public co-operation continued and was greatly appreciated, but despite our every effort, the enquiries that followed only tended to eliminate any newly obtained information from the murder enquiry.

There were many criminals living and working in the Bermondsey and Rotherhithe areas. Many could only be described as violent and nasty habitual criminals. Robberies in betting shops were unfortunately becoming a most popular pastime amongst certain classes of criminals. Not only the police, but the bookmakers themselves were now fast becoming worried as the result of this sudden increase of crimes against their establishments.

On one particular evening, whilst in the murder office mulling over the difficulties that confronted me and my apparent failure to come up with any form of answer, I had an idea.

I remembered an old friend and bookmaker, Jimmy Lane. When I first met Jim, I was stationed at Brixton. He had earned himself considerable respect, which at that time I had some difficulty, in my ignorance, in reconciling with a bookmaker. That respect, I soon learned, had been built up over the years by Jim's readiness whenever any friend or customer fell on hard times, to lend a helping hand. I needed a friend. There was only one thing for it. I must pay Jimmy Lane a call.

He welcomed my call and subsequent visit, and we talked over the case and the efforts I had made to solve it. As time went on he suddenly stopped me short in the middle of one of my explanations. 'Why not offer a reward?' A great idea, and it sounds so easy. I hastened to inform him, however, that the police were most unlikely to do such a thing. That assurance was not necessary. 'John, I want whoever shot Stanley Butcher put where they belong. I am offering the reward, and irrespective of what your commissioner may say, I want this case solved, and solved quickly before someone else gets killed.'

Jimmy Lane started the ball rolling. Our first reward notice mentioned the sum of £2,000. £4,000 appeared on a subsequent circular, but the figure later reached £6,000. It was put up by the association known as The Bookmakers Afternoon Greyhound Service, who were concerned about the persistent number of raids on betting shops and offices, particularly where firearms had been used. This was the first occasion that such a reward had been offered.

Purely out of interest, I shall mention certain names which came up, to indicate to you the difficulties that we met in this case. There was Mr Dick, who, you will remember, talked about a man vaguely described as 'fortyish', a man who walked with a 'wobble'. How on earth can one pick out any person on such a description? Try as we may we were absolutely unable to induce Mr Dick to enlarge in any way on the description of this man.

Also during the course of the investigation we had interviewed three characters whom we were not particularly happy with. Their names were Day, Crane and Baverstock. I think we interviewed them during the middle of February. Day and Crane put forward a most convincing alibi as to their activities on the fateful 3rd February. It was most convincing, perhaps, in afterthought, just a little too convincing, but it completely eliminated them from our enquiries at the time. Baverstock, likewise, had a perfect alibi.

These alibis had been just too good to be true, but on what we had at the time, we could do nothing. In fact, we would have to know a lot more about these people before we could take our enquiries further into their activities. Then, of course, there was this infernal man in his 'forties' who walked with a 'wobble'. None of the trio could fit this strange description, but clearly he was the most important man to find in the first instance.

With our enquiries concentrating on our immediate locality and rightly or wrongly assuming that the villain, or villains, were locals, we concentrated hard on our informants. At the time I had between thirty and forty officers working under me on this enquiry. All were anxious to prove to me that their particular informant would produce the answer to our problem. I knew that I had many informants in the district. It was important for me to get one of them to come up with the answer.

Then it happened, a telephone call. First question: 'How genuine is that reward?' The question was very interesting, so indeed was the accent: true South London, and I could peg it into a half circle of four miles from my office. 'It is very genuine, and I would stake my personal reputation on it,' was my reply. 'I've heard all that bullshit before,' replied the caller. There was no doubt he was very agitated. 'Let us meet,' I requested. 'Where you like, and I shall be on my own.'

We met and accepted each other from the outset. Let me say, however, I have never seen the man since the end of the case. What he said, though, gave me enough information to be able to tighten my

The Stanley Butcher Murder

grip on one area of our division and pay particular attention to names and incidents that our new-found informant brought to my notice. My only worry was that he might have been involved in the murder himself. Thus, before I took one step on his information, I had to eliminate him from this case, if he was innocent, or charge him if he had been involved, even in the slightest manner. Fortunately, he was well and truly in the clear.

Names came quite clearly to our new-found friend: Michael Richard Baverstock, the leader, Peter Crane, Christopher Day and Tony Young, all local lads in their twenties, who would have a go at anything if there was a few bob in it. Then came the interesting one: Danny Duggan, aged about forty-one! Could this be the man whom the very mixed-up Louis Dick had been trying to tell us about? All were apparently regular customers of the Alscot Arms public house in Alscot Road, Bermondsey.

We kept on pressing our man for more information, and our persistence was rewarded. Piece by piece we were putting the puzzle together. We went over and over again with him on every little matter that he brought up. Clearly he was telling the truth. Then he seemed to come to a halt. We did not press him. He was undoubtedly deep in thought. Suddenly, almost as if he had seen something new on the ceiling of the office, he came alive. 'Oh yes,' he said. 'What about the Star of India shooting?' Well, what about it, I almost said. 'The same mob,' he continued. I had no knowledge of a shooting at this small restaurant-cum-café in the Tower Bridge Road. This had to be our next port of call.

Minder Singh, the proprietor of the Star of India restaurant was interviewed. He stated that he had seen Baverstock, Crane and Day with a pistol on different occasions. In fact, he went even further, telling us that Baverstock had fired a small black pistol in the corner of his kitchen during November of the previous year, 1970. We pushed further with Minder Singh for more details, tried and tried again. It was, as we tend to say on this type of enquiry, 'just like pulling teeth'. Then he remembered. Baverstock had returned to the restaurant early in February and asked Singh if he had found the bullet he had fired. What a question! Singh had told him that it had not been found, and he had left the premises. One thing was quite obvious to us. Minder Singh, in common with many other people whom we had met in the area, was clearly very scared of Master Baverstock. He had no desire to talk about him in any way, but we pressed on and pressed hard.

On 22nd February 1971 The Star of India restaurant was searched inch by inch, by a number of my officers, time and time again, but no bullet or trace of one was found. We pressed Singh further. We went over everything we had previously discussed. Finally we advised him in the strongest possible terms that if he thought of any point, even the most minor point, he must contact us immediately. We reminded him that we, the investigators, wanted to hear about these so-called minor points and that it was us and nobody else who would decide whether the particular point should be taken further. As we left his premises, I could not get out of my mind the extremely strong feeling that he was very frightened of something or someone. Was he trying to be too submissive? Was he just being typically polite in his humble attitude. Or was he just relieved that we had left him and glad to see the back of us?

The following morning, whilst sorting through the many messages and actions that had been taking place during the night and early morning, Minder Singh arrived of his own accord at Rotherhithe Police Station, a very welcome guest. To my surprise he brought with him a small collapsible settee. Had he decided to camp outside the police station?

The settee, he explained, had been kept in his kitchen. Indicating a very small hole that was barely visible, he said that this was where the bullet we might be seeking had entered. Exploration of the hole by one of my officers, revealed a ·22 bullet. Ah! Now we were really getting warm. Comparison of the bullet was made with the bullet taken from the body of the unfortunate Stanley Butcher and confirmed that both bullets had been fired from the same gun, the one Baverstock had fired in the restaurant.

Minder produced one of his kitchen assistants, John Joseph Baldesari, who, he assured us, had something of interest to tell us. This man calmly told us that he had seen Day, Crane and Daverstock on occasions in possession of a pistol. He was also present when Baverstock fired the pistol into the settee. To cap it all, he was also present when Baverstock had returned to the Star of India restaurant early in February to find the bullet. According to Baldesari, the pistol was a small black revolver and had the letter 'I' on the handle. He said further that according to Crane it had been made in Italy.

The Stanley Butcher Murder 159

The question now was who to go for first. Of the gang, Young was the weak link. He had ceased to use the Alscot Arms very shortly after the murder. Enquiries to trace him were put in hand. He was tracked to an address in Islington in north London. On 24th February 1971 he was brought to Rotherhithe Police Station. Upon being told that we thought that he had been involved in a murder, he immediately denied complicity. He was not very convincing. After a few more questions, however, he volunteered a statement under caution in which he named Baverstock, Day and Crane as having committed the robbery at 10 Lower Road, Rotherhithe. He even went so far as to say that Peter Crane had been claiming the shooting was an accident and had spoken as to how Stanley Butcher had died. Young admitted receiving £10 from the proceeds of the robbery and named a man called Duggan, often referred to as Danny, who had been present during the conversation. All of the pieces were now beginning to fit together.

The background enquiries that I had initiated earlier were beginning to pay off. Young, for example, had gone to his former employer on 3rd February 1971 and asked for his previous job back. His request had been refused, but he had remained at his previous employer's premises, talking to two old friends. Young left the place with his friends at 5.30 p.m. and they walked towards Rotherhithe tunnel. One of his friends left the company to make his way home, leaving Young with the other person, Peter Hallett. In the vicinity of Rotherhithe tunnel, Hallett left Young on the island opposite the tunnel whilst he went off to collect his van, arranging to pick him up some ten minutes later. Young waited. Then by strange coincidence, and I could put it no more strongly, whilst he was waiting, Crane ran past him. He called out to Crane, but Crane continued on his way, only acknowledging Young's call by shouting, 'Fuck off'.

I immediately instituted a concentrated effort to bring in Baverstock, Crane and Day to the station. As I recall it, it was the 25th February 1971 when the three men were brought in to Rotherhithe Police Station. No trace, however, could be found of the missing link, Duggan.

I interviewed Crane with Detective Sergeant Henry Dowdswell. He made a statement which corroborated everything said by Young. This also confirmed everything that had been said by Minder Singh and his man Baldesari. He described leaving the Alscot Arms after they closed and picking up a piece of wood on the way to the betting shop. He apparently entered the betting shop at about 6 p.m. and told a customer who was in the shop to lie on the floor. This he apparently did without question. Baverstock by this time had gone into the private part of the betting shop and from there he, Crane, heard what he referred to as a crash. Crane then described how he went to the inner part of the office and saw Baverstock, standing with a pistol in his hand and watching the unfortunate Stanley Butcher collapsing on to the floor. At the sight of this Crane undoubtedly panicked. According to him he just grabbed some money and ran. On leaving the betting shop, Crane obviously must have seen Mr Dick standing by his cycle. Then he ran along Lower Road, away from the scene, and in doing so, passed Young. Crane later returned to the Alscot Arms, where the cash taken was shared out. His share for his participation in this awful crime was a mere £30 and a bag of loose silver.

The next most interesting point came from Crane in the course of a conversation some days later. The bullet fired in the Star of India restaurant had to be recovered, because it was fired from the same gun as the one used in the betting shop. This was the gun which Crane admitted handling himself. Very nice confirmation of the laboratory examination. The puzzle was beginning to fit nicely together. The gun, however, was still missing.

I then interviewed Day, with Detective Sergeant Weisham from 'P' Division, who was also on my team. Day gave the impression of being quite frank in his explanation. He told of leaving the Alscot Arms and entering the betting shop with Baverstock. He mentioned that he heard a bang and then saw Stanley Butcher collapsing on the floor of his office with blood coming from his mouth. He also stated that he had opened the till by striking it with a piece of wood which he was carrying at the time. More corroboration. His remarks undoubtedly accounted for the blank entries under the numbers 539 and 540 on the till roll. Was this the piece of wood that Crane had picked up on the way to the betting shop?

The two lads, Crane and Day, gave the impression of being very frightened little boys. It would seem most unlikely that they could have been willing conspirators to murder before the act. A search of their respective addresses revealed nothing of further interest to this particular case, with the exception of a single twelve-bore cartridge found at Crane's home.

The Stanley Butcher Murder 161

Even before interviewing him, it was quite clear that Baverstock was the leader of this little gang of thugs. Upon interview, he projected himself as an arrogant bully, ridiculing any suggestion that this could be murder and attempting instead to put forward the explanation that the killing was an accident. A search of his address revealed a ·22 gas gun, which had recently been fired. According to his mother, she had handled this particular pistol and insisted that it was only a toy that the children played with! Baverstock, of course, denied any knowledge of the existence of this weapon and not knowing the explanation given by his mother, even had the audacity at a later stage to suggest that it had been 'planted' by police.

In his statement which was taken down in my presence by Detective Sergeant Weisham, with Detective Inspector Brothers also present, Baverstock corroborated the statements of Day, Crane and Young. He admitted firing the shot that killed Stanley Butcher, but insisted that it was an accident and estimated that his share of the loot was £60. He also admitted firing the pistol in the Star of India restaurant, but stated that he had given the gun to another person to throw into the river Thames to dispose of it.

On 26th February the four prisoners, Baverstock, Crane, Day and Young, appeared before the magistrate at Tower Bridge Magistrates Court. Here, after a very brief hearing, they were remanded in custody for seven days and each placed in separate cells. As Detective Inspector Brothers and I walked back along the cell passage after placing them in their cells, a conversation commenced between the four men, now isolated from each other. I signalled to Mr Brothers to sit on the floor of the cell passage beside me and I commenced taking down their conversation in shorthand. I directed the detective inspector to watch closely what I did and explained that, although he could not read what was written, he would have to initial each page of shorthand writing, to prove if necessary that he was present when I made them.

The conversation went as follows

Baverstock   'Hey, Chris.'
Day   'Yes. '
Baverstock   'Can you get your head out of the window, my fucking head's too big?'
Day   'I'll try,' – pause – 'Yes, I can get it nearly out.'

Baverstock	'Is there anyone about? Any law?'
Day	'No. No, I don't think so.'
Baverstock	'We've got to get it right about the gun. We didn't put big bullets in it. We only put little ones in it.'
Crane	'That fucking Singh must have grassed.'
Young	'Yeh, it must be down to Singh.'
Baverstock	'Here Pete, don't tell them about the big one.'
Crane	'What one?'
Baverstock	'The big one. You know.'
Crane	'I told them that I had a lump of wood.'
Baverstock	'Good.'
Day	'Here, that Tom was in there last night, I saw him.'
Baverstock	'What, Tom with the arm?'
Day	'Yes.'
Baverstock	'I wonder what he was doing in there. Has he said anything about the bag? What about Danny, they are not on to him, are they? Pete?'
Crane	'No.'
Baverstock	'Chris?'
Day	'No.'
Baverstock	'Tone?'
Young	'No. Here, guess what the big fellow said to me this morning.'
Baverstock	'No.'
Young	'If I could tell him more, he would give me bail next week.'
Baverstock	'You'll get bail anyway. You won't tell him any more, Tone, will you? No more, Tone.'
Young	'No. He said he was going to put a lot of other charges on me.'
Baverstock	'They can't. It's nothing to do with this case.'
Young	'I owe about £150. If my old man paid that up I could get out.'
Baverstock	'Yes, if you could get out you could make yourself busy about all this.'
Young	'Yes'

Pause . . .

The Stanley Butcher Murder

Baverstock 'We'll get about ten years for this.'
Day   'Ten months would be alright.'
Crane   'Ten years?'
Baverstock 'We'll be in patches.'
Day   'Patches. What's that?'
Baverstock 'You know. Patches. You'll be Jack. Here, Chris, there's someone out there.'
Day   'I can't see anyone.'
Baverstock 'We had better bang up.'

With that, this most interesting and instructive conversation ended. This was indeed a bonus and one that I had never expected. Now at least, with a little more effort, I could close this case, place all of the evidence before Her Majesty's courts of law and leave the rest to the judges and the wisdom of their decision as to what to do with these young scoundrels.

We now had the answers to so many of our unanswered questions. Certainly two further suspects had to be seen. 'Tom with the arm' just had to be Thomas David Bushby whose identity we knew, but 'Danny', whoever he was, still had us a little mystified.

Before going further, two points in the cell conversation should be explained. 'Patches' indicated a particular type of prison dress worn by high-risk prisoners. Baverstock was the only one of the prisoners at that stage who might have qualified to come into that category. He was clearly very proud of this and was even expecting to be classified as such. 'Jack' is a shortened form of the Cockney phrase 'Jack the Lad', indicating that the person is a proud man, looked up to by his friends, and does as he feels right regardless of what others think. In this instance my impression was that Baverstock was suggesting that by being in 'patches' they would be the centre of admiration of other prisoners whilst serving their sentence.

Suspicion had earlier been attached alone to a man named Duggan, but the only person who had mentioned him in passing had been Young. Could this be the Danny referred to in the cell passage conversation? Could this also be the 'man who walked with a wobble', referred to by Louis Dick? Bushby had not even been mentioned before, but the bag to which they referred sounded most interesting. We had a hell of a lot more to do yet before we could rest back. Enquiries were therefore placed in hand to trace these two persons.

On 2nd March Bushby was seen at his home address, which was searched. In his room we found thirty-six rounds of ·22 ammunition. Very interesting. He was brought to Rotherhithe Police Station, where he made a statement covering his part in this matter. He related how he was the custodian of a black shopping bag, which, it transpired, contained two sticks, like chair legs, no doubt to be used as clubs, and two pistols, one a Luger, the other a small automatic that had no name on it and looked rather like a toy. He told how the bag was collected from his home on the day of the murder and later brought back to his house in his absence. In some detail, he outlined a conversation that had taken place in the Alscot Arms public house on the day of the murder. This was between Baverstock, Crane, Young and Duggan, when the murder was discussed. Duggan was undoubtedly the 'Danny' referred to. The excitement was gathering. Bushby continued by saying how at 11 p.m. that day he had been told to go and get the bag. As requested, he fetched the bag from his home and on his return to the then closed Alscot Arms public house recalled seeing Day and Crane in a mini-cab outside the premises, with Baverstock, Duggan and Young standing beside it. The firearms were placed in the mini-cab and he was handed back the remaining contents of the bag and told to burn them. For his efforts in this case, Bushby received the princely sum of £2 of the stolen money.

On 3rd March Duggan was seen by Detective Sergeant Henry Dowdswell and other officers at his home. They searched the premises and found a ·38 calibre revolver. Duggan projected himself as a very remorseful individual, who had nothing to say whatsoever. This worried us little, however, in view of the amount of evidence now in our possession, he was taken to Rotherhithe Police Station, very much to his surprise.

The psychological effect of being arrested is an unknown factor. Some immediately turn violent, whilst many accept it apparently quite meekly, either as the inevitable consequence of their previous actions or in the certain knowledge that they can prove their innocence by hook or by crook. Then there is that period following their arrest when they travel to the police station to be detained or charged, a period when the mind works overtime, attempting to find a means of avoiding the consequences of their actions. Alibis are searched, allegations against those arresting them are examined. During this period of time, the person is getting nearer and nearer to the police station and to confrontation with whoever may be in charge of the investigation.

That confrontation, in addition to being something of a trial for the prisoner, is also a trial for the investigating officer, who rarely has any idea just what the prisoner will say. In this particular instance, Duggan quite adamantly was not intending to say anything when arrested, and furthermore insisted that he intended to remain silent. To my surprise and that of all concerned, Duggan insisted on making a statement, telling the sergeant everything that he knew. Even more surprisingly, the whole contents of that statement just had to be true. Duggan detailed incidents and points of interest that could only have been known to those who were actual parties to the murder.

He told of making arrangements to meet Day, Crane and Baverstock outside the betting shop opposite Rotherhithe tunnel, just after 6 p.m.; of seeing an old man – Louis Dick – with a cycle go into the betting shop and come out before they entered. He also spoke of closing a door that was awkward to close. His account of what took place inside the betting shop tallied with that of Baverstock. He described the shooting, taking money from the tills and then leaving the scene because he felt sick about the shooting. He even told of how he disposed of the murder weapon by throwing it into the river Thames at Irongate Wharf near St Katherines Dock, where the Tower Hotel stands. So identical was his statement with the many accounts of other persons involved in this matter that I was satisfied that without doubt we had all the details and evidence possible to obtain, with one exception. To cap it all, Duggan went so far as to mention by way of an afterthought that he had given Bushby £3 for disposing of the bag that had contained the guns, with its remaining contents.

On 4th March I invited Duggan to take me to where he had disposed of the murder weapon. From the details that he had outlined in his statement, I had arranged for some of our friends in the Metropolitan Police Underwater Search Unit to meet me at Irongate Wharf. Here I handed to Duggan a piece of metal of the approximate weight of the murder weapon and told him to throw it into the river from the spot where he had stood on the previous occasion. He did exactly as was asked of him and the spot was marked. Inspector Cotton and his team then explored the murky depths of this piece of water. The maximum depth of water at this point would have been some twenty feet at high tide. Below this, however, was a bed of fine silt, averaging some twelve feet in depth.

An article such as that which we were now seeking does not necessarily go straight down to the bottom. The movement of the tide could shift the weapon well away from its point of entry. Then you have the silt, fine silt that moves about with the tide or is moved by disturbance caused by passing ships. Such a movement would engulf and indeed encourage the weapon to go further and further away from the probing team. Our helpers did everything that they possibly could, but the murder weapon eluded them.

My next step was to contact friends in the Port of London Authority. My liaison here was very good. I had done good work for them in the past and felt that, although this was now something of a scrounge, it was also something that I should at least try. I wanted to borrow a dredger! My Port of London friends were a little taken aback at this request, but of course, this could be arranged. It would have to be paid for, however, and the cost would be in the region of £400 per day, plus £100 for the manufacture of a suitable filter. With the evidence that I already had in my hands, I could not see the Metropolitan Police footing such a bill, but I did not mention this. I told the Port of London people that I would like to speak to the captain of the dredger. He was, of course, only too willing to take on the projected search with his vessel. His honest opinion, however, backed up by his sound knowledge of the particular area of the river, was that the probability of finding the weapon was extremely remote.

I required a more positive answer. 'How remote?' I asked.' Bloody impossible,' was his terse reply. He then backed his statement up by giving me a detailed description of the tidal movement at the particular spot we would be interested in, not forgetting the corresponding movement of the silt at the bottom of the river and his idea of the probable movement of the weapon. We were undoubtedly faced with an expensive, time-consuming task with probably not even a remote chance of being successful. I decided to abandon any further search for the murder weapon.

The six men were all committed to stand trial at the Old Bailey on an indictment charging fifteen counts, including that of murder of Stanley Butcher; robbery; receiving stolen property; firearms offences, and other miscellaneous offences connected with the crime. Baverstock was sentenced to life imprisonment, with the recommendation that he served not less than twenty years. Duggan was sentenced to a total of fourteen year's imprisonment, Day to three year's imprisonment, as was Crane. Bushby was sentenced to one year's imprisonment, whilst Young was sentenced to a period of Borstal training.

As the result of our intensive enquiries to trace those responsible for this murder, we had arrested a further seventeen people for varying offences from robbery to simple theft. Furthermore, by virtue of our enquiries in the Rotherhithe area, not only were the criminal classes being most careful in their activities, but the local inhabitants were beginning to express their gratitude about the work of the police generally. That of itself was a bonus to be savoured.

14
The Murder of Rokaya Bibi Hazari

I had hardly got over the mental strain that goes with a vast and concentrated murder enquiry and disposed of the mountain of paper that accumulates in the course of such a task, when I became involved in yet another such enquiry.

The telephone rang at my home just before eight o'clock in the morning of 22nd June 1971. I was just polishing off a very tasty breakfast before fighting my way through the morning commuter traffic in south London to Southwark.

It was the duty officer at Southwark Police Station on the other end of the telephone. 'Thought I had better let you know, Guvnor. A body had been found on the Thames foreshore, at Rotherhithe. Could be one for you.' I didn't need to know any more. 'Tell them that I am on my way,' was all I said, and all that needed to be said. I bade my wife a hurried farewell and left the house chewing a piece of bread and marmalade as I made my way to Rotherhithe Police Station.

My arrival at Rotherhithe caused a certain amount of confusion. I only called at stations on the division before nine o'clock in the morning if there was a problem of an internal nature or one relating to a serious crime. As far as those on duty were concerned, there was no serious crime, and they were clearly searching their minds to work out what internal problem had brought me into their midst.

'What's this I hear about a body in the Thames?' I asked. 'Oh yes.' There was a noticeable sigh of relief. A body had been found on the foreshore at Cucknolds Reach, in the Rotherhithe area. The Thames Police had taken it to Wapping Police Station on the north side of the river. There was nothing wrong, I was told. I silently cursed the duty

The Murder of Rokaya Bibi Hazari 169

officer who had caused me to rush a tasty breakfast and make my way through the worst of the morning traffic for nothing.

I am not normally given to bad temper, but in this instance I was 'hopping mad'. I decided to vent my feelings on the duty officer who had caused my early arrival. He, however, had little to say. 'I had a feeling' was the limit of his apology, and I must say that it was also his saving grace. I had had 'feelings' about something or other on many occasions. I usually investigated such strange warnings and on a number of occasions those 'feelings' had proved to be a positive pointer.

I returned to my office at Southwark. The Commander wanted to see me. There was nothing unusual about that, he often wanted to see me. His words, however, brought back to me just how important those 'feelings' of my past experience and those of the duty officer that very morning could be. 'I think you had better go over to London Hospital, John. Mr Cameron wants a word with you. Could be a murder.' I needed no further instructions. I knew Professor 'Taffy' Cameron, the Home Office pathologist, only too well, as he had assisted me on a number of previous occasions. He was a most positive thinker, not given to false alarms. I myself was now getting 'feelings' and very strong ones at that. This had to be the body on the foreshore at Rotherhithe's Cucknolds Reach, the one that the Thames Police had taken from the water. I felt quite sure now that the Duty Officer was right. Perhaps now it was I who owed him some apology.

At London Hospital, I began to unravel the story. Kenneth Hawkridge, a tug master employed by Messrs Braithwaite and Dean of Rotherhithe, was in charge of the tug Charlock. That morning he had been on his way downstream to Dagenham when his attention had been drawn to 'something' on the foreshore. He turned his tug round and from a distance of some fifty yards could see that the unusual 'something' was in fact a body. He promptly notified the Port of London Authority Navigation Service by ship's radio telephone. The Rotherhithe area police car arrived at the scene within a few minutes of the call. At almost the same time a Thames Police launch arrived.

The body, that of a woman, was very obviously dead and was therefore taken by the police launch to Wapping Police Station on the north side of the river, following normal practice. There it was examined by Dr David Jenkins, the 'H' Division, police surgeon. He certified life to be extinct, but for reasons not disclosed at the time, insisted that a post-mortem be carried out immediately. What a strange chain of events. The body had been removed to London hospital, and there the wisdom of Dr Jenkins' decision was soon confirmed. Professor Cameron's examination soon proved that the body, that of a young women, probably Indian, had died as the result of asphyxia due to constriction of the throat. Strangulation, rather than a simple drowning.

According to the expert opinion of Professor Cameron, the body had been in the water approximately ten hours before being found. It had been dead, however, for about forty-eight hours. Then, to cap it all, indicating marks on the face and forehead, he was quite firm that these marks had been inflicted before death. There was no indication as to who the woman was. Indian? Yes. Probably about twenty years of age and wearing one very strange item, a most unusual cloth armlet on her left upper arm, probably of religious origin.

My first step was to identify this unfortunate woman. As much as we could say was that she was probably married and in her early twenties. She could have been dropped over the side of a ship in the Thames estuary, having been murdered in a foreign port or on a foreign ship. On the other hand, if she had been murdered in London, she could have been dropped into the river anywhere.

Whilst a search of missing persons reports was in hand, I attempted to ascertain the probable point at which the body had entered the water. The watermen on the River Thames are experts in their own specialised business. I knew a number of these interesting people quite well. I approached some of them with my quest. They were quite enthusiastic to assist. This was their home ground, and they were quick to assure me that they were the only people who might come up with an answer.

I explained Professor Cameron's assessment of the situation to them. The body had been in the water some ten hours. I further explained that by this time I had statements on the subject of wind and weather over the ten-hour period. My new-found helpers finally threw up their arms in horror and were obliged to say that they could offer no suggestion that would be in any way helpful. Now, when confronted by experts, I find it very hard to accept such a response. I wanted an answer, even a negative answer, and if it had to be negative, I wanted an explanation to go with the statement. I persisted and finally got an answer. 'The body could have entered the water five miles east or five miles west of the location where it was found. It could have entered

The Murder of Rokaya Bibi Hazari   171

the water from the north bank or from the south bank of the river, from a bridge, or have been dropped over the side of a ship. Does that satisfy you?' the spokesman asked. The River Thames is very long; at least their assessment kept the scene of the crime within my constabulary area, that is, within the Metropolitan Police District, even if it had been dropped over the side of a ship. I assured them that it assisted me greatly, but I was silently praying as I spoke.

My quest for an authoritative opinion was far from over. I again sought assistance from my old friends in the Port of London Authority. The problem was put to Jim Hordley Potter, a chief engineer with some twenty years' experience with the River Thames and its problems. His answer was to the effect that it was impossible for anyone to state with any accuracy that the body had entered the water at any specific point. As much as he was prepared to say was that in his opinion the body had entered the river on or from the north bank, in an area not far west of the then closed Shadwell entrance to the London Docks: a most interesting assessment, from a man whose knowledge of the Thames tides and eddies was quite unquestionable. Furthermore, it was an assessment which indicated that the body was placed in the water almost opposite the location where it had been found.

Whilst this side of the enquiry was progressing, our prayers and hopes were concentrated on our search to identify the unfortunate woman. It looked as if we were at last on the right track. Rokaya Bibi Hazari, an Indian woman aged twenty-two had been reported missing from her home at 60 Mordaunt Street, Brixton, in south London, on Saturday 19th June 1971, by her husband, Alibhai Ismail Hazari. Could this be our woman? The age was right, and bearing in mind that our dead woman had been in the water some forty-eight hours, this could well be the person we were so anxious to trace.

Alibhai Hazari and his brother, Ahmed Ismail Hazari, were both seen and taken to London Hospital. Here the husband identified his wife quite positively, but I had to say to myself at the time that I felt quite unhappy about his apparent lack of emotion of any kind at the sight of his dead wife. I contented myself, however, with the thought that these people were Indians, and that I had no idea whatsoever just how Asians felt or reacted in such circumstances. The fact, however, that no emotion had been expressed, even a passing glance of sadness, worried me considerably.

Taking the identification further, the husband identified the armlet on his wife's upper arm. He explained that his wife suffered from hysteria and that in view of this he had written to a holy man in India about her condition. As a result, the holy man had sent the armlet, a Talmud, for her to wear as a prevention against this troubling condition. Alibhai Hazari was told that he and all of the other occupants of 60 Mordaunt Street would have to be seen and questioned in relation to the movements of his wife. He was most polite and very anxious to give every co-operation to our request. His sparse knowledge of English, however, left much to be desired. We were going to need an interpreter. Thus far, much of the talking had been done through the husband's brother, Ahmed, who spoke fairly good English. We were dealing with a Moslem family group, the majority of whom were related and whose common language was Gujurati.

I obtained the services of Praful Patel, a Gujurati-speaking Hindu. At the time he was secretary to the parliamentary committee on United Kingdom citizenship, with particular respect to Asians. He was also heavily engaged in community relations work on behalf of the Asian people generally in this country. Praful Patel was a most highly respected man, and I have to say that without his patient and tireless persistence this case could never have been brought to its ultimate satisfactory conclusion.

As we interrogated the family, friends and relatives of Rokaya Hazari, we learned how she tended at times to wear western-style clothes, much against the desires of the family group in 60 Mordaunt Street. We were told how she apparently had many boyfriends whom she met, without telling the family, in Brixton town centre. It was brought to our notice that on the evening of 19th June the family held a party. We never did discover what this party was in aid of. We probed into the reasons for the family party mainly because the family were obviously loath to discuss it, and this of itself was most peculiar. The only interesting point to emerge was that on this particular evening Rokaya had been seen, after leaving the party unannounced, getting into a green Ford motor car that had a white stripe along its side.

Her boy friends were apparently African, European and Mauritian, but all that we had at that stage of the investigation was that she had been noticed getting into this rather unusually coloured Ford car which, furthermore, she had been seen getting into on a number of previous occasions. We had to find it.

After close questioning of all those who had allegedly seen this vehicle, it was established that it must have been a Ford Cortina Mark 1 model, light green in colour, with a cream stripe along its side. A massive hunt was launched to find this car. Enquiries were first made of the Ford Motor Company, where we were informed that no such vehicle had ever been manufactured for sale in that colour. We were, however, told that the particular colour scheme was indeed popular, and that the owners of such cars had arranged to have the stripe painted along the side of the vehicle to suit their own requirements.

An appeal was launched through newspapers, police publications and television. In addition, five thousand posters were prepared and circulated in the Brixton area throughout the Metropolitan Police District and in various parts of the country where there was known to be a Gujurati community. Close to three hundred such vehicles were traced and their drivers or owners interrogated. None answered the very vague description now in our possession of the alleged boyfriend. All were quite positively eliminated from the enquiry.

In addition to the publicity mentioned, on 2nd July 1971 I called a press conference at New Scotland Yard. This was attended by a large number of Indian journalists. The object of the conference was to try to obtain the assistance of Indian newspapers to appeal to their nationals to come forward if they had any information which might assist police. As a result the case received considerable publicity both in this country and in India. One journalist, Ramniklal Solanki, did much to publicise this murder in Gujurati newspapers. He kept in close touch with my office, and it was largely as the result of his enthusiasm in this case that it was ultimately solved.

Whilst all of this was going on, enquiries were being made in Batley in Yorkshire, also in Samrod, in Gujurat State in India, where officers had been sent to further the enquiries. Unfortunately, however, every angle of enquiry seemed to confuse the issue more and more. We found ourselves being very expertly guided away from the Hazari family to all manner of dead-end enquiries.

I sat down in my office and shut the door. I was worried and desperate to discover a lead, a genuine lead. The answer to this whole matter was very close at hand; I knew it, I felt it. It had to be found somewhere in 60 Mordaunt Street. Whilst deep in thought, the telephone rang. It was Ramniklal Solanki. Had I any more information to give him about the Hazari family? I told him that I could give him no more than he already had. He then asked if I had any objection if he went to 60 Mordaunt Street and interviewed the occupants. As things stood at that particular time, I had no objection whatsoever. I did make one proviso, however. He must keep me informed of any conversation which passed between him and any of the occupants that could have even the slightest bearing on my enquiries. To this he readily agreed.

The following morning, 4th August, Solanki telephoned me. The conversation inside the house had obviously tried to evade anything in the slightest way connected with my enquiries. The occupants were willing to talk about all manner of domestic matters and matters touching on their various occupations. Every time, however, that he attempted to lead the conversation in the direction of his particular interest, the murder, he was steered away from the subject by one of the occupants. They just did not want to talk about this terrible affair. Then as he was leaving the house, Ahmed and Alibhai Hazari had indicated to him that they could have told the police who had committed the murder a long time ago, but it was too late now! The murderers had gone back to India. I had a tingling feeling running down the back of my neck. I knew that feeling only too well, it gave me the confidence that told me that once again I was now most certainly 'in business'.

I sat by the telephone for about ten minutes, mulling over the many things that now had to be done. I was also thinking of other things. That duty officer whom I had intended choking off, had had a 'feeling'. I had had a 'feeling' as I had watched Alibhai Hazari identify his wife, but feelings are not evidence. I needed evidence, hard, concrete evidence. The feeling I now had was a lot stronger than those I had previously experienced. I was convinced in my own mind who had murdered Rokaya, but I still needed evidence.

I was getting carried away in my thoughts. Control yourself, John Swain, I found myself repeating quietly to myself. It had to be Alibhai Hazari. But could it be? Then, the more I thought about the case, the more worried I became. Alibhai was such a physical weakling, both mentally and physically. I could not imagine him carrying out this terrible deed alone. Had he been mentally driven to it, he could never have lifted the dead body alone. Alone? Never! To do this deed, he would have needed help, but who?

The suggestion put to Solanki by the Hazari brothers, that two men

The Murder of Rokaya Bibi Hazari 175

had returned to India, was probably the only lead we had in this case to work on. Enquiries were put in hand in an attempt to establish whether two Indians known to the family had in fact returned to their native land after the probable date of the murder, on or before 19th July 1971. I did not believe this suggestion, but if nothing else, I could prove the brothers to be liars, liars, perhaps, with a very urgent cause to lie. These enquiries were carried out in London and in many provincial towns where there were Indian communities. This was something by way of an exercise in psychology, for although we were doing so much that could hardly be expected to produce a result of itself, I knew that information regarding our enquiries would filter back to Mordaunt Street through the Indian grapevine. I also kept to myself the odd pieces of information about the family that I did receive.

The enquiries produced very little, and my superiors' questioning as to how I was getting on with the enquiry were beginning to disturb me.

On 24th August 1971 I arranged for Ahmed Hazari and Alibhai Hazari to be picked up separately and brought to Rotherhithe Police Station to be questioned. Neither knew that the other had been detained. I questioned Alibhai Hazari through Praful Patel, with Detective Sergeant Henry Dowdswell taking notes as we went along. The result of this interview was a little startling.

Alibhai Hazari knew that his wife was going to be murdered and that his brother Ahmed had arranged it months ago, but had told him nothing about it. He was told that he would be arrested and charged with conspiracy to murder his wife, with others. He declined to make a written statement, but wished to give every assurance that he had not killed her. He was taken to the cells by Detective Sergeant Dolan. On the way to the cells, he told the officer that his brother Ahmed had paid two men to carry out this murder.

I then interviewed Ahmed Ismail Hazari, again with Detective Sergeant Dowdswell taking notes. He was told that Praful Patel would act as interpreter, but insisted that he did not need an interpreter. Ahmed denied that he had arranged the murder, but stated that Alibhai had asked him for £50 for two men, who would get rid of Rokaya for him. He said that he gave him the money to end the shame on the family. He was cautioned and asked if he wished to make a written statement, but declined to do so. When asked if he knew the identity of the men who had allegedly committed the murder on their behalf, he replied to the effect that he did not know them, but Alibhai did. When later formally charged and cautioned, he replied: 'I have not committed any murder myself.' A most peculiar remark for an innocent man to make, but it undoubtedly confirmed his previous statement, admitting being a party to getting others to do the killing. As much as Alibhai would say was that he had not done the murder.

One point came home to me very strongly in these interviews, and that was just how visibly shaken both brothers had been when the substance of Solanki's information was put to them – the existence of two Indians who had committed the actual murder and who, according to them, had since returned to India.

It was not until January 1972 that the Hazari brothers appeared at the Old Bailey to stand trial before Mr Justice Mars-Jones. It was here that the court and jury heard the most unusual story of a young Indian woman, born in Burma, who lived in the Gujurat State of India, later to come to England and lived in London, a girl whose father, together with the father of Alibhai Hazari, arranged the marriage of the couple before Alibhai had even seen her. Alibhai then came to England and married Rokaya, and the couple went to live at 60 Mordaunt Street, Brixton, with Alibhai's elder brother Ahmed Hazari and his family. Here they apparently lived together quite happily.

Rokaya gave birth to a daughter, and at the start of their married life all went well. Rokaya, however, began to enjoy the western way of life. She was even at times known to wear western-style clothing, and speak to men of other races and religions. There was no evidence, however, of misconduct of any kind, as understood by English standards. She had nevertheless, according to Ahmed, the head of the family, brought shame on the family by her activities and was therefore told to mend her ways. Her reply was quite simple. She told Ahmed to mind his own business. That reply of itself undoubtedly brought about her death. The two brothers were sentenced to life imprisonment for her murder.

PART FOUR
AT THE TOP OF THE LADDER

15
Detective Superintendent at Southwark

On 4th December 1972, I was promoted to the rank of Detective Superintendent on 'M' Division, the division where I was already serving. This may sound all very grand, but in point of fact it was a case where I just happened to be in the right place at the right time.

On 9th May 1973 I arrived in my office at Southwark a few minutes before 9 a.m. I had become used to the supervisory capacity of my work and gained considerable enjoyment and pride in guiding some of the younger enthusiastic detectives in their work. I had a feeling that this was going to be something of a boring day and settled down to checking through the overnight reports on the various criminal activities that had taken place since leaving the office the previous evening. There was little of interest, and in any event every report had been properly attended to. Certainly none needed my intervention.

A peaceful day ahead, I thought. Probably a boring day, but then an ideal day for a spot of supervision. I settled down to the painful and not particularly satisfying task of selecting which of the seven CID offices on the division I was going to drop in on and cast my eyes over their books and reports. In my heart I was quite happy that all was well on the division, but if anyone was due for a 'spin', it had to be Carter Street, and that only in order of merit.

A WORRISOME SUICIDE

After a quiet cup of tea, I put on my trilby hat and was halfway out of the office when the telephone rang. It was Tom Parry, the detective inspector at Tower Bridge Police Station. 'I hope you are not too busy, guvnor?' was his opening gambit. 'I think we have one over here. Can you come over?' I may have let out a sigh of relief, I am not sure. Of one thing I was sure, however. If Tom Parry wanted me to come over to Tower Bridge, it had to be serious. Furthermore, I knew quite well that whatever it was that had prompted his call, it was undoubtedly a request for assistance. Whatever it was it would certainly be more interesting than carrying out a supervisory visit to a police station purely to justify my existence.

On my journey from Southwark to Tower Bridge, I learned that the trouble was at Rotherhithe. At 6.45 a.m. that morning, Robert Gorringe, a barge builder employed by Talbot Brothers Ltd. of Talbot Wharf, Rotherhithe Street, had opened one of the wharf-end doors and noticed a body lying on the foreshore. The River Thames had receded and there was little doubt but that the body had floated in on the morning or overnight tide.

The body was exactly as had been explained to me. Cursory examination indicated that this was a young man, perhaps in his late teens or early twenties. He was bearded, dressed in a leather jacket and trousers. There was a leather thong around his neck and secured to his left wrist was a pair of police handcuffs. This man could well have suffered a violent death. The matter would clearly have to be investigated as one of murder.

Dr Gorman, the Divisional police surgeon, was the first member of the medical team to arrive on the scene to make an examination. The Home Office pathologist, Dr Johnson, then arrived. He carried out an external examination of the body, took samples of the river water near where the body was found, then supervised the removal of the body to Southwark mortuary. Post-mortem examination of the body by such an expert is expected to come up with sound evidence of the cause of death. To my surprise, however, Dr Johnson was unable to give an exact cause of death until after further minute examination. The words of the pathologist worried me a little. It was so unusual not to have a precise report after post-mortem; though thinking further on the subject, I had to bear in mind that the body had apparently been in the river for about a week.

I was now obliged to regard this matter as murder and to investigate it as such. I therefore opened a murder office at Tower Bridge Police Station and gathered in a group of officers from around the division to assist me in what was clearly going to be a very difficult enquiry indeed.

No correspondence had been found on the body which might have given some indication of the young man's identity or even nationality. Furthermore, the items taken from the dead man and his clothing did not help us very much at that stage. A leather thong had been around his neck, also a yellow metal chain with a medallion appended which bore the Star of David. There was a white metal ring through the lobe of his left ear, but it had no markings. On his right wrist was a Secura-make wrist-watch, but the article that fascinated me, and I thought needed some explanation, was the handcuff attached to his left wrist. The other handcuff of the pair had been open and just dangled from the left wrist. This was a pair of Hiat manufactured handcuffs of the type used by police.

All of this information, plus the description of the young man. as far as we could establish, together with the fact that the body had been submerged in water for about seven days, was circulated by way of the police medium, the press and Interpol, for our man could have come from a foreign visiting ship. Coupled with this circulation was an urgent request for any information that might assist in identifying this unfortunate young man.

I was quite surprised how quickly this circulation produced results. It was not long before we identified our man. For simplicity, and other reasons which I am sure will become obvious, I shall call him 'George'. I was gathering together snippets of information that were coming in from many various angles. I found myself confronted with a picture that was slowly emerging of a disturbed young man who had previously attempted to take his own life.'

'George' had had a homosexual relationship with a male model in Essex named 'Terry'. 'Terry' was traced and decided to be as helpful as he could. He spoke of finding 'George' suffering from an overdose of codeine tablets, of how he had sent for an ambulance and how 'George' had been taken by ambulance to Whipps Cross Hospital in east London, where he was detained. Our enquiries on this point revealed that 'George' had in fact been brought to that hospital on 25th January 1973.

'Terry' went on to mention that during the evening of 21st April 1973 he had visited the Ship and Whale public house in Rotherhithe with 'George', from where, they had continued on to a party at

Lewisham. Here a jealous argument arose between them, which resulted in 'Terry' punching 'George' on the nose and giving him two black eyes. They were both interviewed by police over the disturbance they had caused at the party. They both gave false names, which 'Terry' passed to me. He also mentioned that 'George' had at that time a pair of handcuffs in his waistband. Our subsequent enquiries at Lee Road Police Station, Lewisham, confirmed everything we were told. We continued our interrogation of 'Terry', from whom we learned that 'George' generally wore a leather thong round his neck. We also obtained from him details of a cabaret artist whom I shall call 'Mark' who had been engaged in a double act with 'George' as a female impersonator.

The next step had to be to find 'Mark'. He proved to be very much aware of the association between 'George' and 'Terry'. He confirmed that the relationship had broken up on 30th April 1973. He was even more aware of the earlier attempt by 'George' to commit suicide, when he was taken to hospital. Taking matters further, he mentioned that 'Terry' had fought with 'George' over his possessiveness towards him. His final remark gave us even more to think about. He truly believed 'George' would have another attempt at taking his own life.

Our next visit was to 'George's' address, a basement flat in Leyton in east London. A search of this address confirmed without doubt that 'George' was homosexual. One interesting fact was that the name 'Terry' was painted on the wall of his bedroom. We even found a photograph of 'George' with a pair of handcuffs tucked in his waistband. As the enquiry progressed and expanded from day to day, a distinct picture of an extremely frustrated and disturbed homosexual continued to emerge. He was quite clearly depressed at having been rejected by his friend 'Terry'. At no time, however, was there any evidence of animosity towards the dead man.

On 14th May I was informed by Dr Johnson that as a result of his scientific examination he was now able to give a positive cause of death as drowning. Furthermore, the facial injuries evident had been received well before death. These, of course, were consistent with blows from a fist and could well have been inflicted some seven days before he entered the water. This was clear confirmation of the Easter fight referred to by both 'Terry' and 'Mark'. Dr Johnson also confirmed that the thong had often been worn by the deceased man, and was not connected with his death. I personally could not see this as a case of murder, but I did not have the last word on this point. On Friday 18th May an inquest was held at Southwark Coroners Court, presided over by Dr Davis who concluded, 'It appears from the circumstances of this case, that this young man took his own life. But in view of the fact that there is no evidence to say how he entered the water, the fairest verdict I can bring is an open verdict'. This was a satisfactory conclusion to an investigation which had caused me some near sleepless nights.

This case demonstrated the extremely important work carried out by the men behind the scene, the Home Office pathologists. They are a band of superb investigators, detectives in their own right, a fact acknowledged by all senior detectives, who rely so much on their very specialised knowledge and findings.

A PARTY THAT WENT WRONG

It is always good to see young people getting together for a joyous occasion, to have a party, a celebration, or just to have fun with good friends. The only trouble is that so many of those light-hearted get-togethers end up in disagreement, violence and at times even death.

Such a party took place on 7th September 1973. It was given by Lesley Anne Neenan on her eighteenth birthday. Lesley was a secretary, efficient in her profession and popular with her friends and workmates. Perhaps she was not even aware of the extent of her popularity, for she soon found that the number of friends whom she intended inviting to her party was far greater than she could possibly entertain at her home. This was after all only a small flat in Simlar House, Western Street, Southwark. Lesley was not a person to be put off, however, and approached some of her former employers on the subject.

One of these was Raymond Lee, director of a building company called Interex Interiors Ltd. of 55 Tower Bridge Road. Lesley asked if she could use the first-floor office for her party. Mr Lee, who had considerable respect for her judgement and the company she kept, agreed to the request. He asked her to ensure that there was no mess or trouble from her guests and suggested that she should pay £10 for the use of the room and the cleaner's expenses afterwards. Miss Neenan readily agreed, and invitations were circulated to as many of her friends as she could think of. Probably more than fifty young people were due to attend.

Miss Neenan and two of her friends who were to assist her opened the party at 8 p.m. that night, but the first guest did not arrive until 9 p.m. All went well until about 10. 30 p.m., when there was a violent scuffle in a ground-floor room. There was no apparent reason for this disturbance, and some of the guests parted the combatants. Everyone then settled down once again to more drinking and merriment, and there seemed no reason to expect any aftermath.

Time seemed to pass without further incident and the party could well have gone on until the early hours of the morning. At about midnight, however, Miss Neenan decided, for reasons that we may never know, to think about ushering her guests out of the premises. By ten minutes to one in the morning there was an element of tension amongst those still present. As it was, few were left inside the building, but outside, in Tower Bridge Road, those who had already left were getting into groups on the pavement. There was obviously going to be trouble, and bearing in mind that this was supposed to be a happy birthday party, her own birthday party, Miss Neenan exercised considerable courage. Walking out of the premises, she approached both groups, and pleaded with them to 'Cool it' and make their respective ways home.

Her efforts were to no avail, however, for although it is unlikely that she was aware of it at the time, her erstwhile guests and wellwishers had divided themselves into two distinct and very unsavoury groups, one consisting of local lads from south London – south of the River Thames, the other from East London – north of the river. Most had partaken of more drink than was good for them, and both groups were undoubtedly bent on causing the maximum amount of physical discomfort to each other. In a matter of seconds, the two groups erupted into a general mêlée of violence. Fists, feet, knives and any other article that could be picked up and used as a weapon was taken into immediate use. The result was of course predictable.

The telephone rang at my bedside at about 1 a.m. It was the night duty CID officer speaking form Guys Hospital. His words followed the pattern that I was by now well used to. 'Sorry to wake you, guvnor. We've got a nasty one on Tower Bridge Section. Can you get to Guys Hospital as soon as possible? This looks like one for you.' I was already halfway out of bed. My reply was equally brief. 'I'll be with you in about a half hour.'

There are only two matters that truly wake me up from a sound sleep in the early hours of the morning. They are, either a call to a murder or other serious crime, or a call to a spot of good fishing. Actually, my calls to a spot of good fishing in those days were very rare indeed, but I have to admit that the big fish that I sought on a murder or other serious crime enquiry was always sufficient to get my adrenaline moving.

At Tower Bridge Police Station a number of young people who had been at the party were detained. They could wait. The number one priority was to get to Guys Hospital. The message had been clear to me from my past experience in these matters. Whoever had been detained at Guys Hospital was either dead or dying. If he or she was still alive, the answers to my questions could well be forthcoming and that could cut down considerably the time I would have to spend on this inquiry. Too much time can be wasted, trying to wring answers out of people who from misguided loyalty always seem bent on directing the investigating officer away from crucial issues. Unfortunately, however, I was too late in this instance. Frederick John Winter, an unemployed lad aged twenty years, had died from stab wounds some while before my arrival. Furthermore, the night-duty CID officer had not been able to see the unfortunate lad in hospital because of his condition. Now I had to set about the job the hard way, although I felt sure in my heart that the murderer was already detained, not arrested in the true sense of the word, but in all probability one of the number 'required' to remain at Tower Bridge Police Station whilst inquiries proceeded.

Few of those detained at the police station had any intention of putting me on to the track of the murderer. Nobody had seen anything. In fact, their accounts of what they allegedly saw were so much at variance that the uninitiated could almost be excused for believing they were all innocent bystanders, who should never have been brought to the police station at all.

I had heard it all before. I could feel myself slowly getting annoyed, very annoyed. The hairs on the back of my neck were tingling, and I had to put the brake on my feelings. No good investigator ever permits his temper to take charge. Experience had taught me many things, and one of those was that when one of my 'customers' lost his temper with me, I was always the ultimate winner.

One at a time I had those detained brought to my office. There, by dint of gentle questioning of the type often referred to as 'the Dutch Uncle type' I soon brought out most of the truth of the matter.

Of the total number of invitations sent out, it can be said that only twenty invited guests were at the party. It was estimated however, that over forty people were actually present at the party. About twenty gatecrashers had 'come along for the ride', as they say, and some free booze. Clearly there were two very different groups, those from Stratford and surrounding areas in east London, and the local lads from Southwark and Bermondsey in south-east London.

During the course of the party there had been a couple of minor arguments, which had resulted in fisticuffs, and threats, also of a minor nature. Those incidents had passed off without a particularly worrisome incident, as the result of timely intervention by Miss Neenan. The group from east London, however, had searched around the premises during the party, and armed themselves with knives and other offensive articles that they had found in the kitchen and elsewhere. Why? The reason was never given and never known.

As the guests left the party between midnight and 1 a.m. the east London group had gathered together on the pavement outside and waited for the local lads to leave. Then, at what he must have thought to be the right moment, Alexander Anderson, a fitter's mate, aged seventeen, from Stratford, picked an argument with Harry Abdul Maneh, one of the south London group. Anderson, the undisputed leader of the east London group, had undoubtedly picked on the six-foot tall Maneh to impress his friends. Maneh, however, gave as good as he got. This attack caused the remaining guests to enter into a general free-for-all, with the final result that Frederick Winter was left dying in the gutter, with blood pouring from stab wounds.

The accounts of the mêlée were very much at variance. Everyone, witnesses and participants, had been drinking steadily before the incident. Furthermore, the whole affair was brought to an unexpected end by the arrival of police on a normal patrol. The arrival of the officers quite probably prevented further bloodshed and even death. The mob immediately scattered, leaving Winter bleeding and unconscious in the gutter and the unfortunate patrolling constables with the unenviable task of attempting to gather together as many as possible of those who had been at the party or engaged in this affray.

The movement of the murder weapon, as in so many cases, had to be the key to the whole affair. Fortunately, it was very soon found and

Detective Superintendent at Southwark 187

identified as belonging to Alexander Anderson. When he was in due course confronted with the weapon, and the fact that it was with this knife that Winter had been killed, he admitted ownership of it. He also admitted passing it on to his friends, either Keith Feddon or Tony Brown.

Tony Brown was seen once again. At the outset he was most evasive, but after some obvious consideration, he admitted that he was handed the knife by Anderson and that he had struck the fatal blow to Winter with the weapon. Brown was charged with murder, whilst Anderson and seven of his friends from east London were charged with causing an affray. Affray! This word is so very often bandied about only too lightly. It is, however, an offence under the provisions of the Public Order Act of 1936 and as stated in that Act, is an offence to the terror of Her Majesty's subjects, an offence, moreover, that is taken very seriously indeed.

I enjoyed working at Southwark Police Station. I had had considerable success in the investigation of a number of murders and other serious crimes. I had also built up an extremely useful and healthy network of 'friends'. I say 'friends' because despite their undoubted criminal background, between us we had something of an agreement. Now please don't get me wrong. I had built up a reputation as an investigator of serious crimes in the area, to the extent that I had no time myself to spend on the many minor crimes that were reported daily. These were in any event dealt with by other officers – my junior officers. Information that did come my way during the course of my personal investigations which related to other crimes, generally of a minor nature, I would pass on to one of my junior officers. The resulting rewards were twofold. Firstly, I was happy in the knowledge that the particular officer would bring that enquiry to a successful conclusion and prosecution. Secondly, I knew that when I found myself with the next serious crime to investigate, I would have difficulty in thinning out the numerous volunteers who would wish to join my team.

Much of my success came from the fact that I was apparently only interested in or engaged in the investigation of murder, robbery or serious assault. The petty criminal as you can well understand is rarely involved in that class of crime. I was therefore able to visit a range of public houses where a welcome is rarely extended to police officers, and be accepted by those present. I always conveyed the same message to the 'customers' whom I grew to know: 'I am not interested in whatever 'monkey business' you may be up to, but if I want an answer to a question relating to a serious crime, I shall expect an answer.' This approach had a quite surprising effect. Indirectly I brought about the arrest of many lesser members of the criminal fraternity by passing to my junior officers any information obtained in this way from my visits, the strong point being that I never became personally involved in the case as far as the outsider, or indeed the prisoner, was concerned. Furthermore, when I did put a question to these people, they generally came up with a very helpful answer.

I had resigned myself to the fact that I had reached the climax of my career. I was also resigned to serving out my remaining time at Southwark. I was still often in touch with friends and colleagues serving at Scotland Yard, on the Flying Squad and in other departments. With a touch of sadness, I realised that I had unfortunately long since given up hope of ever returning to the Flying Squad, my first love in the service. I was too old, and that was the end of it.

Having reached the end of this chapter on an almost solemn note, I would like to assure the reader that life rarely had such a sad air, but was generally very satisfying.

WHO WERE YOU WITH LAST NIGHT?

On a very much lighter note, however, consider the following. For reasons that must be quite obvious I have in this instance changed the names of those concerned, so as not to cause them undue embarrassment.

One of the traditions that had always been observed during my service in the CID was the celebration following a long and difficult trial at the Old Bailey. This was something that had become virtually automatic, irrespective of whether the Crown won or lost the case. Let me say, however, that in those rare cases when the Crown did lose, the celebration was more in the nature of a cross between a wake and a very spirited court of enquiry. We just had to find out where we went wrong and in particular how the opposition had managed to come up with answers to questions that we had neither thought of nor discovered during the course of our investigation.

In October 1966, I did lose a case, which caused me and my officers

Detective Superintendent at Southwark 189

a great deal of concern. For a number of reasons, I do not intend going into the full details of the case or naming the very fortunate prisoner. Furthermore, for similar reasons I have named the sergeant in the case 'Fred Hall'. The case itself was one of receiving stolen property knowing it had been stolen, with a street value of some twelve thousand pounds. The arrest was made by the sergeant, one of my officers whilst I was serving on the Flying Squad.

Following the acquittal, my officers and I immediately carried out our own investigation, discussion, analysis, Court of Enquiry, call it what you will, to ascertain just where we went wrong. It was late in the afternoon and we adjourned to the Magpie and Stump, which had just opened. Now the Magpie and Stump is a public house immediately opposite the Old Bailey, a very famous drinking house, often referred to as 'Court Seven' from the days when there were only six courts at the Old Bailey. We could not agree amongst ourselves where we could have gone wrong or just what we had missed out in our evidence or investigation.

We later moved to a watering hole known fondly as 'George the Pole's'; its correct name was the Old Queens Head, in Fieldgate Street, Whitechapel, immediately opposite Myrdle Street, where I was born. Here our dissertations continued until closing time.

Clearly, 'Fred Hall', the arresting officer in this case, was most upset at the acquittal. We went into every detail of the operation that we could think of, but could not fault either our case preparation or evidence. Finally, we had to agree amongst ourselves that although a charge of receiving stolen property knowing it to have been stolen, was a most difficult charge to prove successfully, we had done our best, everything required of us in law, and nobody could ask for more.

We finally left the Old Queens Head and made our respective ways home, all of us, that is, except 'Fred Hall' and myself. He had taken the loss of this case very much to heart and had also taken on board a little more alcohol than usual. I had no intention of permitting him to make his own way home to Palmers Green in north London. Thankfully, 'Jock', one of the squad drivers present, came to the rescue and volunteered to take 'Fred' home, providing I came along as well.

Now 'Jock' did not know exactly where 'Fred' lived in Palmers Green. He knew the road as I did, but did not know the house. I knew the house – I thought! It was one in a terrace of houses that I had visited before on one or two occasions. 'Fred', however, was a little more than fast asleep. He had to be helped into the car, and we made our way northwards. Arriving at the road in Palmers Green, I managed to obtain some form of confirmation from 'Fred'. As much as I could get from him was 'please don't wake the wife'. This he kept repeating. With no desire to draw undue attention to ourselves, we had quite a task keeping him quiet.

At the door, I soon found the house keys in his right-hand pocket. I put the key into the lock and the door opened. I recalled afterwards that at the time I was not sure whether I had turned the key in the lock; then thought that perhaps 'Fred's' wife had left the door on the latch. Most unlikely. More likely, I thought, was that she had not closed the door properly before she retired. This also seemed a little unusual, but we were now inside the hallway.

As for our 'Fred', he was past caring. Then bearing in mind his request not to wake his wife, 'Jock' and I did what we felt was best. Having entered the hallway, we took down some of the coats from the hallstand, cushioned his head on the first step of the stairs, covered him with two other coats and removed his shoes. Finally, and very quietly we left the house, and closed the door, properly.

'Jock' and I left Palmers Green, quietly pleased with ourselves that we had done a good job. We nevertheless vowed that he still owed us both a pint for our efforts on his behalf. Furthermore, we would cash in on that vow later in the day. It was then 1 a.m.

I was in the office at 8.30 a.m. that morning and to my surprise 'Fred' was already there. I thought that he looked a little worse for wear and approached him to inform him that he owed 'Jock' and me the pint for seeing him home, but never got the words out.

'Fred' had been woken that morning at dawn by a woman who was not his wife screaming from the top of the stairs above his head to her husband: 'There's a man in the house'. He knew the voice, and it was not that of his wife. Then he opened his eyes and immediately realised that he was not in his own house. The stairs were on the wrong side of the hall, and there was no hallstand in his hallway. Then a man appeared at the top of the stairs in his pyjamas, carrying a large torch. 'Fred' immediately recognised him. It was his next-door neighbour.

Fortunately for all concerned, 'Fred' was on good 'over the garden wall' terms with his neighbour, and by use of tact the peace was kept, despite the fact that he had quite some difficulty in explaining just what had taken place the previous night, to both his neighbour and his wife.

I did not really know what to say to 'Fred'. I felt like laughing aloud, but this could hardly have helped the situation. I also felt very guilty. I had after all, made the mistake of picking out the wrong house, and even apologies seemed a little out of place. Then in a joking vein I told him that before arriving at the office that morning, both Jock and I had decided that he owed us both a pint for taking him home. Now, in view of what had happened, I told him that perhaps I would buy him a pint instead.

To my surprise, 'Fred' replied that he was unlikely to have any alcohol for some while. His condition the previous night had been a lesson to him. He had never been in that situation before and did not intend getting into such a state again. He then went rather quiet and seemed to be deep in thought. He soon came out of his reverie, however, and was all smiles. He had solved the problem. He and his wife were going to take his neighbour out for a meal at the first opportunity, in an effort to repair their relationship. Perhaps 'Jock' and I would care to foot the bill. I agreed, and some weeks later did foot the bill for the foursome, after 'Fred' had carried out his promise, grateful that this unfortunate incident had ended on a happy note.

16
Back to the Flying Squad

Just before Christmas 1973, Commander Bill Brown, the then boss of 'M' Division, sent for me. There was nothing unusual about this, and I entered his office expecting to be given another assignment or instructions on some matter or other. I found him reading some papers.

I do not recall his actual words, but looking up in a somewhat quizzical manner, he said 'What's the matter, John? Have we upset you or something?' My reply was to the effect that nobody had upset me, followed by the question as to what had given him that idea.

'You are going to the Flying Squad at the end of the month, John. What have you to say about that?' I could hardly believe my ears. I had to say something, but I could hardly find words.

My Commander was not a man to joke on such matters. I was so very pleased. I had enjoyed my service at Southwark, but was nevertheless – and I had to say it – honoured that I had been recalled to the department that I had always held in such high regard. Bill Brown smiled, stood up and shook my hand, saying, 'Good luck, John. We shall be sorry to lose you, but if this is what you want, then you've got it.'

I now had the difficult task of winding up as far as I was able all the outstanding work and cases, which I would be obliged to hand over to my successor. I set about this task with considerable gusto, for the end of the month could not come quick enough for me. Also there was Christmas to think about: office parties, to say goodbye to my divisional colleagues; visits to those 'friends' whom I would now need when I arrived on the Flying Squad. Then of course there was Christmas at my home, and it was going to be very special this year.

COOKING MY GOOSE

My wife and I had moved into a very pretty semi-detached house in New Malden in Surrey. My wife had always fancied a goose for Christmas dinner, and if she wanted one, this year of all years she was going to get one. I knew a butcher in Greenwich market, we had had a pint together in the Admiral Hardy public house on many occasions. As purchasing the Christmas bird was a task that I always took on, I decided I would make a call on him to see what he had to offer.

'George, I want a goose,' I said, and into his cold store we went. There they were, hanging in rows on rails. Now, I know nothing about geese. I am a turkey man myself. I therefore allowed George to pick out a nice-looking bird, and I settled up with him over our usual pint in the Admiral Hardy.

On my arrival home that night I proudly presented my new acquisition to my wife. Now Ursula is usually as pleased as punch with anything that I give her, but on this occasion she did not seem too pleased at all. She made out that she was pleased, but we have been together too long. I tried again. 'You have been asking for a goose. Now you've got one.' Her reply truly shook me. 'It smells a bit funny,' she said. To me a goose and all poultry have a strange smell. I still suffer from sinus trouble a little, and my sense of smell is not good at all. The bird ended up in the refrigerator and that was the end of that – for the present.

The following morning, with my corn flakes in front of me, Ursula went to get the milk from the fridge. Her return to the table was something of a surprise. 'John, come and smell the fridge!' she said. Sure enough there was an unpleasant smell. I was hopping mad. The goose was off, and there was no doubt about it. 'I shall take it back today, lass', I said. 'Don't worry, I will bring home a turkey.' She still wanted a goose, so goose it had to be.

I was on my way to Greenwich just before lunchtime. My butcher friend was surprised to see me and went to a lot of trouble to convince me that goose always smells the same. 'Nothing to worry about at all,' he would have me believe. In the cold store there were considerably less geese on show then the previous day, in fact the rails seemed comparatively empty. This of course prompted the remark, 'You see, John, I sold about fifty yesterday, and you are the only one who has complained.' I was still not entirely convinced, but he had certainly, or perhaps I should say, apparently, done a lot of business with geese since the previous day. I even began to wonder whether the smell was in fact natural.

I was invited to take my pick of the geese on the rails. There were probably fifty or sixty still hanging there. This seemed fair enough. As I examined them I found that I was still not entirely happy about the smell, but contented myself with the thought that goose smells differently to turkey. I chose my bird and made my way back to Southwark. That evening I once again presented the wife with a goose. It was 23rd December when I brought the goose home. It certainly smelt right this time, and after cursory examination by the expert, Ursula, she placed it in the refrigerator, apparently satisfied. At breakfast next morning, there was no adverse comment and I took off to work.

On Christmas morning, Ursula was up with the lark. She even brought me a cup of tea in bed. She was happy and intent on preparing the Christmas dinner of her choice for the pleasure and satisfaction of both of us. We were expecting visitors for dinner. We were not going anywhere, and I was intent on having one of those very rare mornings when I could lie in bed and relax, silently praying of course that I would not be called out to some serious crime or disturbance. I would get up about an hour later than usual, help the wife wherever I could, get the drinks prepared and then look after our guests, who were not expected until about midday.

I was not called out by the service, but the next thing I heard was a horrified shriek from the kitchen. I clattered out of bed, feeling sure that Ursula had hurt herself. The goose was on the table. It had grown fur. Feathers I could understand, but this was too much, a fine white fur or mould, and although it did not smell as strongly as the previous goose, it certainly had a strange odour, a smell reminiscent of smelling salts or ammonia! I was told in no uncertain words just what kind of a shopper I was. I felt like crawling under the table. Furthermore, if I could have got hold of that so-called butcher, George, I would gladly have wrung his neck.

On this special day, I had invited my parents and a favourite aunt who was widowed, to share our Christmas dinner. Now what were we going to do? I felt very small indeed as the wife let go with a few unprintable comments which I knew I was well worthy of, the trouble was that I could not think of anything we could do to save the situation.

To my amazement, Ursula finally quietened down, sat down and roared with laughter. For an instant I was worried. I thought that she had come over hysterical, but no, it was quite genuine laughter. For the first time in my life we cracked a bottle of wine over a breakfast of bacon and eggs and she was still apparently happy. Then to cap it all, she went to the deep freeze, scrabbled around its contents and came up with some pieces of turkey and a tin of turkey. Then turning to me with a smile, she said that it looked as if we would have turkey after all for Christmas dinner.

Before dinner, and with all reverence and humility, we took the carcass of the now pungent goose into the garden and buried it amongst the roses. The nearby bushes looked somewhat wilted, as they normally do at that time of the year. To them at least we had spread a little Christmas spirit, and our thoughts were that perhaps next year the roses would be even better than those of the summer just past.

31st December 1973 was an exciting day for me. I was looking forward to returning to the Flying Squad, and happy in the knowledge that I would be able to see out the last few years of my service doing that which I had always found to be the most satisfying task of all, arresting criminals engaged in serious crime. After the quiet welcome of a not exactly new boy to the department, Commander John Lock sent for me and told me that he was putting me in charge of the Robbery Squad. This was a compliment indeed and my excitement mounted. This was very much a plum job.

Looking round, I felt very confident that I had an efficient team working for me. I was also happy in the knowledge that that confidence would itself support me in my desire to make a success of what would undoubtedly be my final situation in the Metropolitan Police. An element of frustration, however, soon came to light. I found that I was now expected to be more of an administrator than a detective out in the street. I soon learned that I would be working longer hours and with heavier responsibility heaped upon my shoulders than I had previously experienced. As the work progressed, however, I have to admit that I thoroughly enjoyed every minute of what was clearly to be my 'swan song' to the police service.

My Robbery Squad did have a modicum of success. In fact, as I recall it, in the first six months of 1974 we arrested forty-seven persons for ninety-five offences, the majority being charged with either robbery with violence or conspiracy to rob, whilst fifteen were arrested for other miscellaneous offences. Quite a figure you may say, but it is only right to point out that over forty of the robberies were related to a gang specialising in robbing betting shops and small jewellers, whilst fourteen robberies were attributed to one man who wished to wipe the slate clean after we had arrested him for two such offences.

This may sound all very well, but I felt that we could do even better. I had no complaints of the Robbery Squad that I had taken over. My predecessor's squad had taken under their wing the first major 'squealer' on robberies, Bertie Smalls. Bertie had done a fantastic job on the underworld. He had 'put away' so many of his partners in crime that everyone was quite convinced that such a coup could never happen again. Furthermore, there were rumblings in the legal world, questioning the wisdom of giving freedom to such a man, who had taken a very active part in so many serious and violent robberies.

I found myself working late into the night, attempting to bridge that gap, and disconcerted at the thought that we were most unlikely to find another criminal who would 'do a Bertie' and put the Robbery Squad back on the map.

SUPERGRASSES

My impatience was rewarded in the middle of June 1974, when John Lock, my Commander, sent for me. 'Bob Connor's team has arrested a gang of robbers for a robbery at Phoenix Way, as you know. The gang are all in Brixton Prison, and have assaulted one of their number, a chap named O'Mahoney. O'Mahoney is upset about this and has, it seems, decided to tell all. I want you to go to Chiswick Police Station and set up an office and run this one the same as we ran Bertie Smalls.'

I needed no further encouragement. This was exactly the type of break I had been looking for. I had a good team of men who I trusted implicitly. They were efficient and raring to go.

My next stop was Chiswick Police Station in Chiswick High Road. Although I did not know it at the time, I was to remain there, or rather retain an office there, for the next eighteen months. The cooperation received from the Chiswick officers was superb, from the station cleaner to the chief superintendent. We took over the best part of the first floor of the station, and gathered in filing cabinets, copying machines and telephones in a manner that I would never have thought possible within the service. We were short of nothing, but we had to work hard, damned hard. In fact, I truly believe that we kept the legal profession and the courts as busy as we were ourselves.

To give you some idea of the vastness of the job that I took on, perhaps the following will put you in the picture.

From June 1974 through until December 1975, I had the Robbery Squad office operating continuously from Chiswick Police Station. During that time three men asked to come into police custody, strange to say, quite voluntarily. There were times when I looked back over my previous twenty-eight years of service in the police and began to wonder whether I had become involved in an entirely new style of policing. The increase in the number of informers wishing to volunteer their assistance was, to say the least, amazing. They were, moreover, offering far greater assistance than had ever been experienced before. My work was quite obviously adopting an entirely new dimension that prompted me to coin the word 'supergrass' in the course of giving a dissertation on this then very new situation to the Commissioner and other senior officers at New Scotland Yard.

My talk on what was going on at Chiswick was very necessary, for the 'supergrass' was here to stay. Difficulties of an unknown and quite unpredictable nature arose, the nub being that no instructions had been laid down on the procedure for handling these people. The police had large volumes of instructions and legal brains to call upon, but this was a new ball game for them as well.

Bertie Smalls had come and gone. Some peculiar comments had been made in relation to the Smalls affair, comments that could cause me difficulty in what I had before me. Then, as I looked at the manner in which that case had been handled, I got the feeling that I was being told that Smalls was in the past and there would never be another Bertie Smalls for some years. I found this most confusing as I commenced working on the O'Mahoney saga. There was no doubt in my mind that the authorities hoped that whatever comments had been made would be forgotten and that those in charge, both police and legal personnel, would have moved on or retired.

To clarify the point, I must say that the first section of these comments dealt with the wisdom of permitting an extremely active robber to give queen's evidence on a number of serious robberies he had been involved in and then go scot-free. It did not take our legal eagles long to come up with the answer to the question. In simple English, it came down to this. Such persons coming into police custody cannot be promised immunity from prosecution, in fact they will be prosecuted in due course. No promises were to be made as to their ultimate sentence. It was to be firmly understood that this was a matter for the court to make up its mind upon, at the time. It was above all something that police could not and would not make predictions about. As to custody after conviction, they would in all probability be kept in prison custody, where the responsibility for their safety would be a matter for the prison authorities alone.

We, the police, were thus left in a position where we were unable to offer the proverbial 'carrot' to any would-be helper who was arrested. The potential squealer, or supergrass, was therefore left to make his own mind up over the direction he wanted to go. He had to decide very quickly and of his own free will, either to assist police or take the consequences of his criminal actions in the normal way. I must say that on the first confrontation with these facts I found myself wondering whether we would ever be fortunate enough to induce anyone to do a 'Bertie' again. I was wrong.

Maurice O'Mahoney came voluntarily into police custody on 22nd June 1974 and remained with us until 20th September of that year, when he was convicted. Billy Williams volunteered to remain in police custody on 8th August 1974 and remained with us until 9th December of the same year, when he too was convicted. James Trusty, arrested on 5 August 1974, volunteered to become resident at Chiswick Police Station on 18th December 1974 and was with us until March 1975 when he was convicted. Each of these characters had a serious grievance against one or other of his partners in crime. We in turn, knowing this, were able to exploit the point to our advantage.

O'Mahoney was assaulted by some of his partners in crime whilst on remand in Brixton Prison and his girl friend and family were threatened with violence.

Billy Williams was sickened by the cold-blooded manner in which Phillip Trusty had shot Police Constable Clements in the course of a robbery at St Johns Wood in north London. Clements was very fortunate indeed; he only received a shoulder wound, whereas he could well have been killed.

Then there was James Trusty's brother, Phillip Trusty, the man who shot Police Constable Clements. This was the greatest surprise of all, for we believed on good information that the brothers were very very close indeed. Then the truth came out. James had never been in trouble before, whilst Phillip had many convictions. Phillip considered this point quite seriously. With his previous convictions, he knew that he was facing a long jail sentence. His brother, on the other hand, was of hitherto good character and thus stood a very good chance of receiving a much lighter sentence. Rather forcefully, Phillip intimated to James that he should take the full blame for the St Johns Wood robbery and also the shooting of Police Constable Clements. Make no mistake about it, brothers or not, the reputation and previous actions of Phillip Trusty made any threat he might offer a matter of considerable fright. Thus, fearing his brother's threats, James Trusty asked to come into police custody.

At about 6 p.m. on Saturday 1st June 1974, a Securicor cash carrying van was robbed of £13,152.43p by an armed gang in Phoenix Way, Heston, Middlesex, west of London, whilst conveying monies from various pick-up points to its base.

The robbery had been expertly planned, with stolen get-away vehicles placed in various strategic points in and around the area. A stolen vehicle was parked up in a position from which it could be used to ram the security vehicle and bring it to a halt at a position to the advantage of the robbers. Inside a nearby van, the gang had secreted themselves, armed and ready to attack the guards. A shotgun, a hand gun, and various weapons of violence were used in the robbery. A shot was fired, one guard was hit on the head with a hammer, and threats of assault of one form or other, backed up by the various weapons seen, took place before the gang made off with the cash.

It so happened that before this date, Bob Connor, a Detective Inspector in charge of one of the Flying Squad teams, had had his suspicions of the activities of four men who he believed were engaged in robberies. They were Michael Francis Thorne; Maurice Lanca O'Mahoney, Joseph Stephens and Angus George Smith. Information from an informant had led him to believe that these men were planning a robbery of the nature described. It was therefore believed that they would be living from the proceeds of their haul.

Immediately following this robbery, Bob Connor and his team set up a series of observations, and delved deeper into the scant information in his possession. He was determined to ascertain just what the suspects were doing, but they appeared to have truly gone to ground. As opposed to being disappointed, or downhearted, this stimulated Connor and his men to even further exertions, and his suspicion was enhanced by the small pieces of information that he managed to obtain. During the morning of 11th June 1974, a series of searches had been carried out in connection with the Chiswick operation at the homes of the suspects and of their known associates. Thorn, Stephens and Smith, all suspects, were detained and later charged with robbery. O'Mahoney, at that stage, could not be found. Certain known associates were also detained. As it happened, they were not charged with the Phoenix Way robbery, but with other serious criminal offences.

Following the arrest of these people, a great number of enquiries had to be made as the result of the interrogation of those detained. O'Mahoney's current whereabouts were discovered and he was arrested the following day, 12th June 1974. That same day, a cache of arms, ammunition, stolen vehicles and other property was discovered, all of which proved to be 'tools of trade' of this highly organised and very efficient team of robbers. In addition, a small portion of the booty was also discovered. A fifth man, Ronald Cook, was by now also wanted for questioning in respect of other matters, but evaded capture until 5th January 1975.

In O'Mahoney's possession, or to be more explicit, in the flat of his girlfriend's mother, some very interesting articles were found, a shotgun, a pistol, £1,200, part proceeds of the Phoenix Way robbery, also items of clothing which had undoubtedly been used in that robbery. These matters were dealt with at Hounslow Police Station. The four men mentioned were charged with the robbery and duly appeared before the magistrates at Brentford Magistrates Court, where they were remanded in custody for seven days.

Now all robbers are brave men when committing their criminal actions, solely because they have the element of surprise and are armed with some implement or firearm, with which to offer violence and fear to others; whilst the victim is unarmed and going about his normal business. Robbers also have an air of bravado after the robbery, particularly when they are spending their spoils on their usual form of recreation – gambling, women or, as is said in the underworld, just being 'Jack the Lad'.

When robbers are arrested, however, they are entirely different people. They may put up a token resistance in an effort to evade custody, but their successes on that score are very rare indeed. Fortunately for police they are, with very few exceptions, downright cowards. Then, when they find themselves in custody and locked up, they invariably do what they should have done well before the robbery that resulted in their incarceration: they think, and think very deeply indeed. Now for once they have time on their hands and take advantage of it. Their minds are now fixed on one matter in particular, the evidence. Is there a loophole in that evidence? There is bound to be one, and it must be found! Then, during the course of this deep thought, the possibility of any escape route is never overlooked.

In this particular instance, O'Mahoney's confederates for reasons best known to themselves came to the conclusion that his girlfriend must be the weak link in the chain. They, were of course, at the time all locked up in Brixton prison, awaiting the next hearing. They had two lines of action open to them. Firstly they had to make quite sure that O'Mahoney was very much aware that they intended tolerating no weakness in the case from him. Secondly, they had to make sure that his girlfriend was similarly aware that any weakness on her part would be dealt with in the only way approved in the underworld.

The result of this was that one of the suspects, Thorne, a brute of a man, seized O'Mahoney, whilst Stephens, another suspect, attempted to gouge his eyes out with the handle of a toothbrush. This attack took place in prison and was apparently, fortunately for O'Mahoney, stopped by the timely intervention of Angus Smith, the third suspect. At about this time, the wives of Thorne and Stephens, together with Stephens' mother, called upon O'Mahoney's girlfriend and her parents, no doubt at the behest of their respective husbands. In no uncertain terms, both the girlfriend and her parents were threatened with personal violence if they dared to offer to assist police in any way.

It was these two events that influenced O'Mahoney to take the unusual step he did. It was a surprise to police, but an even greater surprise to the London underworld. On his appearance at Brentford Magistrates Court on 21 June 1974 O'Mahoney openly announced in court that he was guilty of the offence charged and wished to be remanded into police custody in order that he could tell the police everything that he knew.

The request was granted, and O'Mahoney remained in police custody until he was finally dealt with. He was sentenced to five years' imprisonment on an indictment charging one count of robbery, one count of burglary and one of attempted robbery. He also asked for ninety-nine other offences to be taken into consideration by the court. The total value of the property involved in the various offences was in the region of £180,000.

I have probably jumped the gun by telling you the result of the case at this stage. Bearing this in mind, however, and the very great number of offences dealt with, you will understand when I say that even the first exploratory interviews with O'Mahoney revealed that he was in a position to give a vast amount of extremely valuable information, which would require a large number of officers to handle the necessary inquiries. The available space at Hounslow Police Station, where the gang were originally charged, was not sufficient to accommodate those who would undoubtedly be required to work on this case. The result of this consideration was that I would have to enlarge my team considerably. In point of fact, I took a total of sixty officers under my wing. They included my Robbery Squad, various officers from the Flying Squad, police officers from other divisions of the Metropolitan Police and officers from Thames Valley Police Force.

Difficulties of course were experienced. The prisoner turned complete informer! Now detained at Chiswick Police Station, and having turned to police for protection against the underworld, they took matters a little further by telling tales on those protecting them, childish tales of little substance, made quite obviously in the hope of obtaining further privileges because they were now important police witnesses. They soon learned, however, that this latest ploy did not work.

O'Mahoney was known to his confederates as 'Soppy Mo'. The reason for this I could never understand. He was undoubtedly a very strange brand of genius and certainly not worthy of such a nickname. Criminal he may have been, but he was also academically quite clever and had a memory that was nothing short of fantastic. We found that he could recall in detail the most intimate points of incidents going back five or six years. Unfortunately, however, his mood changed from one minute to the next.

A separate statement was taken from him in relation to every crime he decided to talk about and this proved to be an extremely time-consuming, if worthwhile task.

It was necessary to take O'Mahoney to the scene of the crime he was detailing, to identify premises, etc. On one such occasion, whilst passing Gospel Oak in north London, he asked the driver to stop the car. He explained that on a piece of grassland, which he indicated, he had buried a loaded pistol some two years previously, his intention at the time being to return and recover it when it was next required. This was quite a large piece of grassland, and although his directions seemed positive enough, short of digging up quite a large area of grass, there seemed little way of checking out his story. Through the good offices of our gadgets department, a metal detector was obtained. Then to our very great surprise, the pistol, wrapped in a weatherproof plastic bag, loaded and in full working order, was found as indicated. It was nine inches below the surface, but so close to the mark made by O'Mahoney that I am quite satisfied that he could have found it himself, had he been free to do so.

A further point of interest that came out from these periodic sorties was the method used by certain criminals in disposing of unwanted tools of trade and identifiable property. He indicated various bridges over the Grand Union Canal and Regents Canal in north London. On this point our old friends the Underwater Search Unit came into their own. I found that some members of the unit remembered their abortive attempt to find the pistol with which Stanley Butcher was murdered, which had been thrown into the Thames. They even indicated that they hoped that the search I was directing them to in this case was not going to be the same. On the basis of past finds on the indication of O'Mahoney, however, I promised them that this search was going to be rewarding. I had a lot of faith in the word of this rascal. The unit did in fact have a field day, in fact a number of such successful days. We found ourselves cataloguing quite a collection of stolen silverware, jewellery, guns and many other miscellaneous articles, all brought up from the bottom of these canals.

Our close interrogation of O'Mahoney produced a host of other matters that had to be investigated. As the result of his information, two hundred and seventy-seven persons were detained. Over one hundred were subsequently charged with serious criminal offences and fifty-nine were under investigation and would in due course be charged.

Needless to say, the successes of the Robbery Squad at this time appeared commonplace. The root of the success lay in the untiring efforts of my team and those whom I had co-opted to assist me when the task became too large for the number of men normally under my control. I would therefore like to quote the words of Sir Carl Arvold, the Recorder of London, addressing me just before sentencing O'Mahoney:

> I would like to commend you and the officers involved in this case. All too rarely do I feel obliged to offer commendation but in this case in particular it is most unusual to hear the accused thank the Police for the way he has been treated and dealt with and I would like to thank you for the excellent work done by you and your officers.

Following the conviction of O'Mahoney, many thought that the job was done. Oh no! It was only just starting. We were in September 1974, and had a large number of people to concentrate on and many more serious crimes to clear up. The task was indeed vast, and I was beginning to wonder whether I would ever be able to complete the work I had taken on before I would be obliged to leave the force at my accepted retirement age (of fifty-five) on 15th August 1975.

Our enquiries continued with the same enthusiasm throughout. CID officers were not entitled to overtime payment in those days and few of us ever thought of seeking it. We were too busy thinking about the next job on the list and ensuring that our supergrasses came up to scratch to worry about time. I say this, of course, for my men. Me, I was getting a little worried. I would never complete this job by August 1975 and I did not relish the probability of having to hand over the hundreds of statements and reports in my possession to a new man. I went to my boss, John Locke, the Commander of the Flying Squad, and told him that there were two points that I wanted him to consider.

Firstly, I did not see how I could possibly complete the amount of work that I had accumulated before I was obliged to retire. I continued with the second point, again before he could say anything, by suggesting that perhaps he could let me stay on for another year. That way I could in all probability complete the many unfinished investigations that were still on the books and would most certainly still be there on 15th August.

To my relief and surprise the Commander agreed to my suggestion, but hastened to point out that the final decision was not his alone. If I wanted to do another year, he would seek advice from above. I could take the matter no further. I therefore retired from his office, with my fingers crossed and in silent prayer. I did not have to wait long for the word. I was told within a few days that my application had been approved, subject to the decision of the Chief Medical Officer. I was also told that an appointment had been made for me to go to see him in two days' time. I reported to the Chief Medical Officer as directed at 9.30 a.m. on the morning in question. I had made arrangements to interview a complainant at New Scotland Yard at 10.30 a.m. firmly believing that the examination would only take about a quarter of an hour. Fifteen minutes! I left the Chief Medical officer's room at 3.30 p.m. that afternoon. I have never had such a thorough medical examination, and believe me I have never been so pleased. His final words to me were to the effect of 'On your way, Mr Swain. I can't find anything wrong with you. You are surprisingly fit for your age.' I now had an extension of service until August 1976.

Many groups of robbers appeared before learned judges at the Central Criminal Court. Our accent every time was on the corroboration of the statements of stories that our new ally the supergrass came up with. I say stories, because some of the descriptions of criminal acts were so unlikely that at the outset we were inclined virtually to ignore them. Fortunately, it was not in my nature to ignore anything these characters told me, and it was just as well. As it turned out, the more fantastic and fictional the description appeared, the more positive was the result of our enquiries. Nothing, absolutely nothing, was therefore ignored.

Our first concern was accommodation, for our police stations are not geared up for the long detention of prisoners. The staff at Chiswick Police Station, however, could not have been more helpful. They continued to rally round in a most creditable manner, despite the difficulties they experienced in this new role of retaining prisoners for longer periods. There was never a hitch. I was fast becoming sure of one very pleasing bonus in this case: if nothing else, the Chiswick operation was doing much to enhance relations between the Criminal Investigation Department and our uniformed colleagues. On this particular point, I made quite sure that Commander Hannan, then in charge of 'I' Division which included the Chiswick sub-division, was well aware of our appreciation of the wonderful work and co-operation were receiving from his officers. I also stressed that the importance of the co-operation could not be emphasised too much.

Corroboration of O'Mahoney's statements proved to be most difficult. Indeed, it was the most difficult part of the whole operation. Many of those interviewed cracked up when confronted with the content of the O'Mahoney statement touching on them and admitted their part in the particular offence under review. Others, more cunning, made complete denials. Notwithstanding this, however, as far as possible no person was charged on uncorroborated evidence and few evaded the consequence of their actions. Even in the face of our successes, however, we were very much aware that so much hinged on the burning question of whether O'Mahoney himself would come up to proof in the witness box. As we progressed, however, and he gave evidence in a number of trials, learned Counsel described him to me as absolutely brilliant. This of course was appreciated, but my worry, nevertheless, was that I knew him to be so much a man of moods. Irrespective of the confidence expressed, he could change in a flash. Anything could happen.

Whilst he was being held in police custody, much was done to relieve O'Mahoney from boredom. Once sentenced, however, he went to Oxford Prison, then to Winchester Prison and finally to Wormwood Scrubs Prison. On each occasion, thanks to the co-operation of the prison liaison staff, he was virtually nursed. His mentality, however, was such that he continually provoked incidents. Oxford could not contain him. He wore out his welcome at Winchester. Finally he came to rest at Wormwood Scrubs, and it was there that he remained on paper until the completion of his sentence. I say 'on paper', because there was still much to do in relation to the many points that arose as our enquiries continued, which needed urgent clarification. For this reason he was brought back to Chiswick Police Station on as many days each week as we could arrange. We put it to O'Mahoney that this was to relieve him from prison boredom. This was not entirely true, but seemed to please him and tended to keep our problem child in a more favourable frame of mind.

As for Williams, he proved to be a cool, calculating villain. Not clever, but certainly cunning. He was no trouble to contain in police custody. The only time he caused us some concern was when he asked for permission to marry his fiancée, who was at that time very pregnant. We need not have worried, however, for the provision for this problem was adequately contained in the Prison Act. Thus, by virtue of the fact that he was our prisoner at Chiswick, having been so committed there by the magistrate at Brentford Magistrates Court, we were able to make the necessary arrangements, on the same lines as would have been carried out by the prison authorities, had he been resident in one of Her Majesty's Prisons.

During his detention, Williams made sixty-four statements respecting forty-eight serious crimes. Some of the culprits had already been arrested, and dealt with or were in the process of going through the courts. When sentenced, Williams asked for thirty-six other offences which he had been involved in to be taken into consideration. The value of the cash and property stolen during the course of perpetrating these offences was in the region of £44,000.

Williams was similarly sentenced to five years' imprisonment and was committed to HM Prison Oxford, where difficulties immediately began to arise. The prison authorities bent over backwards to assist the police in every way, but they had their duty to carry out as custodians of this very strange individual and were already very much aware of the difficulties experienced with the current breed of supergrass.

For reasons best known to Williams, he decided that he wanted to serve out his time in Wormwood Scrubs Prison. The governor of that prison, however, was getting a little fed up with the continued demands of O'Mahoney and quite understandably fought shy of accepting a second problem child. Much as I appreciated the governor's problem, however, I was not a little concerned about Williams. He had intimated to me in a roundabout way that he could well refuse to give evidence against his former associates in crime if he remained in jail at Oxford. He said he had been the victim of jibes and threats whilst at Oxford and didn't know whether he would have the guts to continue and give evidence as was required of him. I knew that what he was saying was not true. To me this was blackmail, pure and simple. Nevertheless, I had to do something. Too much was at stake. I spent some while with Williams, in my efforts to calm him down, and managed to convince him that he was in the best possible place for him.

As it was there were many points in the statements we had taken from Williams that had to be clarified and we were therefore obliged to bring him to Chiswick Police Station on occasion. This, coupled with our previous talk, had something of a remedial effect upon him, but as with O'Mahoney, we often wondered whether he would come up to proof when put to the test at the final trials. Williams did, however, complete his evidence to the absolute satisfaction of prosecuting Counsel. He received fourteen months remission on his sentence, which made him eligible for parole in January 1976.

The third man I have mentioned, James Trusty, although before his arrest a man with no previous convictions, was nevertheless, the brother of Phillip Trusty, regarded as one of the most vicious criminals in London at the time. We were justly worried that he would influence his brother by some means or other not to give evidence.

James Trusty was arrested on 5th August 1974 and was quite content to remain in custody from that date and take his fair share of the consequences, should he be unfortunate enough to be convicted. In fact I am sure that he was resigned to that fact. It was clear, however, right from the outset that the Trusty gang were confident of securing an acquittal by the most devious means. The turnabout came, as I mentioned earlier, when Phillip Trusty, finding that his devious methods had been frustrated, asked his brother James to take the blame for the attempted murder of Police Constable Clements. As it was, James Trusty proved himself to be about the most polite criminal I have ever known. He proved his complete disenchantment with the criminal fraternity by producing in concert with his solicitor and counsel a fifteen-page statement of evidence involving three robberies and a conspiracy to rob, which truly took the feet from under his brother Phillip. For once I felt satisfied that we had a supergrass who would come up to proof.

James Trusty was finally dealt with on 17th March 1975 and served his sentence in Her Majesty's Prison, Lewes. There he became something of a model prisoner and decided to make a study of bricklaying.

At Phillip Trusty's trial, James Trusty had given most damning evidence against his brother and associates. This, needless to say, brought quite enormous pressure upon him by his family. It was to be expected and James was well aware that this would be one of the consequences of his actions. Such were these pressures, however, that it resulted in this quiet and polite individual becoming extremely hostile towards the police.

The magnitude of this case is possibly best summed up in the following list of offences which our three supergrasses, Maurice O'Mahoney, Billy Williams and James Trusty were charged with, and had taken into consideration when dealt with:

Robbery 26
Attempted Robbery 3
Conspiracy to rob 33
Burglary 82
Thefts of lorry loads 2
Miscellaneous crimes 90

You will no doubt have noted that quite a number of conspiracies to rob are recorded as charged or taken into consideration. Make no mistake about it, these were quite definitely robberies that would have taken place at some future date had we not found out about them in advance. The most interesting point was the manner in which these projected robberies were put together and planned. The villains kept extremely thorough observations on these projects, to the extent of taking their wives and girlfriends, even their children or other people's children on these ventures. To the watcher, they were ostensibly shopping, in order to successfully allay suspicion, particularly on the part of any inquisitive passing police officer or private person.

During the course of this saga, we closely interrogated many more people than charged. No snippet of information was ignored, and everything within reason was carded and indexed. There was no secret about the information that we accumulated, in fact we were most anxious to assist anyone in the service with this vast amount of information that we virtually had at our fingertips. The property recovered also caused quite some interest. During the course of these inquiries, we seized two sawn-off shotguns, ten shotguns, some parts of shotguns, such as barrels that had been cut off, one powerful air rifle, nine pistols, three hundred and fifty rounds of live ammunition of miscellaneous calibre, from ·22 up to 12 bore, plus forty-five rounds of blank ammunition.

During the course of investigating the information supplied by James Trusty, he asked us to take him to Teddington Lock on the River Thames, where, he told us, he had disposed of the revolver used by his brother on the Watney's Brewery robbery, at his request. Once again our old friends of the Underwater Search Unit came into their own. I gave James a piece of metal of the approximate size and weight of a pistol as described, handed it to him and asked him to throw it into the water where he had previously thrown the pistol. He did this, and the result was that a diver went into the water and recovered the pistol on his first dive. Cash recovered was to the order of seven to eight thousand pounds. The value of miscellaneous property recovered, however, was far above that sum. We also seized a number of motor cars and on occasions furniture and household equipment that had been purchased with the proceeds of crime. These items were seized for the purpose of disposal in due course in the interest of certain of the losers.

There was great personal satisfaction at the successful completion of this series of jobs. One major problem remained, however: where to house our supergrasses. Individually, they created a formidable problem for the governors of the prison service. Collectively, however, they were an even greater problem. If the trend continues, and I see no reason why it should not, I am quite sure that the Home Office will ultimately be obliged to find a secure wing somewhere in one of their establishments in which to incarcerate these people. This would also enable the police to get the best from them and would take a considerable amount of work away from police officers.

The difficulties of this particular point cannot be swept aside. Consider first the problems we had with O'Mahoney. Following reports sent to the Home Office and backed by very senior police officers, O'Mahoney was transferred in May 1975 to the Special Wing of HM Prison Brixton. Unfortunately, however, the prison authorities did not consider the number of prisoners in custody at that prison awaiting trial on committal as the direct result of O'Mahoney's testimony. The result of this was that by dint of typical prison guile it took those other prisoners on remand a mere forty-eight hours to reduce O'Mahoney, and Williams, who had subsequently joined him, to near mental wrecks. Threats were shouted at our detainees from all directions. Messages in tins were lowered past the cell windows and every form of indignity short of direct confrontation and assault was hurled at them. The result of this was that when O'Mahoney appeared at the Central Criminal Court to give evidence against some of our 'customers', the judge, after hearing of these troubles, directed that O'Mahoney be handed over to the custody of police.

Then outside forces got to work. During a lull in the proceedings, due to the Whitsun recess, another shock was being prepared. An article appeared in the Sunday People newspaper, which projected O'Mahoney in all his glory, mentioning convictions and offences taken into consideration, stating that he had squealed on some two hundred villains and, as was said at the time, 'truly putting the cat amongst the pigeons'. The net result of this was that the trial was stopped. A fresh date was fixed, and it looked as if O'Mahoney would be returning to Brixton Prison. Lord Justice Lawson, however, who made the first direction that O'Mahoney be placed in police custody, asserted that when giving his original direction, he meant that O'Mahoney should remain in police custody throughout the trials. He remained in such custody until finally released on 15th March 1976.

Unfortunately, this was not the end of our troubles. O'Mahoney was finding it more difficult adjusting himself to the outside world, and for the first time he was beginning to realise that the only friends he had, apart from his girlfriend, were the police. This should have worked in our favour, but strange to say, he became even more difficult to contain.

Then there was Williams. Upon his release from prison on 5th April 1976, through the good offices of the police and other co-operative organisations, he was taken to a new home. En route, although undoubtedly suspicious of our reasons for going to the trouble of collecting him from prison and taking him home, he expressed his appreciation of the way he had been treated by police. He furthermore assured me that he would keep out of trouble and in his own way swore an oath that he would never be heard of again by either the police or his old associates.

We parted on extremely good terms, and I felt that at least this one should disappear into the background. Unfortunately, it did not take Williams long to realise that he was sitting on a proverbial gold mine. O'Mahoney was still committed to giving evidence, and Jimmy Trusty was in prison. This gave Williams what is best described as first pickings with the press and anyone else interested. The story that he gave the media was quite startling, far from the truth and suitably garnished in the way that the press know how, to impress their readers. He received from the newspaper concerned a very substantial sum of money, though nobody was particularly worried about that. The trouble was that out of sheer mischief, he lost no time in letting O'Mahoney know that out of this coup he had made some £10,000.

The effect upon O'Mahoney was tragic, in that the vast amount of work put in to investigating the remaining eight cases and preparing the court papers, to say nothing of the time of the Director of Public Prosecutions and counsel, was wasted overnight. Realising the amount of money that he also could have by making similar approaches to the press, he immediately made noises about refusing to give further evidence. These were ignored until early in June 1976, when I again saw him at Chiswick Police Station.

I was so thankful that we had never entered into any type of deal with O'Mahoney and I was certainly not in the mood to enter into one then. I told him that in the light of his previous assurances that he would give evidence in all of his cases, we were entitled to expect him to continue. He was adamant, however, that he would not and could not. In his words, this was because of nerves; because of threats; because of pressures, none of which he would explain. He had decided to stop giving evidence and that, as far as he was concerned, was that. I told him to seriously consider this step and to write a letter to me with his decision. This he agreed to do, and we parted company.

Make no mistake about it, this was blackmail, pure and simple, by O'Mahoney. He had previously asked the authorities to agree to pay him a substantial sum of money out of public funds for the information and evidence he had given and would give in the future. The request, of course, had been turned down. Now he either wanted that decision rescinded, or he would get his cash from the newspapers. This was certainly my way of interpreting this latest ploy on his part. It was also the interpretation put to his words by my senior colleagues.

On 7th June 1976, O'Mahoney attended the office of his probation officer, a person with whom we were always in contact. He said he wanted to send a letter to me. He then dictated the letter to a secretary. The letter was typed, he signed it and on his instructions it was posted to me. It read as follows:

> Dear Mr Swain,
> I wish to inform you that I do not wish to give further evidence re the trials at the Central Criminal Court. I would also wish that the information which I have just passed to you could be given to the Director of Public Prosecutions.
>
> If my short note is not to your satisfaction and to the satisfaction of the Director of Public Prosecutions, then I would be only too pleased to appear at the Central Criminal Court in front of the presiding Judge at any particular trial, when I will give my reasons why I am not giving any further evidence.
>
> Yours faithfully   M. O'Mahoney.

On Thursday, 1st July 1976, three cases were called at the Central Criminal Court. All relied solely upon O'Mahoney's evidence, and in the light of the letter just mentioned, the prosecution was obliged to offer no evidence. O'Mahoney was of course aware that these cases were to be heard and wanted to attend. He was told that he would be taken to court when required. His devious mind, however, produced other ideas. He told representatives of the Sun newspaper, with whom he was negotiating a story on his activities, to be present at court, where they would learn that the paper would now be free to publish his story.

No doubt this ploy would have gone ahead, but for the fact that we had considerable knowledge of O'Mahoney's past activities whilst in our care. The cases were therefore brought on at 10 a.m. instead of the usual time of 10.30 a.m. and by half past ten all of the cases had been completed. The press representative arrived at 10.45 a.m. and was somewhat put out when he realised what had happened. I took the trouble to see him later, however, and explained the position to him. I also pointed out that notwithstanding the fact that O'Mahoney might not give evidence, the remaining cases awaiting trial were still *sub judice* and O'Mahoney's presence at court could still be required either by the prosecution or the defence. The result of that meeting was that the Sun newspaper dropped the O'Mahoney story, at least for the time being. Things were becoming generally unpredictable and we were beginning to wonder 'What next?' Then O'Mahoney made noises indicating that he might change his mind and give evidence. He had said nothing specific, and it was then a matter of waiting until the next trial involving him was called. In the light of his letter, however, the probability was that his credibility as a witness had gone.

With Williams and James Trusty, now released, there was every indication that through the medium of the press they were cooking up a story to assist Phillip Trusty in his appeal. The bonus for them for such an action would be twofold: they could reap a nice cash payment for whatever article they might induce the press to publish; secondly, and more important to them, they could by this means ingratiate themselves to Phillip Trusty, who quite clearly still held both Williams and James Trusty in fear of their lives, even though he was languishing in prison serving a life sentence. The outcome of this latest ploy I never pursued. Time for me was getting shorter each day. I was now in the process of handing over what was left of the supergrass affair to my successor. It was the largest job I had ever undertaken as a police officer, and I was very happy and satisfied with the results I had managed to produce.

PART FIVE

MOVING ON

17
Retirement Time

I was now very near to the end of my service. I had enjoyed my 'swan song' period and the extra year I had been granted. I knew that I had given of my best. Furthermore, I was now receiving words of appreciation from my superiors. The big trouble was that things were now happening so fast that I had great difficulty in keeping up with them. There were things I should have thought of, but had not. I had been so fortunate in having the extra year of service to complete the O'Mahoney saga. I had spent my little spare time in gathering together probable clients for when I retired. Now that period was fast expiring.

With my thoughts fully occupied in a matter that my officers were dealing with, I was walking along the fourth floor corridor from my office to that of the Commander, to report on the current situation. I was suddenly stopped by Brenda. This was quite a surprise. Now Brenda was the Flying Squad Clerk, a very wise woman, whom I had known for many years. It was most unusual for her to stop me. We had a good understanding: she usually would telephone me, and we would call on each other at our convenience. On this occasion she presented me with a list of items of equipment of official issue that I was supposed to have in my possession. Some of the items on the list went back many years, and I had to think very hard to try to imagine where they would be.

Not only did Brenda give me the list of equipment, which I must now locate, but she also reminded me that I had quite a portion of annual leave outstanding, which would bring my retirement date back to 20th August.

Having given my report to the Commander I returned to my office to look out all of the items on the list I had just received. My thoughts, however, were far from concentrated on these items. I had welded together a superb team of detectives and was finding the imminent probability of being obliged to leave the service and the group of officers whom I had begun to regard as my own, somewhat disconcerting. I found it extremely difficult to shake off a feeling bordering on sadness.

I handed over the reins of my team, the Robbery Squad, to my two faithful deputies, Mike McAdam and Dave Dixon. Now I had to set about tidying up the remaining urgent paperwork, organising my retirement party and leaving the service with dignity.

Everything went off smoothly, in fact the only person who was not calm and fully collected was myself. With my retirement party over, attended by a goodly selection of friends, relatives and colleagues, the final moment of truth for any retiring officer is when he hands in his warrant card. In those days the card consisted of a small, black folding piece of pasteboard, or rather pasteboard covered with a black shiny paper, similar to leatherette. On a piece of white paper glued inside, it bore the name, rank and warrant number of the officer to whom it was issued. It bore no photograph. Although it had existed in this form for many years, it was never an impressive form of identity. It was, however, a very prized possession and zealously guarded by all to whom it was issued. Indeed, in the preceding thirty years I had never felt properly dressed without it.

I handed over my warrant card to Commander Neesham. We said our goodbyes and I left his office. As I approached the security officer at the main entrance, on my way out of the building, I found myself wondering whether I had left anything behind at my desk. I even mentally checked over the contents of my pockets. I knew only too well that once past the security post, I would not get back into the building without going through all of the normal rigmarole that any visitor would be subjected to. Me, an ordinary visitor! The thought slowed me down quite considerably. I certainly did not relish having to return and ask the receptionist to arrange for me to be escorted back to what a few minutes earlier had been my personal office.

Once in the street, I turned and looked up at the building I had known so well. John Swain, ordinary citizen, was now one of the many unemployed. But that was not going to be for long!

I had not entirely wasted my personal time, what there had been of it, during the past two years, I had been only too well aware that retirement would face me. It was a subject, a state of mind, even a fact of life that I had never attempted to sweep away from reality. I had therefore faced up to the subject and carried out a spot of research when I could. The problem had been to make up my mind on what exactly I was going to do when that day came along. I also knew that in the past some of my staff had quietly referred to me as a 'workaholic'. I had laughed this off at the time, but now that I came to think about it, I realised that I just have to work at something. Idleness would drive me crazy.

I had given a lot of thought to some of the many jobs as security adviser that had been proposed to me by a number of large companies. I could have signed up with almost any one of them. What put me off for the most part, however, was the probability of having to drive to central London most days and being obliged to hack my way through traffic to get to an office by 9 a.m. or thereabouts; then having to repeat the process in reverse during the heavy traffic to get home in the evening. Not a pleasant thought. Then of course there was the probability of boredom; the same office each day, the same people to work with, almost identical lines of inquiry, if inquiries were in fact involved. The more I thought about it, the more I knew that it was not for me.

I had thought of going into business as a private investigator. The trouble was that the only private investigators I had ever come into contact with were the more disreputable ones, and I had no intention of joining their ranks. I found myself, nevertheless, thinking on lines of taking up this style of work. I needed advice, however.

I decided to go to the one man whom I knew would give me the unbiased advice that I urgently needed. I had always had a good relationship with Special Branch, and whereas I knew CID officers in general would be somewhat biased in their opinion on the subject, there was one man in that department who would be honest with me. I was confident that Vic Gilbert, the Deputy Assistant Commissioner in charge of Special Branch, would give me sound guidance on the subject.

My interview with Mr Gilbert had been most interesting and enlightening. His impression of private investigators was far higher than I would have ever imagined. It is possible that my facial expressions caused him to realise that I was doubting his judgement.

His next remark, however, settled the matter in my mind. 'John, we are a proud and efficient police force, respected world wide, but we have our 'bad eggs'. When they are brought to light and dealt with, the publicity gives us all a bad name. The same applies to private investigators. I think that you would enjoy the work, and who knows, you may even enhance the reputation of that profession in the eyes of the Service. I suggest that you spend some time during the last year of your service sounding out probable clients for the future.'

After talking to Vic Gilbert my mind was made up, and during the run-up to my retirement, that at the time of the interview was one year, and later extended to two years, I was quite busy in my spare time. I secured a verbal agreement with a brewery, a hotel group, a printer, and a former American government investigator, now in private practice, to act as their security consultant, and investigator. When I left the police, I would work from home, whatever hours were required, and wherever required. Furthermore, and the final piece of personal satisfaction, there would be a considerable amount of variation in the work. You will therefore appreciate, that as I quietly made my way home on the night that I left the Yard, I had my future fairly well mapped out.

Despite my confidence that I had made the necessary arrangements for my future activities, I was still in something of a daze that evening. Having recovered from the shock, however, and I do not use the word lightly, of finding myself no longer a member of the Metropolitan Police Service, there was one thing that I urgently needed. Something I needed more than anything else. A holiday. Away from it all, and certainly away from London. I wanted to get away as a private citizen, not as an off duty senior police officer, at the beck and call of the telephone and not having to notify my whereabouts to my superiors in case a big job should break. In short, with no likelihood of being called out of my warm bed in the middle of the night to attend the scene of a murder, robbery, or some other serious incident.

I had no doubts about where to go, or what I was going to do. I told the people who I had agreed to work for that I would commence working for them on the 1st October, 1976. I then went off to Scotland for a spot of salmon fishing. Peter Anderson, probably one of the finest fly fishers in the world, was an old friend of mine. I telephoned him and told him of my intentions, and sought his advice as to the best area to go. His advice was more in line with an open invitation. He had a week free and he therefore invited me to stay with him at his home in Kirkintilloch, just outside Glasgow. From there we could have a few days on the River Tay and other spots near to where he lived.

I was made most welcome by the Anderson family, and spent a very relaxed and enjoyable week with them, and we are still to this day in regular contact. I thus returned home refreshed, with three weeks ahead of me in which to change my mode of life and settle down. I was no longer to be troubled by the ringing of that damned telephone, and that was indeed something that I found difficult to get used to. Telephone calls from now on would be in my own personal interest, and that of whatever clients I had accumulated. Then of course, I found myself able to spend a little more time in my garden, in my workshop, or giving my car that little extra attention it had never before experienced. In my heart I knew that I was going to enjoy myself.

18
Into a New Profession

Upon my return from Scotland, and to reality, I found there was one matter that I was obliged to attend to forthwith. I had to register with the local Labour Exchange at Redhill, which was only a few miles away. I had not reported to a Labour Exchange for forty years, and it felt quite strange standing in line with dozens of other unemployed persons.

The queue was moving slowly, and I could see myself waiting there for an hour or so. Now I am not normally impatient, but I was far from happy shuffling along at about two steps every quarter of an hour.

Then an 'angel' came to the rescue.

A young woman from behind the counter beckoned me over to her. Her opening remarks took me completely by surprise. 'You don't look like one of our usual callers,' she said, 'can I help you?' I explained my situation, that I had retired from the Metropolitan Police on 31st August. She nodded.

I told her that I was going into business on my own account on 1st October. She held up one hand and interrupted – 'I don't want to know about that,' she said. 'Go on'. I then told her that I was reporting in order to register for National Insurance, National Health and whatever else I was obliged to register for. This pleasant young lady, however, was most helpful and took down all my particulars in a most efficient way.

The queue that I had left had not moved, and as I left the building, thanking the young lady profusely for her attention, I was also vowing quietly to myself that I would never return there unless I was truly obliged to do so.

SOUNDING OUT THE FIELD

My work for the hotel group started on 1st October 1978. The group was a subsidiary of a large brewery concern. The object of my work was firstly to ensure that managers were taking all security measures necessary in relation to stocks and staff, then to instil a security awareness amongst them. Many of them had little or no knowledge of the security matters so necessary in controlling staff and stocks when cash was at risk.

There was the matter of staff, particularly bar staff. So many publicans and hoteliers learn all too late about the assortment of ploys adopted by barmaids, barmen and others between taking the order, serving the customer, taking the cash, placing it in the till, ringing up the till and returning whatever change may be due. The devious actions that take place during this very short time have resulted in the ruin of many unsuspecting managers. In this direction, I was able to do much and saved the company a great deal of money.

My success was the result of keeping observation on suspected staff when stock shortages indicated that something was amiss. After a few months, however, I found I was getting known to the staff. This drawback was highlighted when a member of staff who had resigned from one establishment, under pressure from me, turned up at another house under my supervision. He was surprised, very surprised, and left the house without saying a word or asking for his wages! This was a warning I took to heart. I was obliged to take on staff myself in order to prevent a similar occurrence.

One of the many aspects of my new profession of which I had little prior experience, but felt I could do well in and become involved in, was in the purchase and sale of security equipment. I had been spoiled in the police service, in that if I needed an item of unusual equipment, all I had to do was ask for it. If I could prove the need, and the request was reasonable, I generally got what I wanted. As far as I was concerned, now that I was out of the police, I was only basically interested in purchasing equipment for use myself in my business. On the other hand, however, I felt that if I discovered a useful item of unusual equipment, I was not averse to the possibility of getting involved in marketing it.

One such item of equipment was put to me by my American contact in late 1978. He had himself spent quite a while in the UK and was very much aware of the traffic problems in many of our larger towns. Being closely associated with the police during his stays in this country, he was aware of the efforts made by police and traffic wardens to eliminate excessive and unlawful parking of motor vehicles. He pointed out to me that the Paris police had experienced the same trouble on a very large scale and finally managed to cut back that excess by use of what he referred to as 'the Denver Boot'.

I had never heard of this 'thing', whatever it was, and asked him just what this 'Denver Boot' was. He went to a lot of explaining in some depth the details of a large clamp of very heavy construction. This was locked by police to the wheel of an offending motor vehicle, parked by the driver or owner in a dangerous or unlawful position. the vehicle could not be moved. On return, the owner, finding that he could not move his vehicle, was obliged to call the police. He would then have to wait for police to arrive, obviously in their own time. Then on payment of a quite severe financial penalty the clamp would be removed and the driver at liberty to drive his vehicle away. The French authorities had discovered that by use of the clamps unlawful parking had been cut considerably.

My American friend pointed out that no other person in the UK had been approached in respect of the Denver Boot. If I wanted, I could have the sole agency for disposal of the clamp within Britain. I told him that I was interested, but would first need a sample and would then need to sound out the police authorities on the subject before taking the matter further. This was agreed, providing that I could give him an answer within two months.

Now to get such a decision from a government department 'within two months' is virtually asking the impossible, especially in respect of a new item of equipment. I therefore set about getting one of the clamps delivered as soon as possible. I also made representations to get the Metropolitan Police Traffic Department interested.

The distributors of the clamp were the Technology Transfer Group in Washington, USA. A telephone call to them confirmed that they had in fact handed a sample to an American in London. The representative had been asked to do just what I intended doing. The American group, however, had not heard from him and suggested that I made contact and picked up the sample. They gave me the representative's name, address and telephone number. My telephone call to the London-based American was something of a lesson itself. Yes, he had a couple of the clamps. They were a damned nuisance, cluttering up his home and office. 'Certainly you could pick one of them up, but you won't get anywhere with your efforts. I've been trying long enough. They just don't want to know,' I was told.

I had only put the telephone down a couple of minutes before it rang. At the time I was deep in thought. This particular American was well known to me by name. Although I had never met him, he was quite heavily involved in the sale of security equipment. If he could not sell this implement, I would perhaps have similar difficulty. On the other hand, I had already made moves to speak to a senior officer who was involved in the very problem under review. He must know the answer.

These thoughts were flashing through my mind as I reached for the telephone. It was my Traffic Department contact. I put my proposition to him and thought I could hear a faint chuckle at the other end of the line, as I went over the story as put to me. His reply to my dissertation was forthright. 'Good Lord, John, they would never stand for that in this country. Paris, yes, but they do strange things in other countries. Over here, car clamps would cause such an outcry that no political party could afford to back it. Forget it, John. It's just not on.' That was early in 1977, and I quite frankly had a fair idea myself of the feelings within the police service about such a proposition. My friend had only confirmed my own thoughts on the subject.

Confirmed to some extent, yes, but knowing how thoughts on so many subjects had changed over the years, I decided to try other angles of approach. My subsequent inquiries in both parliamentary and police circles produced almost identical replies. Thus, after the first 'knock back' from a colleague whose judgement I thoroughly respect, I had no further confidence in launching the wheel clamp in this country. Undoubtedly my American who had told me that the samples he had were cluttering up his home and office was right. As far as I was concerned, he could keep it. As much as I was prepared to do was to contact the people in Washington and tell them the result of my enquiries.

Having said all that, you can well imagine my personal feelings when about three years later official police wheel clamps, in line with the one known to me as the Denver Boot, appeared in the streets of London.

As time went on, I became quite surprised at the amount of work I was getting from sources I had no previous knowledge of, the result of recommendations and, in instances the outcome of a few contacts that I had accumulated over the years whilst in the police force.

Probably the most surprising came to me in October 1977. I was approached by, of all people, Radio Teilifís Eireann to say a few words on one of their television programmes in Dublin about bank robberies. I had never been on television before, but as there was a fee for my attendance, with expenses paid, I agreed to the request. This was at least a new angle, one I had never explored before. About a month later, I caught the early morning plane from Heathrow to Dublin. I was met on arrival and had a brief chat with the representative who came along. He was not giving anything away, however. It was purely and simply a talk on bank robberies; my experience in the subject would be appreciated.

This sounded all very well, but I knew from my past experience in Eire that English banks differ considerably from the Irish banks. I wanted to speak to the Garda Síochána and then have a look at some of the Irish banks.

At Dublin Castle I was made most welcome. I explained the reason for my visit to Ireland and told them that before I got involved in a television interview on the subject of bank robberies in Ireland, I wanted to have a look inside some of the banks that had been raided. I was aware that in certain cases it had been said that the IRA were funding many of their operations with cash stolen by way of bank robberies. Whilst going over this subject in my mind, I could feel that if I was not careful, I was going to find myself, to use a phrase, 'in the middle' and involved in an interview or line of questioning that would have me criticising the actions of the Dublin police without knowing exactly what I was talking about. Without some personal knowledge of the situation, this was not for me. My visits to the banks and the police headquarters had been well worth while.

At the RTE studios I found myself being made up before going before the camera. This was a new experience for me and something I did not enjoy. I can understand that an actor requires to be made up for a part, because he is to be projected as the person whose part he is acting; by being so made up, he acquires confidence in the part he is going to play. For my part, however, I found that instead of giving me confidence, it made me somewhat self-conscious.

That, of course, was before going in front of the camera. Happily, once sitting before the interviewer, my self-assurance returned. The interview was smoothly and efficiently conducted. I was, however, highly delighted that I had taken the trouble to call on the police headquarters and visit various banks. A Dublin police officer was on the interview with me, and I felt that much of the questioning was worded in a manner that could invite me to criticise the actions of the Irish police. Their apparent inability to get to one of the robberies and capture the robbers before they left the scene was an angle that constantly came up.

By contrast, my criticism was directed towards the bank. Those I had visited had no counter grills. Anyone so minded could just vault over the counter, produce a gun and hold up the cashier for whatever cash was readily available, then make off. Time taken, one minute, or even very much less. With help, all tills could be cleared in about two minutes.

I brought forward the fact that if high grills were installed, similar to those then in use in England, that time needed to carry out such robberies would be greatly extended. It would take the robber a lot longer to get behind the grill. The bank employees would have just that little more time to get to the alarm or telephone. Most important of all, the extra minute or two would give the police an even chance of getting to the scene of the robbery before the robbers had escaped. We had found in England that by installing high grills, most of them reaching the ceiling, robberies had decreased substantially.

I returned to my hotel after the interview and slept soundly after a pleasant meal and bottle of wine. The following morning I was due to catch the 8.30 a.m. plane back to London.

At Dublin Airport, I arrived in good time. My first stop was to the clerk at the Aer Lingus desk to check the departure time of my plane. There was, however, no indication of this. The girl at the desk could not assist me further than confirming that there was an 8.30 a.m plane. She had not at that stage been informed when or if it was going to take off. I found this most peculiar and was shepherded along with other passengers into a corner, seated and told to wait for further instructions.

I had my nose stuck into the morning paper when I became aware that someone was standing in front of me. I looked up. It was one of the police officers whom I had seen the previous day. 'I think you had better come along with me, John,' he said, and I accompanied him to a nearby office. Once inside he said that he thought it better that I should wait there. 'What's the trouble?' I asked. 'A strike,' I was told. 'The loaders have suddenly decided to stage a strike. The trouble is that you might have been the indirect cause. You may have upset someone yesterday.' I still did not see the point and pressed him on the subject. 'If the banks put up those grills and cut off the IRA's source of ready money, you won't be very popular. So the boss told me to make sure that you went on your way safely.'

This was indeed a new angle, which I had not taken into consideration. As it was, the next plane to London Heathrow took off exactly twelve hours after the plane I had been due to catch at 8.30 a.m. that morning. On my return home that evening, I had to admit to myself that I felt strangely relieved as I turned the key in the lock of my front door.

ELECTRONIC COUNTERMEASURES

When I first went into the field of private investigation, I found myself very much drawn towards one side of the business that I had earlier known nothing about: electronic eavesdropping, bugging and telephone tapping. Now I had no intention of getting involved in the eavesdropping side of the business, but the countermeasures truly interested me.

I decided to look into this very interesting subject, but soon found that it was not as easy as one might expect in this country. The principal difficulty was that in order to get involved in the countermeasures to electronic eavesdropping or bugging, one has to have some knowledge of the bugging side of the business. Plenty of people in the business of private investigation are prepared to talk about the countermeasures. The more I spoke to such people however, the more convinced I became the they in truth knew very little themselves about the matter.

Now in order to become a master in countering the electronic eavesdropping menace, you must know exactly what the eavesdropper is up to and precisely what he can do, where he obtains his equipment and how he goes about his task. To a newcomer, however, this information was simply not forthcoming. I was, of course, aware that this type of eavesdropping is illegal, unlawful, unethical and everything else that is wrong. I was therefore obliged to take the problem apart, then go out and attack each section of the question piece by piece.

I found my enquiries leading me to the Paddington area of the Edgware Road in west London. Here in a mews workshop-cum-showroom, I found myself welcomed, but subjected to a fairly high-powered cross-examination as to my finances. Just how much was I prepared to spend? They wanted figures, four-figure estimates at that, before they would agree to show me what they had to offer.

I went along with the questioning up to a point and asked to be shown some of the wares. No, I was told, that was not part of the deal. They could sell me items so small that they could never be discovered. 'How small?' I asked. 'Pinhead size. The size of a bug,' I was told in a most assured manner. I had heard enough. Whatever was used, to my very limited knowledge had to have a power source; a microphone to receive; the ability to transmit; and an aerial. I had made many enquiries on these lines, and no person whom I trusted had tried to convince me that a minute package which could be honestly described as 'pinhead size' existed or could be efficient. Had the man said postage-stamp size, I would have listened further, but I had heard enough from this particular quarter.

Still convinced that I was on the right track, I started to study the oddments of security hardware or 'bugs' that were on sale abroad. Japan seemed to have the lead in supplying circuit boards, with Germany running a close second. The majority of American items proved to contain circuitry from one or the other of these two countries. Having carried out these preliminary enquiries in a none too secretive manner, it did not surprise me when I received a call from one of my first contacts in this field. He was in the process of manufacturing a machine which he was going to call the Scanlock and suggested that I call on him and examine the prototype.

This was exactly what I had been waiting for. I had been introduced to this man by one of my most respected bosses whilst I was still in the police. I was quite sure that this man, whom I shall call 'Len', would tell me the truth, and not go off into the realm of fantasy as others had done during my quest. His interest, in line with my own, was to counter electronic surveillance or bugging, and his machine was made for that purpose alone. Furthermore, there was no doubt in my mind that he was taking into account every means that an aggressive and unethical private investigator might use to obtain the information he was seeking. For my part, my personal interest was stimulated by the fact that none of my former police colleagues was interested in or had any knowledge of this type of approach to private investigation.

I was so impressed by the Scanlock that I purchased one of the first models. Thereafter, by dint of playing hide and seek with the odd 'dummy bug' that I managed to get hold of, I became quite expert in finding bugs. I also accumulated a number of clients, many of whom still call upon me from time to time for assistance, advice or sweeps of certain of their offices.

In this comparatively new line of approach, I have had a fair amount of success. One of the first of these, in January 1978, was something of a put-up job. My electronics friend 'Len' asked me if I would carry out a debugging job for the BBC Science Unit. They were doing a documentary on the use of electronic devices in commercial espionage. I agreed to this and visited my friend's office on the edge of the City of London on 27th January.

My object of going through this so-called exercise was primarily to find out for myself whether the machine, which I had paid a lot of money for, worked under pressure. Here, without doubt 'something' would have been put in place, hence my reason for referring to this piece of work as something of a put-up job. I was asked in this instance if I would give a commentary on my actions, as I went on my search, a commentary that would be recorded as I progressed. Bearing in mind that I was in the presence of the BBC Science Unit members, I was quite sure they would be doing their best to catch me out, if they could. For my part, I hoped they would try, for I wanted to prove my equipment. If I failed, I would get rid of my Scanlock. If I succeeded, I knew that I could go anywhere with my head held high.

Not long after switching on my machine I found a positive trace of a transmitter and tracked it to a position behind a ventilator. This was just too easy, I thought to myself, as I pulled the 'bug' from its position. It was only a momentary thought, however, for when I switched my machine on once again, I found that I was still getting a positive trace of a transmitter. Proceeding onwards with the search, I discovered a 'bug' inside one of the panelled doors leading to one of the offices. Here the wooden strip at the top of the door had been removed, and a hole bored downwards from the top centre. A 'bug' had been lowered down through the hole and secured to the top of the door by a drawing pin attached to the aerial. With the wooden strip replaced, there was no sign of the bug. In the door, however, was a tiny hole of truly 'pinhole' size, immediately opposite the suspended 'bug'. Normally it would pass unnoticed. I was able to locate the hole with my machine and say quite positively that there was 'something' behind the hole that had to be investigated.

Moving onwards, and at first believing that I had found all that was to be found, I picked up yet another trace. This time I was guided by my equipment to the telephone on one of the office desks. This was new to me and quite a difficult place to find such an article as a 'bug'. It was quite obviously placed in a position to which the voice of the subject would normally be directed.

This exercise, unknown to me was later incorporated in a BBC radio programme. I did not hear it myself, though colleagues did, who got in touch with me on the subject. Some of them even called upon me for assistance. This now forms quite a large proportion of the work I am involved in.

My friendship with Tom Duval, who I first met in the Manhattan Club back in 1949, when I was a detective constable at New Scotland Yard, has continued until this day. He had invited me to his home on a number of occasions after his contract in England ended. For my part, however, I was unable to return the courtesy of a visit until 1977.

That year, my business took on a much wider range. Thus, in the interest of expanding my American contacts and seeing for myself just what life was like in the USA, my wife and I took off for Denver, Colorado. There we were met by Tom and his wife Lois and enjoyed a brand-new style of hospitality. We were taken to historical places of interest, but the time passed so quickly that, before we were aware of it, our vacation was over.

THE MISSING AMERICAN GIRL

The following year one of my contact men called me to ask if I was interested in tracing a missing girl. Frankly, I was not, but listened primarily out of respect for my contact, then with increasing interest as the story unfolded.

A fifteen-year old American girl, one of a party of schoolgirls from that country, had disappeared in London, where they had stopped on their way back to America. During their brief visit one of the girls whom I shall call 'Jean' went to the Queens Ice Rink in Queensway, Bayswater, in west London, with some of the members of the group. This was on Saturday 24th June 1978. 'Jean' returned to the rink the following day with two of her friends and another girl from Tennessee, who was also visiting London. Whilst at the rink that day, the girls enjoyed themselves, 'chatting up' various young men. The last time 'Jean' was seen was at 10 p.m. that night. she was then leaving the place with a young man of Arab appearance. She seemed jolly and happy and called to her friends that she would be away for about an hour. She had not been seen or heard of since.

My first impression was that this was a matter for the police. I was assured, however, that the matter had been passed to them to trace the girl and that the American Embassy in Grosvenor Square in London had also been informed. To make matters even more difficult for me, the whole party had now returned home to America.

I could not see what I could do or be expected to do if those two organisations had the matter in hand. I was being told these facts on 3rd July, and by any stretch of the imagination the trail must now be very cold indeed. My thoughts at the time were that if there had been foul play, a victim must have come to light by now. Alternatively, perhaps the young lady had just 'run off' for the hell of it, as so many young people had done to my certain knowledge in the past. In the back of my mind, however, was the knowledge that I was now getting involved with American investigators on other matters, therefore, I should see what I could do on this job.

The age of the girl worried me. She had reached fifteen years only two months earlier. She was well over five feet tall and well built. She was described as a natural leader, secretive, but assertive and good looking. The young man she had last been seen with was believed to be Iranian; he was 5 feet 3 inches tall and called 'Hassan'. I was told he spoke very little English and had been at the skating rink with his mother, sister and brother.

To keep my interest going, I was then informed of the theories that had been put forward during the previous few days. She had gone away voluntarily. Perhaps the motive was sexual, who knows? Perhaps she was unhappy and did not want to be found? Her family and friends who had obviously thought a lot about it suggested she was being held for ransom or had been drugged. The more I heard, the more determined I became to get to the bottom of it all.

Firstly, I needed a photograph of the young lady. This presented no problem and photographs were soon on their way to London Heathrow. Secondly, I needed to pay a call on the Queens Ice Rink, to check out the story presented to me. The manager of the rink, himself an ex-police officer, was most helpful, and with his assistance, the majority of the points we knew were confirmed. The doorman on the night in question even gave me a description of the Arab youth, who had originally been with his own family group, but had gone off with four American girls. He described 'Jean' as very big against the others, despite the fact that they seemed all of about the same age.

Everything sounded a little too good to be true. I had to expand on this information, and for the next few days, long hours were spent in my efforts to trace 'Jean' and her Arab boyfriend. The break came on 7th July. That day a telephone call was made, quite obviously in error, by a member of the Arab youth's family to 'Jean's' family in the United States. Fortunately, the recipient of the call was extremely alert and was able to extract from the caller the telephone number in London from which the call was made. This was relayed to me immediately.

With the number in my possession, I began a series of calls to the subscriber, whoever he or she might be. It did not take long to extract from the various persons answering the telephone the address from which they were speaking. We then went to the vicinity of an address in Hammersmith in West London and caught up with 'Jean'.

The young lady was not entirely happy to see us at first, but we slowly managed to convince her that she should come with us. Our ploy was that some of her family and friends in Kent were worried about her: she should put their minds at rest. She then quite readily agreed to come with us. Our greatest difficulty was in convincing 'Hassan' that it was for the best that he did not accompany her. 'Hassan' referred to 'Jean' as his wife. This was the first time such a mention had been made. Needless to say, this caused us considerable concern.

We questioned 'Hassan' on this point quite forcefully and found ourselves confronted with a marriage certificate, written in an Arabic tongue. This left little doubt in our minds that this fifteen-year-old schoolgirl had gone through a form of marriage with this young man in a mosque in London. Our efforts on 'Hassan' were finally rewarded when we managed to convince him that it was in his own interest that we take his wife to visit her family friends in Chislehurst in Kent. With not a little relief, we took 'Jean' to those friends, happy in the thought that she would be well looked after until she returned to the United States.

Our main worry was whatever action 'Hassan', his friends and family might have in mind. Through our contacts made during the course of this inquiry, we learned that the Arab family were unhappy when 'Jean' did not return to them the previous evening. 'Hassan' had the number of my car, that was obvious. Furthermore, he would certainly recognise me. The question was, what would our next move be? For my part, I had informed the police of the action I had taken. As far as 'Hassan' and his family were concerned, however, they could put the story forward that we had kidnapped the wife of one of them. A very nasty word. I was satisfied, however, that we had acted within the letter of the law.

With the correct name of 'Hassan' now in our possession, as a result of our sight of the marriage certificate, our inquiries brought out the fact that he had made two unsuccessful attempts to obtain American citizenship. The true reason for the 'marriage' was now apparent. With this knowledge in our possession, there was little doubt in my mind that the 'Hassan' family would not take the removal of his so-called wife lying down.

Our Chislehurst friends needed no urging to get the matter moving. Arrangements were immediately made for 'Jean' to return to the USA the following day. With the flight number in my possession, the next morning I put on my tropical suit and a loud necktie, proceeded to Heathrow Airport and waited by the National Airlines desk. Through my contacts at the airport, I had made arrangements for one of my men to take 'Jean' through the back door to the immigration desk. There she was handed over to the Chief Stewardess of the flight taking her home. At last I could relax.

I was still waiting at the National Airlines desk when the flight took off and 'Jean' was on her way home to her parents. I had purposely arrived at this desk an hour before the flight departed. I had told the girl behind the desk my reason for being there and was very relieved when she told me that she knew that something was going on. As she said this she was looking towards four Arab youths who were also waiting near the desk. 'Hassan' was not with the four, but they were all of similar height and age. After about half an hour, I made my way to the restaurant for a cup of tea, only to find that I was being followed closely by the four Arab boys. I returned to the National Airlines desk after finishing my tea, still closely followed by Arab shadows, and left the building only when assured that the flight had taken off.

19
The American Experience

Shortly after the 'Jean' – 'Hassan' affair was over, a good friend of mine, Herb Atkin, got in touch with me from Los Angeles. Herb had been in government service like myself and on retirement had gone into the business of private security. He had charge of the security matters of the pop group known as Led Zeppelin, and on his behalf I carried out a number of inquiries and assignments. Herb was quite obviously delighted with what I had managed to do for him, and upon hearing that I was once again intending to visit Denver later in the year, insisted that I call also at Los Angeles. So insistent was Herb that I visited his city that he even laid on air tickets within the United States and reservations at the Los Angeles Marriott Hotel for the period that my wife and I would stay.

Thus in November 1978 we paid our second visit to Tom Duval and his wife Lois in Franktown, near Denver, Colorado. We did our tours of the Rocky Mountains and even paid a visit to a most memorable viewpoint where my schoolboy hero Buffalo Bill is buried. That year I even got involved on Denver Television in an interview on crime trends. This actually went down quite well, despite my still not being entirely happy in front of the camera. All in all, the company in Denver was superb, but we soon had to make our way to Los Angeles.

There is no doubt about it that Denver was once a very beautiful place. In these days I often wonder. One point that constantly comes up on both radio and television in the Denver area is the density of the 'brown cloud'. When you consider that Denver, known as the Mile High City, is near enough a mile above sea level, fog of any description does not sound real. There is, however, an almost continuous cloud of exhaust fumes over the city.

Leaving the brown cloud of Denver behind, you can well imagine our surprise to find that Los Angeles was almost completely shrouded in fog, nasty brown fog of the type that I had been used to as a child in London. Herb Atkin was there to meet us and made us very welcome. Nothing was too much trouble for him. Our most memorable evening there was our visit to the Marina del Rey, where we had a most excellent meal of shellfish in a restaurant at the water's edge. The fog, however, was so thick that we had to go over to the window before we could see the sea, only twelve feet away.

My business during that year had gathered momentum to the extent that I found that I would have to make certain arrangements. I was getting so many American contacts that I had to have a more positive connection with them, in their own country. To this end, I had made arrangements to meet up with members of the Council of International Investigators in New York. They were at the time holding their Annual Convention, Annual General Meeting and Banquet, at the Biltmore Hotel, close to Grand Central Station.

Before leaving Los Angeles, I telephoned the Biltmore Hotel to confirm our time of arrival and booking. The receptionist was not at all helpful. They had no reservations for us, and in any event they were full up. I attempted to explain that I had their confirmation in writing, but she was not interested in that at all. In something of desperation, I asked to be put through to the convention president, Harry Goff. I had never met Harry Goff and had no idea what sort of reception I would get from him. His wife Eleanor answered the telephone. No, her husband was not in the room. I was beginning to boil. I put over my point of frustration as calmly as I could in the circumstances, then took a deep breath before adding some force to my statement. I did not get that far. 'Mr Swain, you and your wife have a room here. I am not interested in what the hotel say. Be assured you have a room. Don't worry.' We met in New York a few hours later, and the cool efficiency of the Goffs' was demonstrated on a number of occasions. We were now in a big city that neither of us had ever visited before, a city where to my knowledge I had no friends, but I have to put it on record that with one exception, the people whom I did meet were some of the finest investigators I have ever known. Furthermore, many remain close friends to this day.

I was not in the Biltmore very long before a strange incident presented itself. I was approached by one of the members who lived only a few miles from my home. He was inquisitive as to why I was present at the hotel and anxious to give me advice. Being a born listener, I listened. He did not think it was a good idea that I should join the Council. He offered a number of strange and most unusual reasons why I should not do so, in an apparently knowledgeable manner. I could find only one reason for the approach by my compatriot. He was yet another private investigator, who objected to a former police officer entering into the same business as himself. His motive was jealousy, pure and simple.

I remembered then that I did have a good friend somewhere in New York, Bill Kish, a former Legal Attaché at the American Embassy in London. He did not take a lot of locating and the telephone call to him was well received. We met and had a long chat over lunch. The result of that meeting was that I did join the Council of International Investigators and for that matter still carry out work for Bill in this country to this day.

Returning to the Biltmore Hotel, there was yet another surprise in store for me. A man whom I felt I should know, but could not place, stopped a few yards in front of me. He grinned and shouted at the top of his voice 'Johnny. It's been a long long time.' The accent was strange. I knew the face, I thought, but where? Not exactly American, yet hardly Canadian. At the same time there was a touch of Cockney there. This had to be Ken Maslen. We had last met in 1949 or thereabouts. He had joined the Metropolitan Police, but after a couple of years had decided to emigrate to Canada. Life was beginning to become full of surprises. Ken, who had joined the Royal Canadian Mounted Police, had, on retirement from that force, gone into private investigation. His son, like my own son, had followed his father's footsteps and was now serving in the Toronto Metropolitan Police.

Much of my American work had been brought about as the result of joining the Council. Also, within the Council itself, I have had that which I would like to refer to as success. Having supported their activities in Crete, Malta and Portugal, as well as the USA, I was elected their president in 1984.

This may sound all very grand, but in point of fact I had two principal reasons for taking on this one-year presidency: firstly, to show my appreciation for the co-operation and friendship I had received from members; secondly, to bring the Council to London, to give my overseas colleagues an idea of how we operate in this country of ours.

The American Experience

I managed this latter ambition in September 1984, when I organised the annual convention at the Tower Hotel in London. This was attended by somewhere in the region of one hundred and fifty delegates from around the world. The hotel was an ideal location.

It was an arduous task, that kept my wife and myself very heavily occupied, at times until the early hours of the morning. Arduous it may have been but I felt contented in the knowledge that I had extended British hospitality to my colleagues from around the world. In addition, of course, I was satisfied in my heart that I had repaid what I felt was something of a debt of honour to those who had organised similar conventions in other parts, which I had been privileged to attend.

Now all that is left for me to do is to continue with my business and enjoy my home, my garden and my hobbies. My work as an investigator is most satisfying, and I have many good years of work left in me yet, until the time comes when I may sit down once more and write my conclusion to this very small epic.

Since leaving the Police Force, I have travelled the world quite extensively in the course of my business. I have been to Belgium, France, Germany, Italy, Egypt, Spain, India, Japan, China, Hong Kong, Thailand, Canada, Hawaii, and many times to the USA. I generally work on my own these days, and miss the comradeship I had experienced in the Police Force. I had joined the Police after war service, in 1946, and had experienced the challenges and excitement of carrying out the many and various interesting investigations that I undertook prior to retiring in 1976. I would recommend the Police Service to any young person as a career of great interest and satisfaction.